Winning The 3-Legged Race

When Business and Technology Run Together

Hoque
Sambamurthy
Zmud
Trainer
Wilson

Winning The 3-Legged Race

When Business and Technology Run Together

Hoque
Sambamurthy
Zmud
Trainer
Wilson

PEARSON
Prentice
Hall

An Imprint of Pearson Education
Upper Saddle River, NJ • Boston • Indianapolis • San Francisco
New York • Toronto • Montreal • London • Munich • Paris • Madrid
Capetown • Sydney • Tokyo • Singapore • Mexico City
www.ft-ph.com

Library of Congress Cataloging-in-Publication Data

Winning the 3-legged race : when business and technology run
together / Faisal Hoque ... [et al.].
   p. cm.
   Includes index.
   ISBN 0-13-187726-7
   1. Managerial economics. 2. Industrial management. 3. Information
technology--Management.   I. Hoque, Faisal.
   HD30.22.W56 2006
   658.5'14--dc22

                                          2005025624

Publisher: Tim Moore
Executive Editor: Jim Boyd
Editorial Assistant: Susan Abraham
Marketing Manager: John Pierce
International Marketing Manager: Tim Galligan
Cover Designer: Lorenzo Ottaviani
Managing Editor: Gina Kanouse
Project Editor: Michael Thurston
Copy Editor: Keith Cline
Indexer: Lisa Stumpf
Interior Designer: Lorenzo Ottaviani
Information Graphics: Lorenzo Ottaviani
Compositors: Terry A. Kirkpatrick, James Lebinski, and Lorenzo Ottaviani
Manufacturing Buyer: Dan Uhrig

Dedication

To those who are working with us around the globe to advance the science of Business Technology Management.

Contents

Acknowledgments: Authors and Contributors   IX

Preface: Our Journey So Far   XV

Introduction: The Convergence of Business and Technology   XXI

PART I

Preparing to Run Getting BTM on the Executive Agenda   1

1 What Is BTM?   3

2 Strategic Positions   29

3 Making the Right Investments   53

4 Governance: Who's in Charge?   71

5 Is Your Organization Ready?   95

PART II

Leading the Pack Realizing Critical BTM Capabilities   115

6 Buy, Hold, or Sell?   117

7 The Age of Process   135

8 Considering Risk   157

9 Measuring Success   181

Conclusion: Peering Into the Future   205

Profiles: About the Authors and Contributors   213

Index   221

ACKNOWLEDGMENTS

Authors

Faisal Hoque

V. Sambamurthy

Robert Zmud

Tom Trainer

Carl Wilson

Research and Editorial Board

Michael Fillios
Faisal Hoque
Terry Kirkpatrick
James Lebinski
Mark Minevich
Frank Ovaitt
V. Sambamurthy
Robert Zmud

ACKNOWLEDGMENTS

Contributing Authors

Ritu Agarwal
Professor and Robert H. Smith
Dean's Chair of Information Systems
University of Maryland
College Park, Maryland

Anandhi Bharadwaj
Associate Professor of Decision
and Information Analysis
Emory University
Atlanta, Georgia

Michael Fillios
Chief Product Officer, Enamics, Inc.
Executive Director, BTM Global
Research Council, BTM Institute
Stamford, Connecticut

Varun Grover
William S. Lee Distinguished
Professor of Information Systems
Clemson University
Atlanta, Georgia

William Kettinger
Associate Professor
University of South Carolina
Columbia, South Carolina

Terry Kirkpatrick
Editor in Chief
Enamics, Inc.
Stamford, Connecticut

Rajiv Kohli
Associate Professor of
Management Information Systems
College of William & Mary
Williamsburg, Virginia

James Lebinski
Vice President, Knowledge Products
Enamics, Inc.
Stamford, Connecticut

Lars Mathiassen
Professor of Computer
Information Systems,
Center for Process Innovation
Georgia State University
Atlanta, Georgia

Mark Minevich
Chief Strategy Officer, Enamics, Inc.
Executive Director, BTM Global
Leadership Council, BTM Institute
Stamford, Connecticut

Frank Ovaitt
President and CEO
Institute for Public Relations
Fellow, Enamics, Inc.
Stamford, Connecticut

Arun Rai
Harkins Professor, Center for Process
Innovation and Department of
Computer Information Systems
Georgia State University
Atlanta, Georgia

Richard Welke
Professor and Director, Center for
Process Innovation & Department
of Computer Information Systems
Georgia State University
Atlanta, Georgia

Research and Leadership Insights

William Allen
Senior Vice President
Human Resources and
Corporate Communications
Maersk
Madison, New Jersey

P.A.M. Berdowski
COO and CIO
Royal Boskalis Westminster
Papendrecht, The Netherlands

Barbara Carlini
CIO
Diageo North America
Stamford, Connecticut

Lester Diamond
Assistant Director
United States Government
Accountability Office (GAO)
Washington, D.C.

Daniel Hartert
Senior Vice President and CIO
Royal Philips Electronics
Eindhoven, The Netherlands

John Henderson
Richard C. Shipley Professor
Chair of the Management
Information Systems Department
Director of the Systems
Research Center
Boston University
Boston, Massachusetts

Jean K. Holley
Executive Vice President and CIO
Tellabs, Inc.
Naperville, Illinois

Hideo Ito
Chairman and CEO
Toshiba America, Inc.
New York, New York

Kees Jans
CIO and General Manager
Schiphol Airport
Schiphol, The Netherlands

Jerry Luftman
Executive Director and
Distinguished Service Professor
Stevens Institute of Technology
Hoboken, New Jersey

By **Faisal Hoque**

Chairman and CEO
Enamics, Inc.
Founder and Chair
BTM Institute

STAMFORD, CONNECTICUT

Our Journey So Far

As meetings go, it was inconspicuous: A dozen university professors and business executives had gathered in a hotel conference room in Washington, D.C., in December 2004, to discuss their field, managing business and technology together. What was set in motion that day, however, will have far-reaching significance.

It was a year after the founding of the BTM Institute, and these members were meeting to set a three-year research agenda for the emerging management science of Business Technology Management (BTM). The institute had published several management papers on various particulars of BTM, but now those in attendance decided to publish a book. It would be the next step in gathering what we know about managing business technology and pointing to areas for future research.

Although based on research, the book also had to be practical. And so it was agreed that it would contain explicit advice for practitioners on the job and perspectives from executives around the world.

The result is *Winning The 3-Legged Race*.

In the perennial picnic game, teams of two tie the left leg of one partner to the right leg of the other. They must quickly learn to coordinate their movements so that the tied legs stride forward in unison, then the untied legs, then the tied legs. The thesis of this book is that business executives and technology executives must similarly learn to run together. Otherwise, they are likely to lose the race to their competitors.

As a starting point for planning this book, the Institute's Global Research Council used the Business Technology Management Framework created by Enamics, Inc., a company I launched in 1999. The Enamics BTM Framework™ is a comprehensive, holistic approach to managing business and technology. We present it in detail in Chapter 1, "What Is BTM?"

The book is organized into two main sections. Part I, "Preparing to Run," addresses BTM at the most strategic levels, where the board, the CEO, and the entire leadership team must be intensely involved if a company expects to be successful. Part II, "Leading the Pack," delves deeper into specific issues of actually getting business and technology to run together according to strategy.

To the chapters we have added the perspectives of executives and academics around the world. We interviewed them in Paris, Amsterdam, New York, and other cities. Their contributions are labeled "Leadership Insights" and "Research Insights."

The names of these thought leaders are on the back cover. If you were to add up the years these accomplished people have devoted to studying, teaching, and practicing the management of technology, it would be many, many times greater than the 50 or so years we've had information technology.

Each chapter begins with a summary that places the subject in context. An "In Brief" section summarizes the chapter at a high level. Each chapter concludes with an "Executive Agenda," where the chapter's subject is translated into specific action steps. You can use these chapter elements, along with the subheads and call-outs, to get a quick overview of the subject matter.

In the introduction and conclusion, two prominent CIOs reflect on the need for a standard for business technology management, much as other fields such as finance have standards of practice. This is the goal toward which the BTM Institute is working. Surely at this stage in the field's evolution, we can agree on what works and what does not. The power of this technology is so great, the change it is forcing, not only in business but in every other human endeavor as well, is so sweeping, that now is the time to settle on how best to use it.

The first of many steps leading to this book came in the summer of 1999, when I was working on my first book, *e-Enterprise: Business Models, Architecture, and Components*. A fundamental argument in it was that technology is meaningless if you do not know how to manage it. This realization came from working for large corporations, as well as from being an entrepreneur and having these corporations as customers. This was a genuine and unmet need, one I wanted to address. I couldn't imagine then how far that desire would lead.

What I had witnessed in company after company was how haphazardly people managed technology, particularly technology spending. The business principles they applied in other areas were not being applied to technology. They would not think of building a new plant without understanding exactly how it would benefit the business. But technology? In many firms, it was bought and deployed on a hope and a prayer. This was the era of dot.com exuberance, of course, and there was a madness loose in the land, but I had seen this problem in earlier, quieter years.

People were looking at pieces of a solution—the concept of portfolio management was getting attention, for example, as were various methods for measuring the ROI in information technology. But no one was looking at the problem holistically. The term alignment was growing in prominence, but not many firms knew how to get there. One or two management enthusiasms of the month would not be the answer.

I became convinced that business executives and technology executives still viewed each other across a chasm, even if they were now sitting at the same table. Only when they took off their business or technology hats and worked together to build the business could they succeed.

How would they do that? They needed a set of ideas, a framework of concrete practices and procedures that would turn the amorphous concept of alignment into reality. I started Enamics, and we began to research and develop this framework. We called it the Business Technology Management Framework. After several years, we took on a limited number of customers to test it in practice—if it had no commercial value, it would be nothing more than a nice theory. As it turned out, the framework was greeted with enthusiasm by executives wrestling with real-world problems.

The framework was a fundamentally different proposition for them. Every management team has pretty much been creating its own approach and practices. Sometimes they worked, and sometimes they did not. Now, with the BTM Framework, the management of technology had a chance to become a science that would replace trial and error. BTM aims to unify decision making from the boardroom to the IT project team. BTM provides a structured approach to such decisions that lets enterprises align, synchronize, and even converge business technology and business management, thus ensuring better execution, risk control, and profitability.

Three years after the formation of Enamics, we published a book on BTM, *The Alignment Effect*. This began to attract attention among university professors who were teaching the management of technology. Today, more than a dozen universities use the book in their courses.

Enthusiasm among professors and industry practitioners was strong enough that, in 2003, we created the BTM Institute, a nonprofit organization that could pull together the work of many academics, provide feedback from executive practitioners, and develop a research agenda to create a standard for BTM—much like Carnegie Mellon's Capability Maturity Model, which is a standard for process improvement. This book is the institute's first major publication.

The institute has become a global community, with members in Asia, Africa, Europe, and the United States. Technology has so infiltrated our world, changing societies and economies, that the need for managing it intelligently has become a global concern.

I returned to Washington recently to meet with Harriet Mayor Fulbright, chairperson of The Fulbright Center, which has a rich legacy of international educational exchanges and a worldwide community of scholars and alumni. She has joined us in promoting the education of a new generation of leaders in Business Technology Management.

A few weeks before, I had spent time in Sweden with Dr. Michael Nobel, chairman of the Nobel Family Society. The family has long been associated with innovations that not only have commercial value but also promote human welfare. He has joined us, too, seeing in BTM a transforming potential rivaling any other field of science.

The interest of these two distinguished people was unimaginable when we started, and it is unprecedented. What they could see, I'll confess I didn't when I started this quest: Technology informs and influences and improves every aspect of our lives.

Our hope is that this is the beginning of a revolution in the management of business and technology together across the globe, and that what we are learning will not only benefit us all today but influence leaders of the future, as well.

We have created wonderful technology. Now we must understand how to use it.

By **Carl Wilson**

Executive Vice President and CIO
Marriott International, Inc.
Co-Chair
BTM Global Leadership Council
BTM Institute

BETHESDA, MARYLAND

The Convergence
of Business and Technology

Two cheers for creativity. It has a place in almost any business process.

As a basis for repeatable value creation, however, the art of the individual began falling from favor in mass manufacturing a century ago. In service provision, defined processes and standards became core management tools decades ago. In financial reporting, those companies that exercised too much creativity in recent years are regretting it.

Too many business executives seem to understand that real management standards and repeatable processes provide the key to value creation almost everywhere—except in information technology.

Unfortunately for you, if your executive team still doesn't get it, there is a growing danger that a competitor does. Some leading companies are starting to understand that business technology is no longer just a cost center run by people who may be little understood by management. It is not just experimentation or R&D on new information-based products or services. It is not a back-office function unrelated to how the company actually makes money or deals with customers, suppliers, and employees. It is central to business success and needs to be understood and managed that way.

Your business runs with comprehensive decision processes and standards in manufacturing, sales, service provision, accounting, human resources, and many other functions. Therefore, you may assume that's what it means when you hear "best practices" in the context of information technology. Unfortunately, it does not.

Indeed, the absence of standards and structured decision making is why most companies have yet to derive real, repeatable business value or advantage from business technology investments. Expensive failures have led many observers to question whether business technology can ever produce a defensible long-term competitive advantage.

Yet today, it *is* possible to subject business technology to a comprehensive set of management processes and standards. Furthermore, this is not a technology issue. It is a *business* issue, and it will not see resolution until enterprises have a fundamentally better way to manage technology's contribution to the value chain.

The "whole brain"

In the early 1960s, Roger Sperry and Ronald Meyers discovered the split-brain effect, revealing that the two hemispheres of the brain are responsible for different modes of thought and action. The right side specializes in visual and global processing, the left side in analytic and linear processing. The two sides are wired together by a thick structure of nerves, the corpus callosum, which integrates communication and function. Without the corpus callosum, the two hemispheres would quite literally suffer a disconnect that would make it impossible to work as a coordinated whole brain.

The business and technology sides in many companies still behave like two separate hemispheres of the same brain. The business side processes information and determines action in terms of revenue targets, products, customers, suppliers, organizational capabilities, and the like. The technology side processes information and determines action in terms such as applications, systems, data, and throughput. There has been a traditional bias exhibited by the "dollars and cents" half against the "engineering" half. The business doesn't always understand its other half and typically expects the technology side to behave and act exactly like itself.

But the technology side cannot disregard its engineering nature any more than the right side of the brain can disregard its creative nature. Nor should it if a company intends to maximize its overall business performance. For example, while any company should expect its marketing department to implement appropriate cost controls, it would never expect marketing to be less creative. An uncreative marketing department is oxymoronic; so is an un-engineering IT department.

That doesn't excuse IT from following good financial or management practices. Conversely, a senior business executive must make the effort to understand and help direct the role of technology in the business, although no one expects the business person to understand the intricacies of the company's technology infrastructure or to drive decisions related to it.

(However, I do have to say that in my own company, Marriott International, I consider it a major mark of success when a tech-oriented question comes up at a strategic planning meeting and one of my business counterparts is able to answer correctly! And since securities analysts and ratings agencies also understand today that the technology strategy and the business strategy must be tightly interwoven to produce real results, CIOs will increasingly find themselves in front of financial and investor audiences answering questions about the business.)

Working together

Indeed, companies should strive for a more "whole-brained" set of behaviors, norms, and practices. The business and technology halves need a unifying *management* system that can connect them and facilitate their coordination as a whole.

This connective tissue is BTM, which addresses business and technology as a holistic, structured management system. BTM standards cover critical capabilities and a BTM Maturity Model to identify areas most in need of improvement, establish the starting point, and specify the correct path for change.

The key to institutionalizing these principles and capabilities is that they be ordered by a set of robust and repeatable *processes*, executed by appropriate *organization structures*, informed by useful *information*, and enabled by the right *technology*. Simply defining processes is insufficient. Many organizations maintain a set of documented standard operating procedures that are honored only in the breach. That's because they run counter to organizational interests, or the right information isn't available, or they are so difficult to comply with that they are unlikely to be repeated in approved form.

In this book, readers are introduced to essential BTM capabilities from the four functional areas of BTM that are critical for successful integration and the conversion of business technology investments into business value:

- **Strategy & Planning.** This includes the capabilities of *Business-Driven IT Strategy*, *Strategic Planning and Budgeting*, *Strategic Sourcing and Vendor Management*, and *Consolidation and Standardization* that collectively determine technology focus and operational intent, establish a joint business-technology agenda and necessary management oversight, and induce shared accountability.

- **Managing Technology Investments.** This includes the capabilities of *Portfolio and Program Management*, *Approval and Prioritization*, *Project Analysis and Design*, and *Resource and Demand Management* and their role in managing information and decisions on corporate assets and activity to achieve business objectives.

- **Strategic Enterprise Architecture (SEA).** This functional area includes capabilities of *Business Architecture*, *Technology Architecture*, *Enterprise Architecture Standards*, *Application Portfolio Management*, and *Asset Rationalization* that define and integrate the business architecture (processes, organization structure, facilities and information) and the technology architecture (applications, data and systems infrastructure) to execute the business strategy.

- **Governance & Organization.** This includes the capabilities of *Strategic and Tactical Governance*, *Organization Design and Change Management*, *Communication Strategy and Management*, and *Compliance and Risk Management*. As a whole, these BTM capabilities tightly integrate with the three other functional areas to structure and manage the business technology organization, allocate investments, manage enterprise risk, and ensure that business objectives are both enabled and shaped by business technology.

Each of these four functional areas, as described in Chapter 1, "What Is BTM?," has different implications regarding what processes, organizational structures, information and technology are needed. Without a single, comprehensive management science by which enterprises can manage technology in lockstep with the business, value and competitive advantage will remain hostage to market and institutional vagaries.

After 30 years in business technology leadership, I am absolutely convinced that it's no longer enough to talk about aligning technology with the business anymore. To create an environment where technology helps shape (rather than simply enable) strategic choices, leading enterprises are working to synchronize (rather than simply align) their business and technology decision making. And in the best-managed modern enterprises, technology will converge with the business as completely as, say, sound financial management.

Winning the race

Thus, the path of progress will move from alignment to synchronization to true convergence of business and technology. Increasingly, this will be the source of all dramatic competitive successes in today's marketplace. That's why we call this not business and technology, but Business Technology Management. To reinforce this new way of thinking, in this book, we will use the term business technology to refer to the application of IT to deliver a business capability or automate a business operation.

In a three-legged race, a well-coordinated team can achieve astonishing speed across the picnic ground, beating other teams by many yards. The competition may look awkward, but winners never do.

So it is when business and technology run together.

Preparing to Run

Getting BTM on the Executive Agenda

1

chapter

What Is BTM?

In Brief

The BTM Standard provides a set of guiding principles that create a seamless management approach that begins with board- and CEO-level issues and connects all the way through technology investment and implementation.

The Standard identifies 17 essential capabilities grouped into four functional areas: Governance & Organization, Managing Technology Investments, Strategy & Planning, and Strategic Enterprise Architecture.

The BTM Maturity Model identifies areas most in need of improvement, fixes the starting point for the enterprise, and specifies the path for change.

The right way to approach BTM implementation is iteratively. An enterprise must determine where it is in order to focus on specific priorities, design and implement specific capabilities against those priorities, and then execute and continuously improve.

Over the past few years, a standard for the management of business technology has emerged—a repeatable set of processes, defined in terms of 17 business capabilities, that lead to intelligent and consistent business technology management. This chapter sets forth the particulars of this Business Technology Management (BTM) Standard and argues that it is not only a solution for the problems that plague technology deployment, but also a competitive advantage for firms that adopt it.

In today's world, to manage the business well is to manage technology well. And vice versa.

By now, we certainly know what happens when business and technology are managed on two different tracks. Companies devote half of their capital investments to technology and often just can't shake that sinking feeling that something is wrong.

Hundreds of millions spent by big-name companies on enterprise resource and customer relationship systems have been wasted; nobody thought to redesign underlying work processes or to make sure employees understood what was happening and why. Huge business technology expenditures to lubricate the supply chain of a global apparel maker managed only to wrap that chain around the axle, leaving the company worse off than if it had done nothing at all. As one CEO said in exasperation, "Is this what we get for our $400 million?"

Such expensive failures have led many observers to question whether information technology can ever produce a defensible long-term competitive advantage.

Unquestionably, there have been enough successes to whet the appetite for the rewards of getting it right. In the late 1990s, for example, Herman Miller began offering small businesses no-frills, quality furnishings delivered quickly at a reasonable price. It established a new operating unit, Herman Miller SQA ("Simple, Quick and Affordable"). By applying business technology exceptionally well, it reduced an industry order cycle of about 14 weeks to about 2 weeks. Sears Home Services consolidated all of its information systems to manage its 12,000 service people. Everything is automated and wirelessly connected. The result is huge savings in parts management, huge increases in productivity of their service people, and significant increases in customer satisfaction.

But on the flip side of exceptional success lies precipitous (or perhaps worse, incremental and undetected) failure. The results have been manifest in productivity shortfalls, imposed workforce reductions, damaged corporate reputations and downward market valuations.

These outcomes threaten to marginalize technology's role in value creation at the very time that it should be brought closer to the business than ever before. Instead, we are seeing chief information officers reporting to the CFO rather than the strategy office or CEO. More symptoms: a headlong rush to outsource business technology, and choke-holds on technology spending, without any truly strategic understanding of either move. With that often comes a pattern of serial CIO—and maybe CEO—replacement, which virtually guarantees that short-term thinking will rule. What appears at first blush to be the fault of the technologist ("Can't you make this stuff work?") is really a failure to unify business and technology decision making.

Key Terminology

This book develops a new model for managing business and technology. It uses terms that may be new to some, and it uses familiar terms in specific ways that reflect this new model. Here are the most important:

IT, IT assets, and information technology are equivalent terms. They all refer to tangible items ranging from hardware to software to telecommunications to personnel. IT can be thought of as being composed of technology-related goods and services that are typically purchased in discrete quantities. By itself, IT offers only potential value. IT investments and IT capital are investments directly tied to the purchase of IT.

Business technology is the application of IT to deliver a business capability or automate a business operation. Business technology can be thought of as the result of configuring, implementing, applying, and using IT to produce a business result. Business technology investments and business technology capital are investments related to the creation, use, and maintenance of business technology.

Business Technology Management (BTM) is a management science applied to business technology that unifies and improves decision making. BTM provides a structured approach that lets enterprises align, synchronize, and even converge business technology and business management, thus ensuring better execution, risk control, and profitability. BTM investments are investments related to the creation and realization of BTM capabilities.

A Business Technology Management (BTM) capability is a specific competency defined by four critical dimensions: Each capability is ordered by *repeatable processes*, executed through appropriate *organizational structures*, and enabled by the right *information* and *technology*. There are 17 capabilities grouped into four functional areas: Governance & Organization, Managing Technology Investments, Strategy & Planning, and Strategic Enterprise Architecture.

Companies can move beyond alignment

For many enterprises or operations, *alignment* of business technology with the business has been considered the Holy Grail. Alignment can be defined as a state where technology supports, enables, and does not constrain the company's current and evolving business strategies. It means that the IT function is in tune with the business thinking about competition, emerging threats and

Figure 1.1 Alignment, Synchronization, Convergence

The three states of alignment, synchronization, and convergence demonstrate different relationships between business and technology.

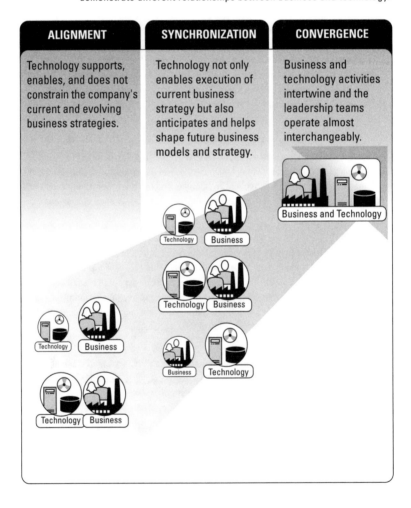

ALIGNMENT	SYNCHRONIZATION	CONVERGENCE
Technology supports, enables, and does not constrain the company's current and evolving business strategies.	Technology not only enables execution of current business strategy but also anticipates and helps shape future business models and strategy.	Business and technology activities intertwine and the leadership teams operate almost interchangeably.

opportunities, and the business technology implications of each. Technology priorities, investments, and capabilities are internally consistent with business priorities, investments, and capabilities.

When that's the case, the company has reached a level of BTM that relatively few have achieved to date. Alignment is a good thing, and sometimes sufficient to serve a particular business situation.

But there are higher states to consider (see Figure 1.1), and for some enterprises, synchronization of technology with the business is the right goal. At this level, business technology not only enables execution of current business strategy but also anticipates and helps shape future business models and strategy. Business technology leadership, thinking, and investments may actually step out ahead of the business (that is, beyond what is "aligned" with today's business). The purpose of this is to seed new opportunities and encourage farsighted executive vision about technology's leverage on future business opportunities. Yet the business and technology are synchronized in that the requisite capabilities will be in place when it is time to "strike" the strategic option.

Business Technology Management (BTM) is an emerging management science, grounded in research and practice, that aims to unify decision making from the boardroom to the project team.

Finally, there is the state of *convergence*, which assumes both alignment and synchronization, with technology and business leadership able to operate simultaneously in both spaces. Essentially, the business and technology spaces have merged in both strategic and tactical senses. A single leadership team operates across both spaces with individual leaders directly involved with orchestrating actions in either space. Some activities may remain pure business and some pure technology, but most activities intertwine business and technology such that the two become indistinguishable.

Is this actually possible? Quite so. Examples are abundant for alignment, less so for synchronization, and still fairly rare for convergence. More important, however, how does an enterprise decide what state it should be pursuing, and how does it get there?

The role of BTM

Business Technology Management (BTM) is an emerging management science, grounded in research and practice, that aims to unify decision making from the boardroom to the IT project team. The standard described in this book and put forth by the BTM Institute provides a structured approach to such decisions that lets enterprises align, synchronize, and even converge technology and business management, thus ensuring better execution, risk control, and profitability.

Companies have employed a number of methodologies and techniques to improve business and technology alignment. Although many of these methods have acknowledged strengths, they represent piecemeal solutions.

Disparate islands of practice exist within the technology management domain (see Figure 1.2), particularly in the areas of operations and infrastructure. These range from the Software Engineering Institute's Capability Maturity Model (CMM) to PMI's Project Management Body of Knowledge (PMBOK) and the IT Infrastructure Library (ITIL) for services management. However, none of these approaches focuses on integrating and enabling the capabilities necessary to achieve strategic business technology management and the sustainable value that follows. But the danger of relying solely on downstream technology management methodologies is that by the time misalignment becomes apparent, it may be irreversible.

The BTM Standard provides a set of guiding principles around which a company's practices can be organized and improved. It builds bridges between previously isolated tools and standards for business technology management. Essentially, BTM sits strategically above operational and infrastructure levels of technology management. The standard aims to create a seamless management approach that begins with board and CEO-level issues and connects all the way through technology investment and implementation.

The BTM Framework identifies 17 essential capabilities grouped into functional areas: Governance & Organization, Managing Technology Investments, Strategy & Planning, and Strategic Enterprise Architecture. These capabilities are defined

Figure 1.2 **Other Management Frameworks**

BTM integrates and enables the capabilities necessary to achieve strategic business technology management.

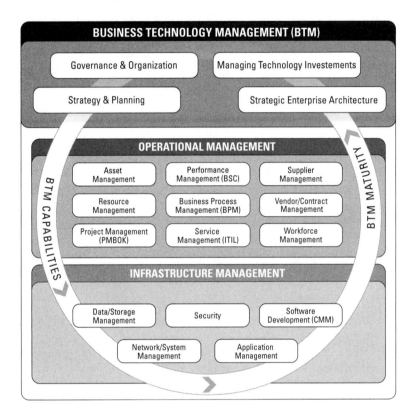

and created by four critical dimensions: processes, organization, information and technology (see Figure 1.3).

BTM has four critical dimensions

As illustrated in Figure 1.4, the first dimension for institutionalizing BTM principles is a set of robust, flexible, and repeatable processes. Simply defining these processes is insufficient, however. To effectively implement BTM requires that processes be evaluated to ensure the following:

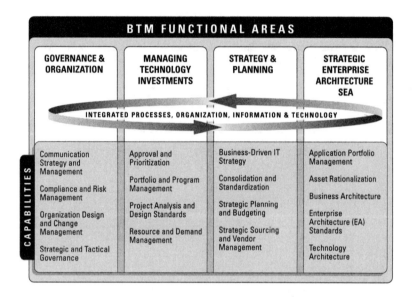

Figure 1.3 The BTM Framework

The 17 BTM capabilities are defined across four functional areas.

- General quality of business practice—Doing the right things

- Efficiency—Doing things quickly with little redundancy

- Effectiveness—Doing things well

Management processes are more likely to succeed when they are supported by appropriate *organizational structures* based on clear understanding of roles, responsibilities, and decision rights. Such organizational structures generally include the following:

- Participative bodies, which involve senior-level business and technology participants on a part-time but routine basis

- Centralized bodies, which require specialized, dedicated technology staff

- Needs-based bodies, which involve rotational assignments, created to deal with particular efforts

The right set of structures will vary according to an enterprise's value discipline, its primary organizational structure, and its relative BTM maturity. Centralized bodies, such as an Enterprise Program Management Office (EPMO), tend to require specialized, dedicated staff. Participative bodies, such as a Business Technology Investment Board, are ongoing, part-time assignments for their participants—the key stakeholders. Needs-based bodies—functionally specialized groups such as project teams—tend to be rotational assignments created in response to particular needs. These bodies set direction, guide specific business technology activities, and systemically execute against approved plans.

Valid, timely *information* is a prerequisite for effective decision making. This information must be delivered in a way that is comprehensible to non specialists and, at the same time, actionable in terms of informing choices that matter. Useful information does not just happen. It depends on the interaction of two related elements: data and metrics.

Data must be available, relevant, accurate, and reliable. Metrics distill raw data into useful information. Thus, metrics

Figure 1.4   Critical Dimensions of BTM

The four critical dimensions of BTM are processes, organization, information, and technology.

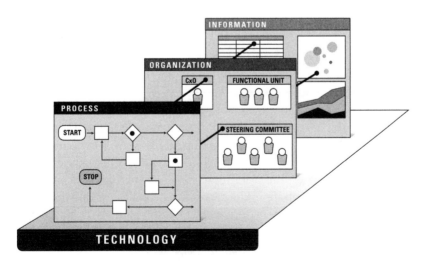

need to be appropriate and valid for strategic and operational objectives. Internally, they should be comparable across the enterprise and across time; and externally across industries, functions, and extended-enterprise partners.

Management processes based on flawed information will fail when confronted with conditions that exploit the flaws. As an illustration, consider a major retailer of auto parts that spends millions acquiring and analyzing customer data to determine where their customers live. The retailer then sites new stores in strip malls near these neighborhoods only to be disappointed to discover the new stores' sales *lag* the older stores. As it turns out, "where the cars *live*" is a poor predictor of success compared to "where the cars *work*." Locating stores along major routes to and from primary employers would produce much better results. As this example illustrates, flawed information need not be incorrect—just inappropriate for the intended use.

Effective technology (that is, management automation tools) can help connect all the other dimensions. Appropriate technology helps make processes easier to execute, facilitates timely information sharing, and enables consistent coordination between elements and layers of the organization. It does this through the following:

- Automation of manual tasks

- Reporting

- Analytics for decision making

- Integration between management systems

The simple addition of technology to automate existing processes leaves most of its potential value untapped. The largest gains result from the optimization of processes, organizational structures, and information flows. The complexity of managing the business technology function and increasing demands of an ever-evolving business climate require more information transparency and operational synchronization than basic computing tasks can provide. The appropriate use of technology should not only ease the development and reporting of information needed to fuel management processes across the organization, but also to achieve consistent horizontal and vertical management integration.

A BTM capability is therefore defined as a competency achieved by applying well-defined processes, appropriate organizational structures, information, and supporting technologies in one or more functional areas. Successfully implementing any of these capabilities will move an organization closer to the goal of business and technology unification. This progress accelerates as each additional capability is realized and continuously improved.

The 17 capabilities are interrelated and interdependent or "networked." All of them should be implemented to maximize the business value of technology investments. But doing so requires a carefully orchestrated approach with top-down and bottom-up support. It also involves business and technology groups in equal measure—plus hard work and time, of course.

Leadership Insight

P.A.M. Berdowski on Synchronization

P.A.M. Berdowski is the COO and CIO of Royal Boskalis Westminster, a dual role that gives him a unique perspective on managing business and technology together. In an interview, he explained his company's strategic view of business technology.

"We're In It Together"

When P.A.M. Berdowski joined Royal Boskalis Westminster, the big international dredging company in Holland, in 1997, he encountered a sprawling and struggling operation. The company had harbor and waterway projects underway in 50 countries, but it was trying to coordinate everything from human resources to vessel maintenance with antiquated systems. The company's business technology assets were home built, were not standardized, and could not talk to each other. And they were 10 years old.

In recognition of the strategic value of business technology, Berdowski was named COO and CIO, a novel blending of roles. "This was essential to the changes we needed to make," Berdowski said in an interview. "You will encounter resistance to new ideas. People will say, if you do this you will destroy the business, and it is almost impossible for IT people to overcome that resistance. In my position, I could balance the competing ideas. I'm not saying you should ignore problems. But I could say to my business colleagues, listen guys, at the end of the day, we're in it together. I'm responsible for running the business. Trust me, this is the best solution. It's not them, it's not us. We're all together."

This was a deliberate decision to move Boskalis beyond alignment, where the IT department supports the business, and even beyond synchronization, where business and technology executives share in leading the company forward. This was convergence, where business and business technology become one and the same.

Technology becomes strategic
Berdowski and other executives realized that their ambitious growth goals would require significant change. "We came to the conclusion that we had to completely reengineer our model," Berdowski says. "We had to completely reengineer from a business point of view, but as a consequence of that, we had to also reengineer from an IT point of view. We believed that by optimizing our operational strength in this way we would also by definition strengthen our competitive edge.

"Information and communication technology (ICT) was an important cornerstone in improv-

ing our competitive edge. So I lifted the whole issue from the level of technical operational people to the strategic. This is one of the key elements in the strategy. This is one of the key factors for success. If you really want to achieve 20 percent growth in the next five years, technology becomes a strategic issue."

Strategic to Berdowski means that the board plays an active role. "If you're really convinced that IT is critical for the future of your business, you have to understand why that is. You hope the board has a view on their business, a view on what they want to reach in the next five years. I'm not talking about financial goals. At the end of the day, it's an outcome in specific business goals. What is happening in the market, what are your competitors doing, how can you beat your competitors? What is the essence of your business as far as people and equipment are concerned, but also systems? How can IT help you really improve your competitive edge? For us, that was a very important starting point. In some industries, IT is purely cost. Boards have changed. They no longer have a view of operations. They look at financial markets. A lot of board members don't run their businesses any more. I see situations in which IT has become a budget issue but not a business issue."

"We did it, guys."
The company first looked at its

business architecture, then its technology architecture. "We started by defining the essence of our business model," Berdowski says. "Then we translated that into the essence of the kernel we needed in four layers to make sure 20 critical processes were congruent. It didn't mean they were exactly the same. But we made sure that where you needed the same type of information it was well defined. How do we define a supplier, an invoice, what country codes do we use? Simple things, but you can spend lots of time getting everyone lined up."

Berdowski wanted a more integrated system. "We can use different types of systems as long as they all fit into the same model from a business point of view and from an IT point of view." When he started, 30 of the 40 people in ICT were building homemade systems. That has been turned completely around.

He worked from a blueprint, but wasn't a slave to it. "It's good to know where you're going but to be flexible in getting there. We take a lot of time to decide what we want. We never start an IT project if we don't know what we want. Nobody gets a green light to step into any IT project if it's not well defined."

This year Berdowski invited his four top people to a dinner to celebrate what they had accomplished, starting back in 1997. "Eight years later," he said to them, "and we did it, guys."

These 17 capabilities are grouped into the functional areas described in more detail next: Governance & Organization, Managing Technology Investments, Strategy & Planning, and Strategic Enterprise Architecture (see Figure 1.3).

Governance & Organization

This functional area is focused on enterprise CIOs and business executives concerned with enterprise-wide governance of business technology. The capabilities that must be developed to support this functional area ensure that required decisions are identified, assigned, and executed effectively. Necessary capabilities also include the ability to design an organization that meets the needs of the business, manages risk appropriately, and gives proper consideration to government, regulatory, and industry requirements. Four capabilities constitute the Governance & Organization functional area:

1. The *Strategic and Tactical Governance* capability establishes what decisions must be made, the people responsible for making

them, and the process used to decide. This relates to a full range of business technology governance issues, investment decisions, standards and principles, as well as target business and technology architectures.

2. The *Organization Design and Change Management* capability establishes the makeup of work groups, defining and populating levels, roles, and reporting relationships to enable technology-based business initiatives. This capability also supports structuring and administering organizational and individual incentives as well as designing programs to foster quick and effective adoption of change.

3. The *Communication Strategy and Management* capability establishes overall strategy and tactics for creating broad-based understanding and getting actionable information throughout the organization. In particular, this capability facilitates the management of communications associated with large-scale change programs and business-technology synchronization.

4. The *Compliance and Risk Management* capability ensures that government and regulatory requirements are understood and met with regard to business technology initiatives and that appropriate risk mitigation strategies are in place.

Managing Technology Investments

This functional area focuses on the Enterprise Program Management Office (EPMO) and other technology and business executives who are concerned with ensuring selection and execution of the right business technology initiatives. The capabilities that must be developed to support this functional area ensure that the organization understands what it owns from an IT standpoint, what it is working on, and who is available. The organization must make certain that business technology investment decisions are closely aligned with the needs of the business and that technology initiatives are executed using proven methodologies and available technology and IP assets. Four capabilities constitute the Managing Technology Investments functional area:

1. The *Portfolio and Program Management* capability identifies, organizes, and manages existing IT assets and projects. This

capability is focused on effective program monitoring and execution. This includes the development of enterprise project and asset portfolios along with appropriate reporting.

2. The *Approval and Prioritization* capability determines the criteria used for evaluating alternatives, specifying the evaluation process, and prioritizing technology investments. The creation of enterprise business cases and the definition of appropriate selection criteria and mechanisms are thereby enhanced.

3. The *Project Analysis and Design* capability drives technology-enabled business improvements and leverages re-usable IT assets. This allows the integration of Enterprise Architecture (EA) and governance with a system development life cycle (SDLC).

Research Insight

Professor John F. Rockart on Leadership

John F. Rockart, Senior Lecturer Emeritus of Information Technology at the Sloan School of Management at MIT, has been a student of technology management for nearly half a century. In these excerpts from an interview, he relates how business technology's role in the organization has evolved.

"We've Come a Long Way"

History of business technology
"I've been observing IT since 1957. In the early days, the late 1950s and early 1960s, the field was not a field. It was a simple back-office functional area often run by somebody who came out of the accounting department and who was working either with punch cards or the first rudimentary computers. At that point, this person reported two or three levels down from the CFO.

"As the technology got better and better and better, slowly but surely, IT took over just about everything in the accounting department. Then came order entry procedures and basic transaction processing. At this point, the CFO became much more involved. It was not really until perhaps the past 20 to 25 years that line management has started to get somewhat involved. It was in the early 1980s that I, and some others, started to call on line management to take a stronger role.

"Starting about that time, it

became important for the success of the business for IT to be involved heavily in major transaction processes. However, these could not be designed or implemented well without a full understanding of what the business was all about and how the business operated. And that understanding really had to come from business executives.

"In the mid 1980s, we started to talk to business leaders about this need and found some receptive, but not many. For about the next 15 years, we talked about starting a course called "IT for the Non-IT Executive," because we recognized the importance of line leadership. But we didn't get much of a reception. It's really been in the last five, six, seven years that non-IT execs have started to say, 'I really have to understand IT.' As a result, one of the most popular executive courses at MIT right now is 'IT for the Non-IT Executive.' We offer it three times a year for 75 to 100 people each time.

"Many management teams, but far from all, have now caught on to the fact that IT is just one of the tools in the business. Twenty years ago, as a line manager thought about his strategy, he focused on three major assets—people, money, and machinery. Today, since IT is now in many companies more than 50 percent of the machinery, the focus is now four-fold—people, money, machinery, and IT.

"No executive today would turn to the CFO and say, 'I don't understand this money stuff. Take care of it and keep me out of the loop.' Or turn to the head of HR and say the same thing about people. But some managers today are still effectively saying this sort of thing about IT. There are far fewer of them. This doesn't happen in most major companies any more, but you still find it in small and even some midcap companies. However, this attitude has significantly changed over the last 20 years.

The need for convergence

"One thing that is very clear to me is that the BTM approach, not just alignment, but synchronization, is correct. I would hope for convergence some day. Given the need for convergence, there is a significant need for more IT education of line managers. It's also a reason that, at MIT, a number of the courses in the master's program I taught were aimed at line managers or potential line managers. Students now want to understand enough about IT to get heavily involved, although they only know the basics about technology itself.

"If this is to be successful—and I refer to the entire IT revolution we're undergoing that will make companies much more competitive—the degree of understanding of the business by IT and the degree of understanding of IT by business has clearly got to be better than it is today. I think we're a lot better today on the understanding of business by IT, certainly in major companies. I watch time and time again where the fundamental choice of who is to be the CIO is based on how good a business person the candidate is. We're still probably far less from there on the other side.

"We've come a long way from the day in which a data processing manager ran IT to a day in which there is a shared understanding at the senior executive levels that there needs to be a very close convergence between the business leaders and the IT leaders, that they each need to be, to some extent, the other guy. The IT guy has got to be a business leader and the business leader has to understand IT. We're not at the point where each can do the other's job. We're still a long way away, and we will never close that gap because there's a need for expertise on each side. In some companies, we're coming very close to what I would call the ideal roles, dual roles to make IT work effectively in the organization."

4. The *Resource and Demand Management* capability is used to quantify, qualify, and manage business technology demand and resource requirements. It supports and promulgates the process for categorizing and prioritizing business technology requests to ensure that they are consistent with required business capabilities, priorities, budgets, and capacity. This capability also guides the allocation of high-value scarce resources.

Strategy & Planning

This functional area focuses on enterprise CIOs, divisional CIOs, and business executives who are responsible for the efforts to synchronize business technology with the business. The capabilities that must be developed to support this functional area ensure that a target set of applications will meet the needs of the business and reduce overall complexity. In addition, annual planning and budgeting must incorporate elements of business technology strategy and other evolving needs of the business. Four capabilities constitute the Strategy & Planning functional area:

1. The *Business-Driven IT Strategy* capability articulates required business capabilities and the technology plans to enable them. This allows an organization to translate business strategy into specific required business capabilities. It defines principles to

guide decisions on applications and infrastructure and supports plans for moving from as-is to target architectures.

2. The *Strategic Planning and Budgeting* capability is necessary to define and link plans and budgets to strategy and enterprise architecture. Goals, milestones, and contingencies are identified and highlighted, as are planning assumptions and prerequisites.

3. The *Strategic Sourcing and Vendor Management* capability deals with creating and managing relationships with those vendors best suited to an organization's strategy. This includes identifying areas of strategic opportunity for outsourcing, co-development, and vendor selection.

4. The *Consolidation and Standardization* capability integrates accumulated or acquired IT units and assets to ensure consistency with an organization's strategy. This delivers improved performance by rationalizing the number of projects, assets, sites, and processes. It also extends to identifying which assets to eliminate, consolidate, or enhance, and which to standardize on.

Strategic Enterprise Architecture

This functional area focuses on the Office of the Chief Technology Officer and business and technology executives who are concerned with the overall architecture and standards for the enterprise. The capabilities that must be developed to support this functional area ensure that appropriate information and documentation exist to describe the current and future-state environments. Also, it is necessary to verify that business and technology people can implement strategies and plans and make recommendations simplifying the existing business technology environment. Five capabilities comprise the Strategic Enterprise Architecture functional area:

1. The *Business Architecture* capability is used to describe the business strategies, operating models, capabilities, and processes in terms actionable for business technology.

2. The *Technology Architecture* capability defines the applications and technical infrastructure required to meet enterprise goals

and objectives. This includes the creation of application models, data models, and associated technical infrastructure models for the enterprise.

3. The *Enterprise Architecture (EA) Standards* capability is necessary to define standard business technology applications, tools, and vendors. This capability centers on the delivery of EA guiding principles, plus assessing and defining other governance requirements. Also included are standards for IT vendors and reusable assets, including design patterns and services.

4. The *Application Portfolio Management* capability is employed to establish and manage portfolios of applications, consistent with IT strategy, and to achieve target architectures and maintain standards.

5. The *Asset Rationalization* capability applies enterprise architecture and standards to simplify the infrastructure. This reduces complexity and cost by controlling the number of applications and systems.

The BTM Maturity Model measures a firm's progress

Given the interconnectedness of the 17 capabilities and the importance of approaching them on a clear priority basis, it is critical that an organization understand its maturity relating to them. The BTM Maturity Model (see Figure 1.5) defines five levels of maturity, scored across the four critical dimensions described previously: process, organization, information, and technology.

A maturity model describes how well an enterprise performs a particular set of activities in comparison to a prescribed standard. This instrument assists in levying a grade based on objective, best practice characteristics. A maturity model also makes it possible for an enterprise to identify anomalies in performance and benchmark itself against other companies or across industries. The measurement of BTM capabilities through the BTM Maturity Model identifies areas most in need of improvement, fixes the starting point for the enterprise, and specifies the path for change.

Figure 1.5   The BTM Maturity Model

The BTM Maturity Model identifies areas most in need of improvement, fixes the starting point for the enterprise, and specifies the path for change.

	Process	Organization	Information	Technology
LEVEL 5 (Maximum BTM Benefit)	Continuous process optimization, experimentation, and innovation	Evolving organization structures, roles, and decision rights; synchronous collaboration	"Intelligent" decision-making/ information routines; experimental benchmarking	Consistent, coordinated use with complete, related integration
LEVEL 4	Repeatable, predictable, and consistent process execution; fully integrated across the business	Fully implemented structures with all roles executing to defined responsibilities; fully functioning COE	Data and metrics integrated across the business; use of both internal and external benchmarking	Full automation and coordinated use with partial, related integration
LEVEL 3	Core processes are defined and documented with some integration between key process areas	Some structures exist, with related roles executing per defined responsibilities and decision rights; sequential collaboration; COE or equivalent	Appropriate data sharing and use; integrated operating metrics and use of internal benchmarking	Automation of appropriate tasks/functions with some coordinated use
LEVEL 2	Some core processes are defined and documented	Structures and related roles/ responsibilities are identified and defined	Defined and consistent information policies and measurement criteria	Partial or sporadic automation of appropriate tasks/functions
LEVEL 1	Unstructured and ill-defined processes with no process integration	Missing structures and unidentified or unclear roles/ responsibilities/ decision rights; ad-hoc collaboration	Data and metrics are in isolated pockets and are ill-defined	Lack of required automation for appropriate tasks/functions

Left axis (bottom to top): Learning & Defining → Developing & Executing → Improving & Evolving

Right axis (bottom to top): Alignment Threshold → Instances of Synchronization → Potential Convergence

A growing body of BTM Institute and Enamics research shows that at level 1, enterprises typically execute some strategic business technology management processes in a disaggregated, task-like manner. A level 2 organization exhibits limited BTM capabilities, attempts to assemble information for major decisions, and consults IT on decisions with obvious business technology implications. Enterprises at level 3 are "functional" with respect to BTM, and those at level 4 have BTM fully implemented. Organizations achieving level 5 maturity are good enough to know when to change the rules to maintain strategic advantages over competitors who themselves may be getting the hang of BTM.

The evidence shows that enterprises at lower levels of maturity will score lower for business technology productivity, responsiveness, and project success than enterprises at higher levels. As BTM maturity extends past level 3, the resulting synchrony of business strategy and technology delivery makes the enterprise more agile and adaptable. For such companies, changes in the business landscape impel appropriate adjustments to strategy and corresponding action without major disruptions or anguish.

Leadership Insight

Hideo Ito on CEOs

In these excerpts from an interview, Hideo Ito, Chairman and CEO of Toshiba America, Inc., explains how a CEO must think about business technology.

The CEO's New Imperative

"For a long time, Toshiba—and many companies in Japan, Europe, and the United States—didn't think of IT strategy when we thought of business strategy. IT was always just information processing, something done in a back room.

Today, IT strategy should be part of the business strategy, a major element of strategy and planning.

"To lead a company, the CEO needs to understand how IT affects business decisions. For example, it's necessary in collecting all the data the CEO needs for reviews. But, more than this, the CEO needs to know how IT plays a role in all of the organization's processes, from the customer through production and logistics.

"Today, however, the maturity of IT management is at the infant level. All too often we have an IT expert in the company who notices something new and thinks it will be beneficial and asks for money to produce it. But these decisions should be much more systematic. I don't like to confess that many companies, as we, are still dependent on the technology person's capability—for good or bad, we don't know.

"We used to view logistics separately; it was just trucks and customs. But now, it's integrated; it's a very important part of our business. If managed well, it can save time and money. Now IT has to be viewed the same way, as an integral part of the business.

"But, unfortunately, managing IT is still an art, not a science."

Emerging opportunities are sensed and addressed more quickly. Project execution to deliver new capabilities is more sure-footed. As joint management of business and technology improves, the maturity of the enterprise is reassessed to focus the next set of priorities. As gains result from BTM, remaining weaknesses become more obvious and the business case for addressing them becomes more compelling.

BTM can be implemented in five steps

But where to start? The job of implementing 17 BTM capabilities and measuring progress using the BTM Maturity Model can seem overwhelming. After all, every enterprise starts from a different place, with existing investments in systems and business processes that make starting over virtually impossible.

So don't start over. Start anywhere.

The right way to approach BTM implementation is iteratively. Fundamentally, an enterprise must determine where it is in order to get focused on specific priorities, design and implement specific capabilities against those priorities, and then execute and continuously improve.

You not only can, but you actually must begin by recognizing where the enterprise stands with regard to BTM maturity. Only by respecting what is can you make real progress toward what is to be.

Then you cycle again, using five steps to continuous BTM improvement (see Figure 1.6):

1. Establish a Baseline (assess BTM maturity levels, confirm opportunity areas, identify high-priority functional areas and key stakeholders).

2. Educate and Align (educate key stakeholders on BTM capabilities, review baselines, and develop consensus on roadmap).

3. Diagnose and Design (analyze and define the scope of the problem, identify relevant components of the BTM Framework, design processes, organization, information, and automation).

4. Realize and Mobilize (implement the design with best practice templates, operationalize repeatable decision-making processes).

5. Optimize and Maintain (fine-tune management processes, update information, and ensure decision quality).

The flexibility of this approach provides multiple points of entry into a BTM roadmap, with or without previous BTM experience. This eliminates any need to completely recast the existing approaches in an organization. BTM maturity initiatives are easily blended with and serve as a supporting framework that can organize and improve existing practices. Incumbent tools and standards for technology management are integrated into the holistic BTM Framework.

The flexible nature of BTM and its implementation cycle easily interfaces with external sources such as compliance studies, management consulting engagement outputs, and audits. Regardless of the source, virtually any baseline or starting point will support the identification of target activities appropriate to an organization's current environment and its state of business and technology synchronization.

As a company approaches the successful conclusion of a BTM improvement cycle, it will be simultaneously planning the evolution of its BTM maturity. This is accomplished by observing results and preparing to establish the next performance baseline. Ultimately, a company operating in the "execution and improvement" zone will seek to revisit their baseline and to determine areas of focus for the next cycle of BTM progress.

Figure 1.6 **A Step-by-Step Approach to BTM**

There are five steps to continuous BTM improvement.

IMPLEMENTING BTM CAPABILITITES

GOVERNANCE & ORGANIZATION
- Communication Strategy and Mgt.
- Compliance and Risk Mgt.
- Organization Design and Change Mgt.
- Strategic and Tactical Governance

STRATEGIC ENTERPRISE ARCHITECTURE (SEA)
- Application Portfolio Mgt.
- Asset Rationalization
- Business Architecture
- Enterprise Architecture (EA) Standards
- Technology Architecture

MANAGING TECHNOLOGY INVESTMENTS
- Approval and Prioritization
- Portfolio and Program Mgt.
- Project Analysis and Design Standards
- Resource and Demand Mgt.

STRATEGY & PLANNING
- Business-Driven IT Strategy
- Consolidation and Standardization
- Strategic Planning and Budgeting
- Strategic Sourcing and Vendor Mgt.

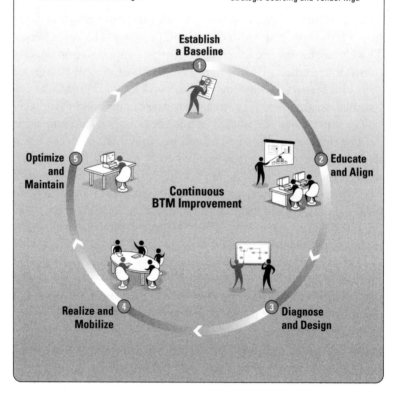

Establish a Baseline ①

② Educate and Align

③ Diagnose and Design

④ Realize and Mobilize

⑤ Optimize and Maintain

Continuous BTM Improvement

Smart enterprises today are rightfully pursuing alignment of technology with the business, and that in itself is no small achievement. But for some, the right level is really synchronization, where technology shapes (not just enables) strategic choices. And at the highest level of achievement, business and technology leadership actually converges, reflecting an executive and management team that has achieved an extraordinary level of cross-understanding and vision for the future.

The BTM Standard supports enterprises at all three levels. Assembling the components of Business Technology Management as described previously yields unprecedented capacity and opportunity for success in a marketplace where competitive advantage is increasingly defined through technology.

Business technology budgets are so big today that they obviously cannot be ignored by any senior management team. There are those companies with executives who will wring their hands, clamp down with arbitrary spending caps, demand a quick fix such as outsourcing, and call for the head of the CIO. Within a short while, they will cycle through those steps again, since nothing there addresses the core issue: You cannot spend (or slash) your way to business technology excellence and congruence with the business. That demands intelligent application of technology, with spending determined by strategic business needs, not by arbitrary benchmarks.

In fact, there are companies whose executives are beginning to see that business technology investment must be accompanied by appropriate BTM investment. This new kind of capital includes the processes, organizational structures, information and technology required for unified business and technology decision making. This new kind of company will move beyond alignment, where technology supports but never goes beyond immediate business needs, to synchronization and convergence, where technology helps shape new opportunities and in fact cannot be separated from the business.

You had better hope that company is your own, and not your competitor.

2

chapter

"The elevator pitch to a CEO is: Take a hard look at the companies in your field that are surviving and doing well. All of them today have outstanding IT, operated effectively, which is a product of significant cooperation and understanding between line executives and IT executives."

—Professor John F. Rockart, MIT

Strategic Positions

In Brief

Only when a firm matches the level and mix of business technology and BTM investments to its strategic positioning can it know whether it is spending correctly.

Business technology is often critical in establishing or sustaining a strategic position; not understanding its roles across a firm's product-markets can lead to inappropriate levels of investment.

Scholars studying how firms or networks of firms evolve their strategic positions have observed that two very different types of strategic actions are necessary: exploitative and exploratory.

Building lean or agile organizations requires substantial investment and carries strategic risks. It is important to realize that not all firms need to be lean or agile and that it is possible to exhibit both leanness and agility.

Investing in business technology[1] should begin with the organization's strategic position. These positions are often crafted without a clear understanding of business technology's potential to influence or execute them. Mischaracterized as merely being "IT strategy," efforts to guide the potential contributions of business technology are relegated to the back office where they frequently comprise little more than architecture, platform, and standards mandates. Even purported "business and IT alignment initiatives" often involve more reconciliation of separately crafted strategies than synchronization of business technology with business needs.

This chapter examines several common strategic positions and shows how business technology can support each. It shows why determining the appropriate level of business technology investment is made easier by several of the BTM capabilities,[2] including Strategic Planning and Budgeting *and* Strategic Sourcing and Vendor Management.

We argue that only when business technology investments are tied directly to business capabilities that enable a firm's strategy can an organization be sure it is investing correctly. Contributing authors for this chapter are Michael Fillios, Chief Product Officer, and James Lebinski, Vice President of Knowledge Products, at Enamics, Inc.

"Are we investing too much or too little in IT?" All too often, business technology executives answer this question with comparisons to a generic peer group—an approach that can prove increasingly counterproductive the more distinct a firm's business strategies and tactics are from those of the peer group members. Only by matching the level and mix of business technology investments to its business strategy can an organization be sure it is investing correctly.

Moreover, only part of these investments should be for IT assets[3] such as hardware and software or their application. Equally important is investment in the BTM capabilities needed to manage the complex relationship between business technology and business needs. This means developing the processes, organizational structures, information, and automation necessary for choosing the right technology and implementing it effectively. Without this, investments in hardware alone offer little or no value, and efforts to assemble supporting business technology often are disconnected from the enterprise business strategy. A firm seeking strategic value from its business technology must ensure that its IT strategy respects and supports the business strategy.

> *A firm seeking strategic value from its business technology must implement BTM capabilities to ensure that its IT strategy respects and supports the business strategy.*

To understand how business technology can become an integral player at the strategic level, it is helpful to briefly review the basics of strategy. A firm fabricates a strategic vision and assembles the competencies enabling it to occupy a niche in a product-market. Typically, this is done through competencies in cost leadership, product/service leadership, and/or customer leadership in a product-market.[4]

If a firm is alone in a product-market niche, this extraordinarily favorable situation typically does not last long as competitors respond to the above average returns. It is crucial, therefore, to both establish a profitable strategic position and sustain it. With today's globalized—and, hence, increasingly competitive—marketplaces, this is more difficult than ever.

A simplified view of what occurs is depicted in Figure 2.1. Business strategists discover profitable opportunities—new market spaces or gaps in existing market spaces—by considering (1) signals regarding product/service, customer, technology, socioeconomic and cultural trends; (2) competitors' current and future strategic positions; (3) the firm's internal competencies; and (4) recognition of the competencies it might gain access to through partners.

Figure 2.1 **Establishing Strategic Positions**

Companies discover market opportunities by considering internal competencies and external signals.

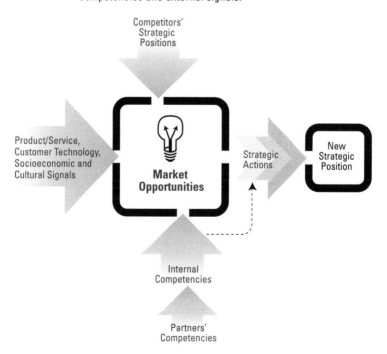

A firm's initial position in the product-market must then be regularly augmented such that it continues to offer a value proposition beyond those provided by competitors. As is explained later in this chapter, business technology often plays a critical role in establishing a strategic position or in sustaining it once established; not understanding these roles across each of a firm's product-markets can—and often does—lead to inappropriate levels of business technology investment. By giving visibility to the particulars of a firm's business strategy and the technology resources deployed to achieve it, BTM[5] allows firms to gain that understanding.

> **BTM capabilities serve as a strategic enabler of multi-firm partnerships. Failing to understand the role served by business technology can result in inappropriate levels of business technology investment.**

Invariably, today, strategic positions are forged not by single firms but rather from leveraging the distinctive competencies of a number of firms (see Figure 2.2). The BTM capability of *Strategic Sourcing and Vendor Management* recognizes this, and defines the approach for creating and managing these relationships. This includes identifying areas of strategic opportunity for outsourcing, co-development, and vendor selection. By each strategic partner nurturing its distinctive competencies to world-class levels and by tightly coordinating partner activities, these networks of cooperating firms, or "value nets," can continuously improve their value propositions or engage radically transformed or newly created product-markets.[6]

Firms engage in two general types of strategic actions

Scholars studying how firms or networks of firms develop their strategic positions have observed that two very different types of strategic actions are necessary: exploitative and exploratory.[7] Exploitative actions refer to continuously improving the competencies associated with an existing strategic position. The string of initiatives taken by Wal-Mart during the 1990s to drive costs out of its supply chains is an example. Exploratory actions, on the other hand, refer to discovering new strategic positions or new

Figure 2.2 Value Nets

Strategic positions are often forged by coupling the competencies of multiple firms.

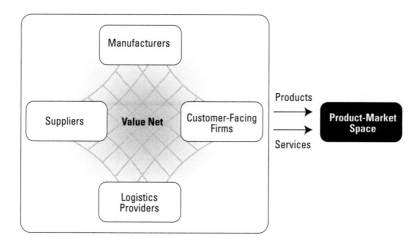

competencies that might be instrumental in creating radically transformed or new strategic positions. An example is the string of anything-but-systematic initiatives taken by Dell during the 1990s in arriving at its Direct Model.

Exploratory strategic actions create new product-markets. After a new product-market is created, firms with favorable strategic positions in it strive to exploit their position to sustain it. Known and unknown competitors, however, engage in exploratory actions to supplant this position. If an exploiting firm is inattentive to the behaviors of exploring firms, it can be locked out of these emerging but highly attractive product-market niches.[8]

Exploitation: being lean

Exploitation has been a hallmark of industrial competitiveness over the past two decades, encompassing movements such as Total Quality Management, Lean Manufacturing, and Six Sigma. With such initiatives, the intent is to delight customers by eliminating defects and waste (in materials, methods, processes, time) and thereby delivering high-quality products and services at low cost and in a timely manner. Through such regular, incremental improvements, favorable strategic positions can be continuously refined, enhanced, and sustained.

Generally, a firm becomes lean by accumulating experience, data, and knowledge about the work environment and exploiting these to improve efficiency and effectiveness.

Exploration: being agile

Concern with exploration has intensified along with the increased competitiveness of the global economy and the increasing rates of scientific progress. With increased competitiveness, it becomes difficult to sustain a favorable strategic position as existing competitors are motivated to quickly match or best the position and as new competitors are motivated to enter the product-market. With increased scientific progress, the technological basis of a favorable strategic position is more quickly eroded. By being agile, a firm is able to sense and respond to competitors' strategic moves within existing product-markets, as well as sense and respond to environmental signals arising from shifts in customer desires or in new technologies. Firms demonstrate strategic agility in four major ways:

1. They continuously scan their environment to identify threats to existing positions and opportunities to forge new positions.

2. They regularly engage in strategic experiments. That is, they implement small-scale strategic initiatives to perturb internal or external work environments to gain experience with emerging technologies, work practices, product, or service concepts, customer segments or product-markets.

3. They devise adaptive business architectures so that their competitive assets (as well as those of partners) can be realigned quickly—shutting down activities, commencing new activities, or shifting resources among activities.

4. They learn to radically renew the competencies that characterize their competitive nature.

BTM informs and enables a firm's strategic investments

The *Strategic Planning and Budgeting* capability can prepare an organization to examine how it will use business technology to enable its exploitative and exploratory strategic actions. This is illustrated in Table 2.1 for four classes of business technology investments focused respectively on a firm's transactions, decisions, intellectual capital, and relationships. Understanding these classes of investments helps in understanding how BTM contributes to the forging of exploitative and exploratory strategic actions.

Table 2.1 **Enabling Strategic Actions Through Business Technology Investments**

Firms exploit four types of business technology investments to support strategic positions.

Area	Transaction Focused	Decision Focused	Intellectual Capital Focused	Relationship Focused
Definition	Enhances the quality of ongoing transactions	Enhances the quality of ongoing decisions	Enhances the quality of organizational intelligence	Enhances the quality of relationships across the firm and across the extended enterprise
Exploitative Strategic Actions	- Speed - Reliability - Volume - Cost	- Speed - Volume - Completeness - Reliability	- Codifiability - Accessibility - Transferability	- Reach - Velocity - Depth - Customization
Exploratory Strategic Actions	- Reach - Breadth - Visibility	- Distributed - Multiple perspectives - Local autonomy	- Reach - Breadth - Distributed - Multiple perspectives	- Adaptability - Breadth

Transaction-focused investment facilitates exploitation by handling business transactions (both within an enterprise and with external parties) faster and more reliably (that is, fewer errors or steps), thereby increasing productivity and responsiveness as well as lowering costs. Transaction-focused investment facilitates exploration by increasing both the number of potential parties with whom transactions can be executed and the potential types of transactions that can be handled, as well as by increasing the visibility of transactional events across the extended enterprise. This last point has become extremely important today with most firms finding themselves having to expose data about key business events—orders, deliveries, low inventory levels—to customers or suppliers and likewise expecting their strategic partners to do the same. With increased information visibility across supply chains and value nets, business models and value propositions that were unimaginable only a few years ago have become the norm.

Decision-focused investment facilitates exploitation by enabling decision automation through the embedding of decision rules within software as well as by providing employees with enhanced information and proven decision filters for decision situations that are not automated. Decisions are made faster, more reliably, and more completely, thus increasing decision quality and responsiveness as well as employee productivity. This lowers costs and better aligns products and/or services with customer requirements. Decision focused investment facilitates exploration by enabling decision authority to be distributed more widely, by increasing the number of perspectives brought to bear on a decision, and by allowing more discretion to employees closest to a decision. Emerging opportunities are more likely to be recognized, interpreted from a variety of perspectives, and acted on.

Intellectual capital-focused investment facilitates exploitation by codifying, archiving, making accessible, embedding in processes and decision schemas, and transferring across the firm the knowledge that has been acquired and created. This use of knowledge regarding the firm's product-markets, as well as the assets and activities needed to enhance strategic positions in them, produces deeper, more consistent thought, purpose, and ability across the firm. Intellectual capital–focused investment facilitates explo-ration by extending a firm's "intelligence at the edge." It does this by enhancing sensing and interpretation, increasing the number and variety of accessible external sources of knowledge, increasing firm-wide visibility into what is happening at the firm's edges, and enabling specialized knowledge sources to be easily estab-lished, promoted and accessed.

Relationship-focused investment facilitates exploitation by tight-ening relationships across a firm and between a firm and its trusted partners. Within a firm, it provides collaborative work environ-ments in which the insight of all employees involved in fashion-ing and maintaining a strategic position can be brought to bear without regard for time, location, or positions. Externally, it cre-ates resilient links with partners that enable the firm's ability to

Research Insight

Professor John Henderson on Business Architecture

John Henderson, the Richard C. Shipley Professor of Management and Faculty Director, Information Systems Department, at the Boston University School of Management, conducts research on the strategic impact of tech-nology. In this excerpt from an interview, he discusses how some companies gain a competitive edge using technology.

The "Edge" Organization

"The companies that have sus-tained strong performances—Kraft, P&G, Wal-Mart, BP, UPS, Progressive—have had strong IT organizations. They have committed to technology and evolved their capability to manage information technology strategically, and they have continued to stay in front.

"It's because they have good leadership. Leadership is a differ-entiator of companies. Technology is not a differentiator. It's about the effectiveness of the leaders on both the IT side and the line side.

Emerging architectures
"We're moving away from a busi-ness architecture defined by processes toward an architecture that combines both process and infrastructure. It is defined in terms of things like the ability to inno-vate, adapt, and respond to the marketplace.

"A business platform that allows

you that agility requires you to have both some centralized control over shared services and decentralized management of market-based capabilities. It requires a lot of shared vision among the leadership. At the end of the day, you measure your success on your ability to acquire or absorb innovation. For example, if your business platform allows you to spin off companies or to acquire companies and to do that in a way that meets the economic expectations of the investors, then you have achieved IT and business alignment.

"It means that you have the ability to launch products and services in the marketplace with faster cycle times. You have the ability to cross-sell or integrate your product portfolio to a customer. In the old days, business architectures were market based— meaning my architecture recognized that I had businesses and processes lined up with markets. My architecture had notions of channel and geography in it. Today, I see more and more the notion of a business architecture being my ability to drive innovation and to be agile in the marketplace. I call them edge organizations."

The story at Sears
"An example is Sears Home Services. It had a business architecture defined in terms of geography, meaning regions and districts, an organization structure on top of that and an information system set up to support that business architecture.
"They consolidated all the

information systems in one location. They dispatch and manage 12,000 service people daily, delivering parts directly to the home of the service person. And they have automated the customer transaction system. So the Sears person drives into the driveway of the customer and flips on his 802.11 mobile WiFi. He gets out of his truck with a laptop connected to the truck, and the truck's connected back to headquarters, and when he does a purchase or a parts order, it's real time in front of the customer, directly connected to the ERP systems of the business.

"It's a good example of an organization that at one level became more centralized, because they brought the information flows into a centralized organization. But on another level, they became extremely decentralized. They drive everything at the edge of the organization. Every service person works out of his house and can coordinate with people adjacent to them to adapt to a change in a customer need. It's neither centralized nor decentralized—it's an information-enabled edge organization.

"It's not technology that drives the success. It's the fact that they've created a completely different business model. Everybody at the edge of the organization knows as much about the customer as anyone at the central part of the organization, and they know at the same time.

"The role of leadership in that organization is different. On the business side, one of the things that happened was a significant delayering. Supervisors became coaches who recognize patterns and create conditions for success. Individuals at the edge became more responsible. The leadership is more about thinking through conditions and products and capabilities needed to succeed than it is the day-to-day supervising of activities.

"The result? They've had huge savings in parts management, huge increases in productivity, and significant increases in customer satisfaction. Over the last ten years, it has gone from being one of several players to being the dominant service provider in the United States. It's gained huge market share."

work with them and understand them better. Relationship-focused investment facilitates exploration by broadening relationships across a firm and with partners and allowing them to be easily formed or disbanded. As a consequence, a breadth of assets, skills, and competencies become available to identify, assess, and act on opportunities. Just as important, those associated with underperforming positions can be reassigned or eliminated.

To illustrate the many and varied roles served by business technology and supporting investments, consider the action initiated by Herman Miller in the late 1990s to stake a strategic position in an underserved market—that of offering small businesses no-frills, quality furnishings delivered quickly at a reasonable price.[9] In accomplishing this strategic initiative, Miller established a new operating unit, Herman Miller SQA (Simple, Quick and Affordable), and introduced a flurry of innovations that have since migrated into the parent company:

- Local dealers are provided with innovative 3D visualizing tools and product configurators that are used in consulting with customers about a potential order—furniture, design styles, fabrics, wood finishes, space layout, and so on (decision-, intellectual capital-, and relationship- focused business technology investments).

- When the dealer and customer have reached agreement on an order, the software creates an order list with all parts and the final price (decision- and transaction- focused investments).

- As soon as the order is accepted, it is sent via the Internet to a Miller SQA manufacturing facility, where it enters production and logistics scheduling systems. Within two hours, the dealer and customer receive confirmation of delivery and installation dates (decision-, relationship-, and transaction- focused investments).

- Miller SQA's supply net transparently links its many suppliers to its operations, streamlining purchasing, inventory, and production processes. Here, the 500 suppliers are provided visibility into the data in Miller SQA's systems and are expected to automatically send more materials when needed (decision-, relationship-, intellectual capital-, and transaction-focused investments).

> *Success comes from imbuing assets with firm-specific structure and content, embedding these in business architectures enabling business strategies to unfold, and managing these assets with BTM.*

By applying business technology exceptionally well in both exploitative and exploratory ways, Miller SQA reduced an industry order cycle of about 14 weeks to about 2 weeks and, in the process, redefined what was required for competitive success in this product-market niche.

At first glance, the Herman Miller example belies the notion that technology assets are, for the most part, commodities. However, with a deeper look, it becomes clear that success was achieved from more than IT investment alone. True success came from imbuing these assets with firm-specific structure and content, and by embedding these within business architectures enabling business strategies to unfold, and by providing careful management of these assets through a well-honed set of BTM capabilities. In this way, these "commodities" can be transformed into value-adding assets.

How does a firm like Herman Miller determine appropriate investment levels? One approach to answering this question begins with the firm's strategic learning orientation.

Firms can have two types of strategic learning

Statements extolling the desirability of being lean, being agile, or both reverberate throughout the business press and strategic consultancies. However, building lean or agile organizations requires substantial investment and carries strategic risks. A lean firm can become blind to the emergent opportunities that eventually overtake a favorable strategic position; an agile firm can lack the discipline required to sustain a favorable strategic position.

It is important to realize that not all firms need to be lean or agile. Figure 2.3 provides a way to think about this based on the organizational learning orientation (that is, the types of learning behaviors emphasized and required by the nature of the product-market within which a firm has taken a strategic position). Two very distinct strategic learning orientations exist:

- Single-loop learning refers to the efforts taken to continuously monitor performance against plan, learn from deviations, and embed this learning in action. Single-loop learning is most effective for a relatively stable business environment where new understanding can be accumulated and aggressively applied in improving performance. Such a learning orientation is necessary in furthering exploitative, or lean, strategic actions. For example, single-loop learning has been turned into an art form by firms such as McDonalds, whose business model involves determining the most efficient operational processes within a fast-food environment and then replicating this best practice across all it retail outlets.

- Double-loop learning refers to continuously challenging assumptions about a given operating area and quickly adjusting operating practices when the assumptions are proven invalid. Double-loop learning is most effective for a relatively dynamic business environment. Such a learning orientation is necessary in furthering exploratory, or agile, strategic action. For example, double-loop learning has been turned into an art form by firms such as Benetton, whose business model involves understanding the frequent shifts in global and local fashion trends in order to quickly emphasize hot product lines, drop cold product lines, and design new product lines in response to current or emerging tastes.

Figure 2.3 **Strategic Positions Vary with Market Conditions**

Different levels of product-market competitiveness and stability require different strategic positions and levels of business technology investment.

Four categories of product-markets are depicted in Figure 2.3. Note the dollar signs, which indicate the relative business technology investment required to maintain strategic positions in each.

The status quo cell in Figure 2.3 is intuitive. If a strategic position enjoys little competition and exhibits stability over time, then few, if any, strategic actions need to be implemented to sustain it. Historically, firms in highly regulated industries or isolated geographic areas enjoyed the luxury of holding a status quo market position. It is not that being lean or being agile is "bad" for firms in this status quo cell, but rather that the significant investments required to become lean or agile are not necessary. Finally, the fourth quadrant—"leagility" (that is, lean *and* agile)—at first glance might seem contradictory. Given these very different firm behaviors (each of which require distinctive business architectures), can a firm be both lean and agile? Manufacturing theorists argue that with appropriately designed business systems, it is quite possible to exhibit both leanness and agility.[10] The manufacturing solution involves designing decoupling points into supply chains such that upstream from the decoupling points processes are lean, whereas downstream processes are agile. In other words, upstream work processes are highly optimized and tightly integrated; however, downstream processes are customized and only loosely integrated via selective data sharing with other work processes. For example, if assembly is postponed until customer orders are received, then customized assembly operations can respond to specific customer requests; but the upstream inbound logistics and component manufacturing activities can be very lean. Thus, activities prior to the decoupling point are "push driven" by forecasts and designed to be as efficient as possible, whereas activities after the decoupling point are "pull driven" and designed for customization and responsiveness.

Leadership Insight

Christopher Wrenn on Culture

As Managing Director and COO of HVB Americas, with responsibility for business technology, Christopher Wrenn helped create a cultural change at the bank that encourages business and technology executives to work in harmony.

Beware the Cocktail-Party Solution

To support a new business vision, HVB Americas, the New York-based branch of Germany's second largest bank, began investing in information technology in a big way in 1998.

As it did, Christopher Wrenn, Managing Director and COO, with responsibility for business technology, was very careful about requirements definitions. "We were not going to have any cocktail-party solutions," he said in an interview.

"We have all experienced the Monday-morning meeting in which somebody reports that, at a cocktail-party, they talked to a person who has the solution to all our IT problems. They say, and by the way I already called the vendor, and he's coming this afternoon. The vendor may have a great solution, but there's no way anything but a small subset of our requirements was talked about at that cocktail party."

Many people—in business, operations, finance, and compliance—need to contribute requirements for any application, he says. "If it's just the business person, the other users are unlikely to get what they want. So we started bringing all the players to the table. The interesting thing is that we created a culture in which everybody is talking about the same problem. And they began working together. Suddenly, we had technology people learning about the business and the operations and we had the business and operations people learning about the technology."

In this cultural shift, technology became an integral part of the business. "And now if we get involved in any kind of technology project here, people automatically know the drill. They watch out for each other. 'Oh, if I do this, it affects that guy.'"

A need to grow

The HVB Americas investment in technology began because the bank wanted to expand its higher margin businesses by offering more structured capital market products. The Americas operation was seen as a crucible for developing these new products.

But nearly everything in the Americas branch was manual. "When we started, we had a variety of disparate systems," Wrenn says. "Everything was so manual we couldn't expand our business without adding headcount. Take

foreign exchange, one of the most commoditized products. Any one transaction could have been entered manually in up to seven systems. Imagine how cumbersome and error prone that is. Expanding that business would have meant just adding people to do the work in a low margin business. So we had to find a way to connect all these systems so that we only have to input it one time. And it flows straight through, front to back."

The "Big Dig"

The work moved on to money markets, then lending products, and is now moving into securities and derivatives. "In some cases, it was like paving over the cow path," Wrenn says. "The processes weren't all that bad. But in other cases, we needed to do a lot of process re-engineering. That's because people were missing at the table and not all their requirements were understood and delineated. We went from paving a cow path to the 'Big Dig.'"

One thing in HVB's favor was its four-member management committee, of which Wrenn is a part. It meets weekly, and IT is a recurring topic. "So IT receives senior management attention," Wrenn says. "It's not just those guys down in the basement running computers." IT reports monthly on the status of every project.

The benefits of its technology initiative have been tangible. Eliminating manual inputting of data has reduced errors, saving time and money. The quality of data has improved significantly, leading to fewer compliance and reporting problems.

All told, he estimates that the bank has saved approximately $3 million a year.

"You need to look at IT as a precious resource, and if you have a business vision, you've got to have someone monitor that resource and use it to drive your business vision. If the senior people don't recognize the importance of that, if they don't get involved, then they do so at their peril."

In this new culture, everyone sees himself or herself as a technologist, Wrenn says. "But I'd rather have that problem than one where you just throw it over the fence and hope those guys in IT come back with something, And then you blame the IT guys when it doesn't work. That's crazy."

Applying similar architectural design principles, Figure 2.4 depicts how a firm might fabricate a very exploitative architecture consisting of common, tightly coupled data, decision, and process structures but then insert decoupling points to a variety of loosely coupled architectural environments that allow for more exploratory strategic actions. Consider, for example, the business architecture supporting a technical call center. Most customer support calls involve either quite routine problems or are from customer segments providing low profitability margins. As a result, very lean, automated business architectures are commonly applied via an archived problem solution repository accessed directly by customers via a Web interface or through customer support representatives following tightly written scripts. However, the processes used in dealing with unusual, highly technical problems or from customer segments providing high profit margins are typically decoupled from this very lean business. Although the investment in designing, implementing, and evolving such ambidextrous business architectures is high, the advantage of being able to maintain favorable strategic positions in competitive, dynamic product-markets far outweighs the cost.

Figure 2.4 **A "Leagile" Architecture**

A firm can have an exploitative architecture with "decoupling" points for explorative activity.

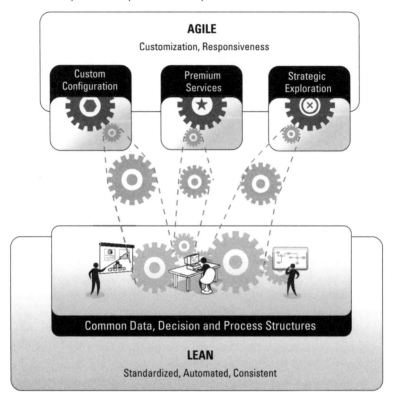

Business technology investment changes with strategic positioning

The heated debates throughout the 1990s regarding the "IT productivity paradox" seems to have dissipated with the general acceptance of two insights:

1. IT assets (hardware, software, communication networks, and so on) *by themselves* add little, if any, economic value.

2. The added-value nature of IT assets materializes through their *appropriate* use in fabricating business platforms that deliver products or services and business solutions that address emergent opportunities and problems. An appropriate use of business technology reflects (1) that investments are based on sound business cases; (2) that complementary investments (in data collection and organization, business process redesign, employee skill development, employee incentive structures, and so forth) are executed; and (3) that the business technology-related activities associated with investment initiatives are themselves well executed. For these three conditions to be met, a management standard, such as the BTM Standard fusing business and technology acumen, must exist.

> *In applying business technology to develop or sustain strategic positions, firms may very well be underinvesting or overinvesting in IT assets, business technology, or BTM capabilities, or all three, even though they might benchmark well with other firms.*

An additional insight follows directly from the recognition that there are actually three forms of investment—IT assets (for example, hardware and software), business technology (applying these IT assets to meet business needs), and BTM (managing business and technology together)—and the realization that different product-markets are likely to involve very different levels of investment.

Desired levels of investment in IT assets, business technology, and in BTM capabilities vary depending on the strategic learning orientation of the targeted product-market. As a result, in applying business technology to develop or sustain strategic positions, firms may very well be underinvesting or overinvesting in IT assets, business technology, or in BTM capabilities, or in all three, even though they might benchmark well with other firms.

Figure 2.5 contrasts IT, business technology, and BTM capability investment levels across the four product-market situations. As might be expected, the lowest investment levels would be seen with firms focused on maintaining the status quo, and the largest would be seen with firms having to build the ambidextrous business architectures associated with leagility. The investment in IT assets and business technology required by a lean strategic posture is likely to be greater than that to maintain an agile posture because the emphasis on optimizing work processes via common process and data models requires substantial investment and reinvestment in interoperable technology platforms. However, investments in BTM capabilities are very likely to be greater for firms building and evolving agile strategic postures because of (1) the firm-specific, action-specific nature of the roles served by business technology in enabling strategic actions and (2) the requirement that management capabilities—in particular, BTM

Figure 2.5 IT/Business Technology and BTM Capability Investment Levels

The ratio and relative level of investments in IT, business technology, and BTM capabilities will differ depending on a firm's strategic orientation.

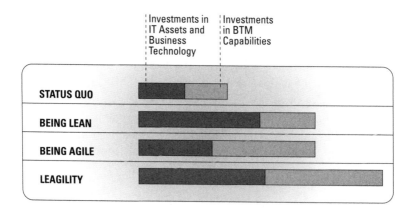

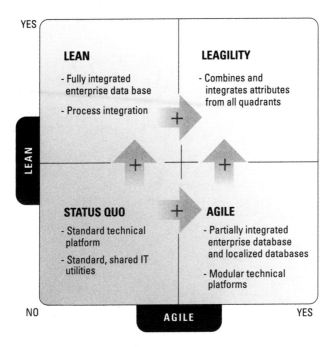

Figure 2.6 **IT and Business Technology Investment Mixes**

The types of IT and business technology investments will vary depending on a firm's strategic orientation.

capabilities—be exercised across a constant stream of new product-market positions and innovative strategic actions.

Figures 2.6 and 2.7 depict how investment levels in IT/business technology and BTM capabilities might be expected to differ in supporting these four product-market situations. In Figure 2.6, the lowest level of investment is had with the lower-left cell (neither lean nor agile) and the greatest level of investment is had with the upper-right cell (both lean and agile). Also, the arrows in the figures indicate that the investments in a target cell (for example, upper left) also include the investments in a source cell (for example, lower left). In Figure 2.7, an organization operating in the status quo quadrant will typically focus on the highlighted BTM capabilities, while prioritizing the development of others.

Operating in, or moving toward, the agile or lean quadrants requires that the organization expand its focus to include additional BTM capabilities, while still prioritizing the development of others. Finally, moving toward the Leagility quadrant means that all of the BTM capabilities must be developed to achieve and maintain this strategic orientation.

As a firm discovers through BTM the right level and mix of investments, it will also discover whether its IT function has the depth and expertise to deliver what is expected—a large and complex firm requires a higher level of sophistication in its technology. Size and complexity also suggest much greater potential benefit from effective BTM.

Figure 2.7   BTM Capability Investment Mixes
How a firm prioritizes its investments in BTM capabilities will vary depending on its strategic orientation.

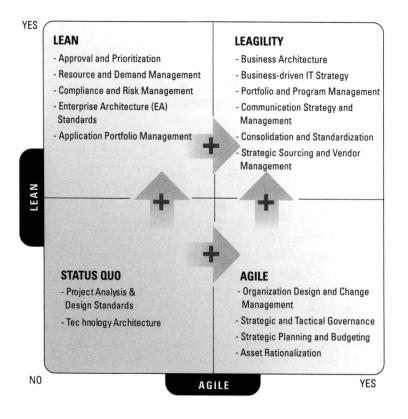

Strategic Positioning

▶ **Review** your firm's strategic position, as well as your business strategy and IT strategy formulation activities. Are marketplace and competitive analyses part of these activities? Is the role of business technology prominent in these analyses? Is strategic experimentation used to better understand the roles served by business technology investment in acquiring and sustaining favorable market positions?

▶ **Determine** how IT and business technology investments are handled in your firm's strategic planning and budgeting activities. To what extent do investment levels across operating units reflect the role that business technology actually serves in enabling strategic positions? To what extent do investment levels across staff or support units reflect the role that business technology actually serves in enabling these units to accomplish their mission? Are the baselines for such analyses founded on historical grounds, industry benchmarks or carefully selected (that is, strategically and operationally comparable) peer groups?

▶ **Assess** the existence and maturity of BTM capabilities across the enterprise. Which BTM capabilities, given the role that business technology serves in enabling your firm's strategic posture, need to be maintained at world-class levels? Has sufficient investment in BTM capabilities occurred at an enterprise level and within each business unit?

▶ **Answer** these questions: Is your business strategy and strategic position well communicated and understood across the organization? Are your organization's business strategies reflective of exploitative strategic actions, exploratory strategic actions, or both? What roles do your business technology investments play in enabling these strategic actions?

▶ **Develop,** after these questions are understood, an appropriate mix of the various kinds of business technology to advance your firm's strategic agenda. Technology thus becomes a significant tool for the CEO and the board.

Notes

1   See the "Key Terminology" section in Chapter 1.

2   Ibid.

3   Ibid.

4   Treacy, M. and Wiersma, F. D. *The Discipline of Market Leaders: Choose Your Customers, Narrow Your Focus, Dominate Your Market.* Addison-Wesley, 1995.

5   See the "Key Terminology" section in Chapter 1.

6   Premkumar, G., Richardson, V. J., and Zmud, R. W. "Sustaining Competitive Advantage through a Value Net: The Case of Enterprise Rent-A-Car." *MISQ Executive* (December 2004), 189–199.

7   O'Reilly, C. A. III. and Tushman, M. L. "The Ambidextrous Organization." *Harvard Business Review* (April 2004): 74–81.

8   Christensen, C. M. *The Innovator's Dilemma: When New Technologies Cause Great Firms to Fail.* Harvard Business School Press, Boston, 1997.

9   Prahalad, C. K. and Ramaswamy, V. *The Future of Competition.* Harvard Business School Press, Boston 2004; Rocks, D. "Reinventing Herman Miller." *Business Week.* On-Line, April 3, 2000.

10 Van Hoek, R. I. "The Thesis of Leagility Revisited." *International Journal of Agile Management Systems* (Vol. 2, No. 3, 2000) 196–201.

3

"If you take Dell and Wal-Mart and Cisco and a few other companies that have excelled in the use of information technology, you quickly conclude that just because everyone has access to the same tools and technology, you don't get the same results at all; in fact, you have vastly different results."

—Michael Dell, Chairman, Dell, Inc.

Making the Right Investments

In Brief

A business-driven IT strategy articulates the business capabilities required for success.

This clear understanding of business requirements dictates the technology plans and appropriate business technology investments to execute the firm's business strategy.

Aligning business technology investments with business strategy is done by focusing on the type of value that the firm seeks to create.

Decisions on business technology[1] investments require structured thinking about business goals. BTM provides an approach for this through its Business-Driven IT Strategy capability.

This chapter shows how this BTM capability[2] aligns the enterprise business strategy, enterprise IT strategy, and IT function strategy to enable corporate goals and deliver desired levels of stability and agility. Contributing authors for this chapter are Varun Grover, William S. Lee Distinguished Professor of Information Systems at Clemson University; Michael Fillios, Chief Product Officer; James Lebinski, Vice President of Knowledge Products, at Enamics, Inc; and Arun Rai, the Harkins Chaired Professor, Department of Computer Information Systems from the Robinson College of Business at Georgia State University.

Business technology executives have different notions about technology strategy. Most of these notions are wrong.

For some, it means high-level summary statements about the direction of IT. For others, it consists of a tactical set of plans around a major application suite, such as an integrated enterprise resource planning (ERP) application. These limited views represent the conventional wisdom across most industries and within most organizations. They have little or nothing to offer when it comes to creating and sustaining true alignment (let alone synchronization or convergence) of business and technology.

BTM solves this problem by providing a holistic, comprehensive approach. The *Business-Driven IT Strategy* capability focuses on using business technology[3] to enable the business models and competencies required to execute the business strategy.

Business strategy must start at the top, with the board of directors, executive committee, and office of the CIO being the key stakeholders. Without this level of involvement, management teams are far more likely to experience business technology-related failures, and then to focus more on the symptoms than on the root cause. When you hear that "IT just doesn't understand the needs of the business" or "they don't deliver" or "what they're giving us we don't need," you're seeing the symptoms of an organization without a business-driven IT strategy.

Required business capabilities must be identified

A business-driven IT strategy begins by articulating capabilities necessary to achieve the business strategy, and then the technology needed to enable those capabilities. Intimate knowledge of the business architecture, operating models, capabilities, and processes are actionable inputs for an astute Business Technology Management[4] team. In fact, true business-driven IT strategy incorporates three critical elements: enterprise business strategy, enterprise IT strategy, and IT function strategy (see Figure 3.1).

The *Enterprise Business Strategy* outlines the strategic goals, imperatives, and initiatives that the company is pursuing, including specific business capabilities that make it all happen. There may be an overarching business strategy for a group of business units (for example, shared services across multiple business units); however, each business unit is likely to be pursuing strategies specific to its segments as well.

Figure 3.1   Business-Driven IT Strategy

A Business-Driven IT Strategy incorporates the enterprise business strategy, enterprise IT strategy, and IT function strategy.

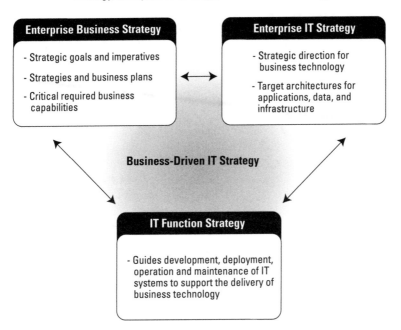

The *Enterprise IT Strategy* outlines the strategic direction for business technology. It specifies a plan for deploying the technology to meet business capability needs and to support the business strategy. It can actually help shape the enterprise business strategy when enabling technologies are available to create sustainable competitive advantage.

The *IT Function Strategy* outlines how the IT function develops, deploys, operates, and supports the IT systems needed to deliver business technology. Consequently, it is driven by both the Enterprise Business Strategy and Enterprise IT Strategy. In turn, these higher-level strategies may be limited or enabled by the capacity and abilities of the IT function. The function level includes IT assets that support processes and infrastructure across organizations and locations, including centralized IT groups, satellite IT groups, and people performing IT roles in the business user areas.

In thinking about business technology investments, a basic four-step process should be followed (see Figure 3.2). Defining

Figure 3.2 **The Four Steps of Business Technology Investment Decisions**

Determining business technology investments must begin with a solid understanding of an organization's strategy, goals, and objectives.

Business Technology Investment Decision Making

Define firm strategy, goals and objectives by considering

- Short and long-term strategy and objectives
- IT enablers
- Posture and levels of stability or agility required

Determine required business capabilities

- Specify capabilities needed to meet goals and objectives and execute strategy
- Identify potential business technology enablers

Identify and prioritize required capabilities to be pursued

- Evaluate capabilities
- Identify deficits
- Prioritize remediation or development

Define/select IT investments

- Create high prioritiy capabilities
- Adopt a portfolio approach
- Manage primary and secondary capability development

Types of Business Technology Enabled Capabilities to Pursue

Externally Focused

Internally Focused

Exploitative Capabilities

- Improve existing ways of working
- Processes enhanced through business technology
- Business technology enabled leverage of knowledge assets and relationship capital

Explorative Capabilities

- Identify new marketplace opportunities
- Create value through business technology
  - New products and services
  - New ways of working with customers, suppliers, and partners

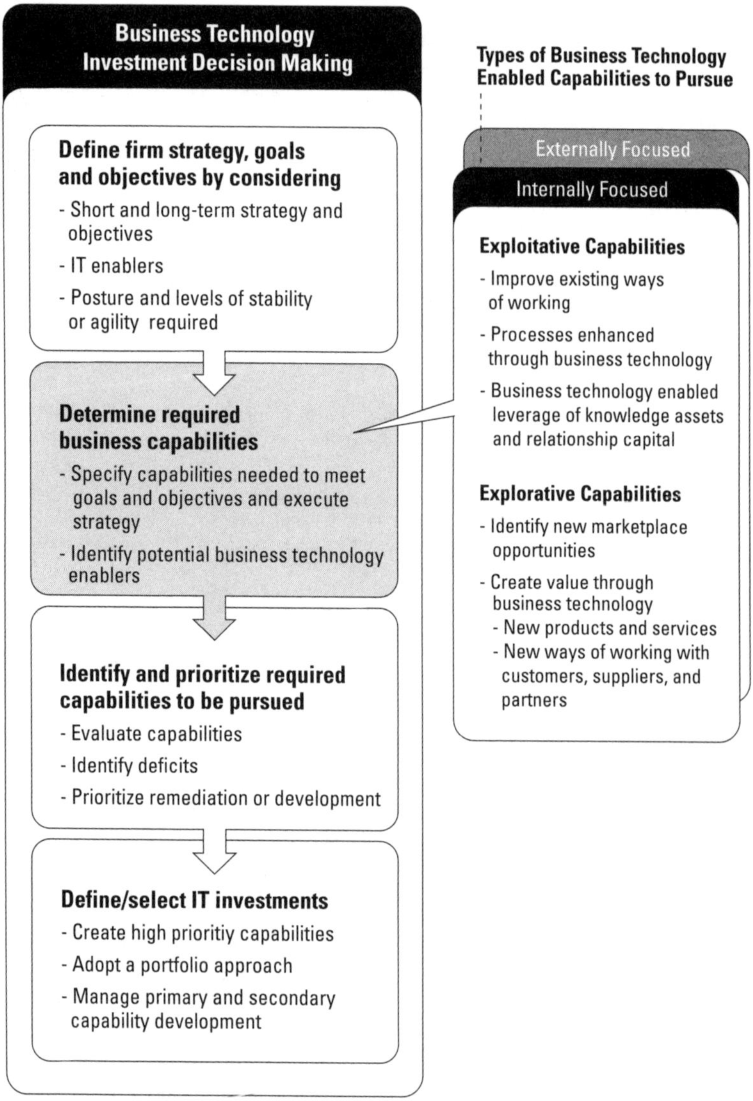

and selecting business capabilities are the most critical decisions a firm can make with regard to business technology investments. Selecting the right capabilities is also a very complex undertaking, requiring a thorough analysis of the business.

Required business capabilities start with strategic positioning

Chapter 2, "Strategic Positions," described various product-market conditions, the ways in which organizations learn about and respond to these conditions, and the characteristics of leanness, agility, or even "leagility." All of these factors impact investments in business technology because they are central to defining required business capabilities. Defining these capabilities, however, also requires the selection of "value disciplines" for the organization as well as the "value type" it is looking to create.

Value discipline refers to the primary advantage the company seeks to achieve in the marketplace. The choice of a value discipline shapes the company's subsequent strategies and underlying

Leadership Insight

Daniel Hartert on CIOs

Daniel Hartert, SVP and CIO at Royal Philips Electronics, who has five divisional CIOs reporting to him, says it is essential that CIOs understand how to contribute to a firm's strategic decisions.

IT *Is* the Business

Daniel Hartert joined Royal Philips Electronics as CIO in 2002 and a year later was named to the Group Management Committee, the highest consultative body in the company. From that perspective, he makes a wry observation about CIOs and other CXOs.

"You go to so many CIO conferences and all you hear is, what is the role of the CIO? I can't stand it anymore," he said in an interview. "In finance, are they discussing in their conferences the role of the CFO? No. They see themselves as part of the business. And chief marketing officers. What is the role of the CMO? How can we align with the business? No. They are the business. For me, it is the same thing—IT is part of the business."

Unlike other companies, he says, "In Philips, IT is recognized as essential to reaching company targets." Each of the company's five product divisions has a CIO, and Hartert wants them to play a strategic role. "Not CIOs who have to manage people running PC support. We need people who can join management discussions, contribute to strategic decisions, who can really help show their colleagues in management new ways to leverage technology to do more on the business side. When it comes to commodity services, I don't expect CIOs to run that. We can outsource it. Where IT provides the value, where it comes closest to the business and business processes, there I need the brightest people."

CIOs, he says, should be able to think as entrepreneurs but also know how to execute. "They can't be just idea generators. They must know how to adapt business processes to make ideas work. The CIO has to be aware of what's going on in the technology world, but it's more important to know how to use technology for the business." At Philips, IT projects are managed as a portfolio, with each linked to business strategy and scored in terms of its business benefits.

Hartert thinks the disconnect between CIOs and other CXOs has several causes. For one thing, it does not help when a CIO comes into a company and undoes everything his predecessor did.

Then there is the CIO's perception, which is also reality to some degree, that everybody on the other side does not understand what he or she is doing. "And to some extent, it's correct. HR people really don't need to know how IT works. They should measure it by results. But IT is the big unknown, and because of that, CIOs are often defensive. And when they are defensive, they start to talk their own language. Then they see themselves as people who understand how it works but aren't able to explain it. And a lot of CIOs really don't have business experience. They were always supporting the back office in the basement somewhere. That doesn't train your brain."

operating model. Using a model developed by Michael Treacy and Fred Wiersema in *The Discipline of Market Leaders*, leading companies keep their edge by picking one discipline and executing primarily toward it. Examples include the following:

* *Customer intimacy*—Enabled by cultivating close and long-term customer relationships driven by intimate knowledge of customer requirements, creating a dependency of customized service and support, and a focus primarily on customer retention and satisfaction. According to Treacy and Wiersema, a company that delivers value through customer intimacy does not deliver what the market wants, but rather what a specific customer wants. Therefore, the company's greatest asset is its customer loyalty.

- *Operational excellence*—Enabled by offering a combination of quality, price, and ease of purchase that no one else in the market can match. The focus is primarily on executing extraordinarily well, guaranteeing low prices and hassle-free services, standardizing, and simplifying. Operationally excellent companies not only promise the lowest total cost, according to Treacy and Wiersema, but are able to do it 365 days a year.

- *Product leadership*—Enabled by focusing primarily on innovation and development of products that push performance boundaries. The organization invents, develops, and markets with tremendous speed, making its own products obsolete. A product leader's proposition to customers, according to Treacy and Wiersema, is best product, period!

Increasingly, companies are finding that they have to excel in multiple postures to maintain industry leadership.

Value type refers to the nature of the value that a company seeks to create. There are stability and agility dimensions to business value creation. *Stability* refers to the extent to which operations can be made efficient, effective, and predictable. *Agility* refers to the extent to which the organization can identify new opportunities and seize them by responding appropriately (see Figure 3.3).

The following example applies the concept of using a value discipline and desired value type to identify potential business capabilities and business technology enablers. Building on the example presented in Figure 3.2, Figure 3.4 shows that if this customer-intimate organization seeks to support stability, its value discipline dictates a need to improve part of its overall supply chain (that is, working better with suppliers) as well as customer relationship management or CRM (that is, its processes for resolving customer issues). Its agility-related value discipline involves acquiring new marketing representatives, monitoring the external environment, and using advanced pricing techniques.

In this example, the organization's quest for customer intimacy involved performing a broad-based, root cause analysis on its entire portfolio of related assets and activities to confirm the real reasons that a particular business capability did not exist at the required level. In the preceding example, a root cause analysis revealed that the business technology investments needed to go beyond the simple implementation of new business applications and warranted an improvement in the underlying infrastructure. Identifying the right technology enablers is therefore a critical piece of the overall puzzle.

The stability and agility-related business capabilities in our example are generated by very specific exploitative or explorative business technology enablers. As discussed in Chapter 2, business technology can enable two different types of business capabilities: exploitative and explorative.

Figure 3.3 **Value Disciplines and Value Types**

Organizations focus on selected value disciplines and seek to create corresponding value types.

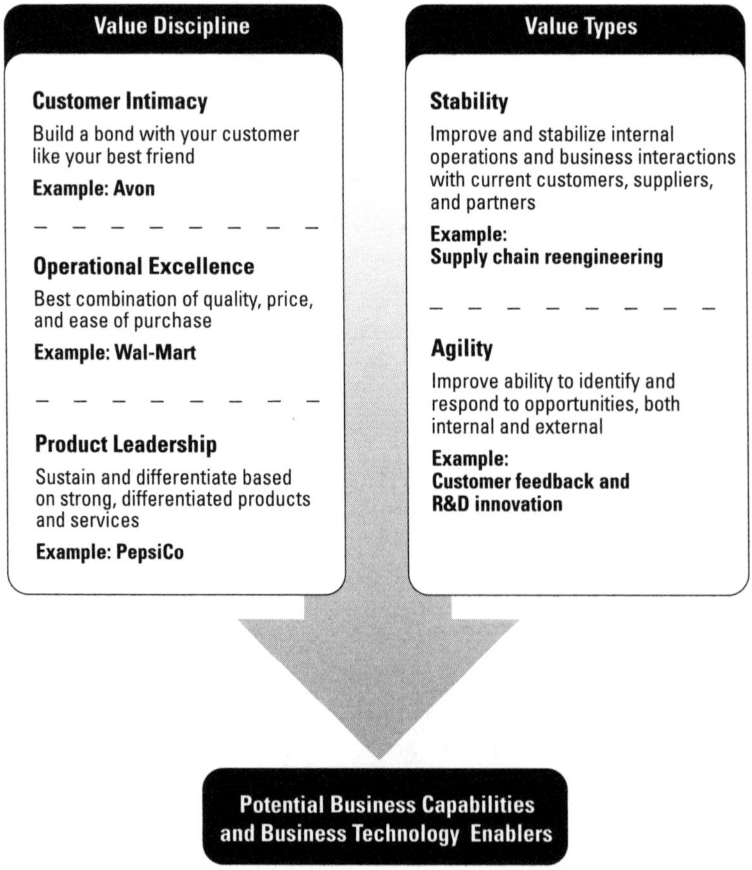

Value Discipline	Value Types
Customer Intimacy Build a bond with your customer like your best friend **Example: Avon**	**Stability** Improve and stabilize internal operations and business interactions with current customers, suppliers, and partners **Example:** **Supply chain reengineering**
Operational Excellence Best combination of quality, price, and ease of purchase **Example: Wal-Mart**	**Agility** Improve ability to identify and respond to opportunities, both internal and external **Example:** **Customer feedback and R&D innovation**
Product Leadership Sustain and differentiate based on strong, differentiated products and services **Example: PepsiCo**	

Potential Business Capabilities and Business Technology Enablers

Figure 3.4   **Value Discipline Choices and Investments in Business and Technology**

Business capabilities and business technology enablers are derived from decisions about an organization's value discipline and value type.

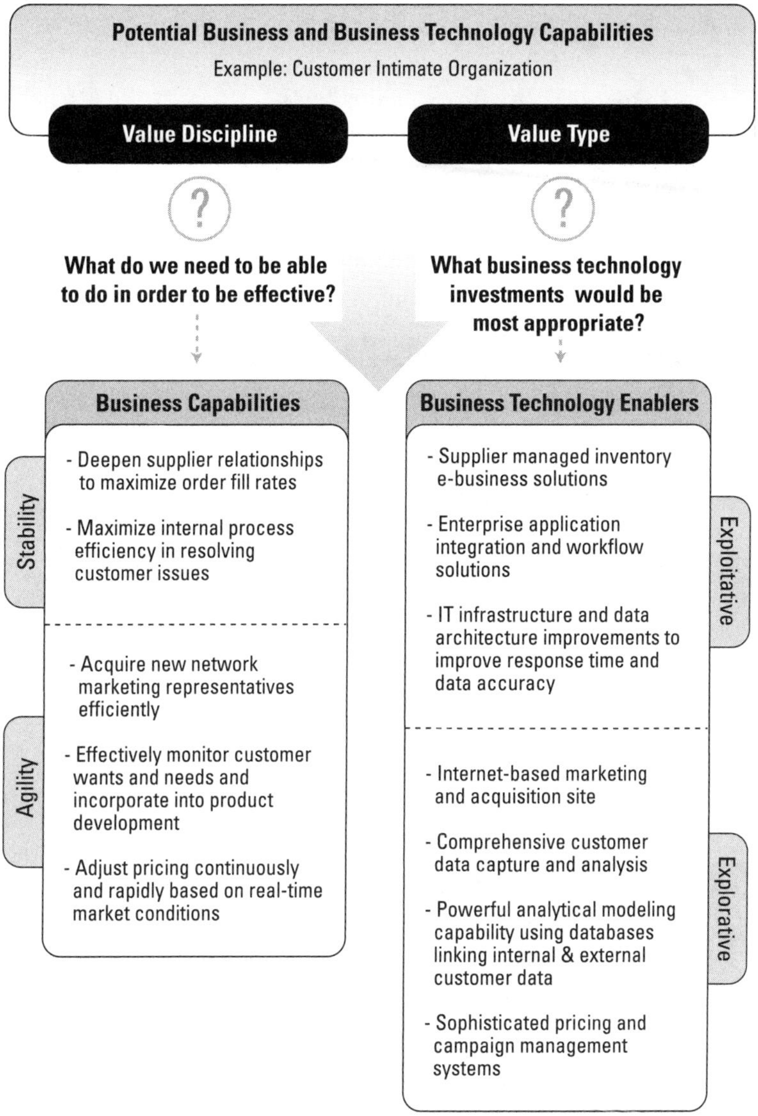

Potential Business and Business Technology Capabilities

Example: Customer Intimate Organization

Value Discipline   **Value Type**

What do we need to be able to do in order to be effective?   **What business technology investments would be most appropriate?**

Business Capabilities

Stability

- Deepen supplier relationships to maximize order fill rates

- Maximize internal process efficiency in resolving customer issues

Agility

- Acquire new network marketing representatives efficiently

- Effectively monitor customer wants and needs and incorporate into product development

- Adjust pricing continuously and rapidly based on real-time market conditions

Business Technology Enablers

Exploitative

- Supplier managed inventory e-business solutions

- Enterprise application integration and workflow solutions

- IT infrastructure and data architecture improvements to improve response time and data accuracy

Explorative

- Internet-based marketing and acquisition site

- Comprehensive customer data capture and analysis

- Powerful analytical modeling capability using databases linking internal & external customer data

- Sophisticated pricing and campaign management systems

The exploitative enablers identified in the previous example include, among other things, improvements to the underlying infrastructure. The explorative capability examples, by contrast, focus on the innovative application of business technology that results in previously unavailable business capabilities.

Exploitative capabilities leverage stable platform resources

The exploitative capabilities evidenced in Figures 3.2 and 3.4 can best be described as structured activities involving process, knowledge, and relationships. They create desirable outcomes in the form of predictable behavior with respect to key performance indicators of core processes. These key performance indicators can include response time, quality, and customer service, among others.

Leadership Insight

Steve Matheys on Convergence

Steve Matheys recently became Executive Vice President of Sales and Marketing of Schneider National—after a stint as CIO. With the CEO, also a former CIO, and Matheys' replacement, the company's top executive team will have three people with CIO experience. That is, almost by definition, "convergence."

The Three CIOs

When you see a big 18-wheeler rolling down the highway, you might think that the only information technology on board is a CB radio.

If it is a Schneider National truck, however, the driver will have a mobile communication terminal connected to the company's Green Bay, Wisconsin, headquarters for two-way communication. There will be a satellite tracking device attached to the trailer so that headquarters knows, within 50 feet, where every one of its 48,000 trailers is. Another device sends back data on engine performance. A sophisticated system processes all this and outputs 10,000 load assignments daily.

If this isn't enough indication that IT is at the heart of the company's operations, consider this: Schneider National's CEO, Christopher Lofgren, and Steve Matheys, Executive Vice President of Sales and Marketing, both previously served as the CIO.

"We are becoming a converged company," Matheys said in an interview. "The CIO reports to the CEO and is part of the executive team with a shared set of responsibilities. That brings the process and technology needs to the executive team unfiltered. It creates business-oriented discussions with the opportunity to do something with technology to change our approach in the marketplace. Those are intertwined conversations within Schneider's executive team."

IT prowess has given Schneider a marketplace edge; it is the largest truckload carrier in the United States. "Do I think IT has contributed to our growth and to our position in the marketplace? Absolutely," Matheys says.

"IT has created a competitive advantage that the marketplace recognizes. Although we have a rich history in the application of technology, it's always been driven by the business needs. How do we face our customers differently? How do we make ourselves easier to do business with? How do we drive out costs? It has never been just because someone was enamored with the latest technology craze."

Senior business leaders are integrated into steering committees to influence technology decisions. A major business processing reengineering effort started in 2001 and

overseen by business managers became a requirements generation process for the technology side. "So, it's putting those two pieces of the puzzle together on the front end in a very organized and managed fashion to feed this technology engine " Matheys says.

Typically, in the room for the presentation of a business case for a new technology implementation will be a product manager, a process manager, and eight business leaders. "There really isn't a true technician in the room," Matheys says.

Matheys says the marriage of business and technology at Schneider happens naturally. "A lot of folks would be surprised at how advanced some of those discussions are for something that would look to an outsider like just a transportation and logistics company. Why would you have that much of a technology orientation in your executive team meetings when you run lots of trucks on the highway? Well, there's a tremendous opportunity to improve the way we do business with our customers.

"The global environment creates a need for products to originate in far away places and arrive at locations scattered throughout the country, and the common ingredient for managing this is information. And this can be enhanced technologically."

In seeking to maximize an exploitative approach, organizations must rely on core business technology capabilities that are well integrated across the enterprise and leverage these stable platform resources. Ignoring this requirement has been the root cause of many of the notable failures in e-commerce. Such failures can be traced back, for instance, to the treatment of e-commerce Web sites as outside of the scope (not integrated with) of an organization's core operations. To illustrate this, consider a firm that articulates a multiple-channel strategy to interface with its customers. If the firm elects to implement a customer-facing Web site as an appendage, orders will not flow seamlessly through an end-to-end process. Without investments in the e-commerce engine and a commitment to enterprise-level integration of that platform, the result is operational inefficiencies. Operational inefficiencies can also result from a failure to harness organizational assets for core operations. This will not only result in delays but also require numerous corrections, manual interventions, and updates—all of which will result in poor product and service delivery.

> *A well-articulated business-driven IT strategy will recognize the uniqueness of exploitative and explorative capabilities, and will balance these with the desired strategic positioning of the organization.*

Conversely, the initiatives undertaken by DHL provide a good illustration of IT-enabled exploitative capabilities for value creation.

DHL, in seeking its own version of exploitative capabilities, focused on integrating business technology with its knowledge and relationship assets. It adopted a Web-based solution that enables agents, partners, managers, and other users to maintain a single view of all customer information, gain instant access to organizational knowledge, and efficiently interact with customers across multiple communication channels. It has led to vastly improved capabilities in DHL's customer service.[5] Similarly, 3M invested in creating online access through its corporate intranet to the company's enormous volume of customer content. As a result, 3M now has superior capability to service its customers who no longer need to wait while service representatives research their inquiries.

Given this discussion and these illustrations, we can conclude that exploitative business technology enablers can take the following forms:

- *Business technology and business processes*—Business technology can leverage and enhance process investments by streamlining and refining processes across the firm's internal and external business network. Common strategies include automating process tasks, increasing end-to-end process visibility, and enhancing the velocity of information transfer for improved process coordination and control.

- *Business technology and knowledge assets*—Business technology can leverage and enhance knowledge assets by codifying tacit knowledge, creating knowledge maps, identifying expertise, and broadening access to knowledge modules and decision schema that are distributed across the firm's internal and external business networks.

- *Business technology and relationship assets*—Business technology can leverage and enhance relationship assets that are distributed across the firm's internal and external business network by facilitating communication, brokerage and integration of expertise, and reducing coordination costs for relationship management.

Explorative capabilities and the dynamic leverage of options

In contrast, the examples in Figures 3.3 and 3.4 present business technology-enabled explorative capabilities, which are activities involving the configuration of technology and business resources that enable agile and novel responses to unpredictable business conditions.[6] These kinds of responses are required for the development and introduction of new products and services, definition of new customer and supplier segments, and determination of new ways to work with partners.

An illustration of explorative capabilities comes from the Southwest Bank of Texas, which uses "responsive innovation" to meet customer needs. When commercial customers asked for a more flexible and secure online processing system for credit card and check payments—one that the customers' own IT groups could manage—the bank's IT Application Development group responded in just three months. The group built templates, Web services, and a software development kit. Now, the bank's customers can extend payment processing to their own e-commerce applications, complete online transactions using the bank's "transparent" payment-processing system, enhance transaction security, brand their sites, switch payment-processing service providers, and better control the payment process.[7]

As a second illustration of explorative capabilities, take the case of Advance Transformer, a company specializing in commercial lighting products. It began its most recent transformation in 1999, when, weighed down by an aging IT infrastructure, it

Leadership Insight

Alain Poussereau on Alignment

Alain Poussereau, an experienced business technology executive named best CIO in France in 2001 by EURO CIO, has his work cut out for him now. As head of the IT department of the country's retirement branch, he must meet growing citizen demands for services with shrinking resources.

Seeking Agility

As one of the largest and most complex government agencies in France, the retirement branch employs more than 10,000 people, with approximately 2,000 of them in the IT function. The branch is now undergoing a major business and technological transformation. The organization has a CIO for each of its 20 regions.

"As with many other public and private entities, the branch, Caisse Nationale d'Assurance Viellesse (CNAV), has been focus-ing on delivering more and more services by information technology," Alain Poussereau, who heads the IT division, said in an interview. "We must provide these services to meet the growing needs of our citizens." For example, citizens want to get quick and accurate information on their accounts through the Internet.

At the same time, however, Poussereau faces a looming personnel problem. More than 6,000 employees will retire from the branch between now and 2012. As this occurs, the workload is expected to increase by 50 percent, due to the baby boom generation reaching retirement.

"These two constraints, along with the change management implications, will have a material impact on our eight-year plan," Poussereau says, "resulting in the need for cost savings and operational efficiency throughout the branch." And so one key objective is to increase overall productivity by 25 percent. A main contributor to these productivity increases will be the improvements in processing retirees, from claims to payments; this is the central activity of the branch.

Consequently, the branch is aggressively developing a technology architecture to achieve agility, flexibility, and simplicity in processing the huge number of transactions it faces—with the goal of reducing costs. Simultaneously, it is rationalizing its applications and developing a migration strategy to move toward the target architecture.

To accomplish his objectives, Poussereau has adopted a portfolio approach to managing technology investments. "As we migrate toward our target architecture, our portfolio of technology invest-

ments will be allocated equally for enhancements and maintenance. This will enable us to manage our investments at the branch level and also manage to specific targets for each of the regions," Poussereau says.

Achieving the strategic objectives of the branch requires more than just alignment. According to Poussereau, who works very closely with regional CIOs and CEOs, "Our strategic planning process not only ensures that IT is supporting the business objectives, but in several instances, IT is driving them." For example, he introduced a CRM solution to power a Web site FAQ. And his department implemented technology that allows citizens to find answers to everyday questions, such as about hospitals and housekeeping services.

"Although we are a government agency," Poussereau says, "we face many of the same issues as corporations—pleasing our customers, keeping our costs under control, understanding what the new technologies have to offer. We can only be successful when we manage our 'business' and our technology together."

launched an overhaul that swapped its mainframes for a client/server environment. This jump-started a supply chain reengineering and service management process that continues to improve corporate performance today. The new computing architecture was far more flexible and efficient—a crucial factor, given that Advance Transformer needed to trim its staff by 10 percent in 2000. But it was only the first step in the process. To align IT with the business, Advance Transformer added a suite of management software that dynamically linked its IT resources with business imperatives. Now, Advance Transformer can quickly pinpoint potential hardware or network glitches—for example, an over-heated server in its Mexico facility, a storage device reaching capacity in its Texas warehouse, or a router causing delays at its Atlanta office—and make adjustments before they interfere with business.[8]

As a final illustration of explorative capabilities, consider the case of ING Financial Services. Formed through a number of acquisitions, the company now has 27 business lines, with divisions located across the Americas. ING found itself in a poor situation with regard to data integration, which inhibited its ability to manage its network of relationships. The company responded by building five integration hubs that align with and serve its institutional, retail, broker, and corporate financial business lines. Now, 30 percent to 45 percent of common components and servers, software assets, data models, and best practices are reusable within the company's five hubs. That means IT can take a cookie-cutter approach with the code it uses to move data from one database to another, or with the rules it uses that govern how that data moves within the network.[9] This allows it much more flexibility to explore and exploit business options.

Ultimately, a well-articulated business-driven IT strategy will recognize the uniqueness of exploitative and explorative capabilities, and will balance these with the desired strategic positioning of the organization. An ideal profile will include investments targeted at both platform capabilities (exploitative) and options building (explorative). Such firms will operate at higher levels of BTM maturity, and changes in the business landscape will trigger updates to enterprise business strategy and flow smoothly to a business-driven IT strategy and corresponding IT function strategy, resulting in the real-time identification of necessary actions and the ability to execute changes without organizational disruption or major anguish.

Business-Driven IT Strategy

▶ **Ask** what specific business technology capabilities must be put in place for you to meet your short-term and long-term business goals and objectives. A mature business-driven IT strategy is the most effective way to ensure that IT understands the specific business needs and enables the business strategy.

▶ **Prepare** the processes that need to be put in place to improve communications and educate the organization about each component. Creating an effective strategy requires careful and complete communication, and the integration of the enterprise business strategy, enterprise IT strategy and IT function strategy.

▶ **Decide** what internal and external capabilities you need to execute on defined business strategies. What is the relative priority of stability and agility with regard to the business capabilities we need to have in place? Prioritizing and focusing investments starts with understanding the type of value to be created. Enabling stability and/or agility will require different levels and types of investments. Further, consideration must be given to the nature of this investment mix as it relates to supporting explorative and exploitative activities.

▶ **Understand** and specify the business value disciplines and value types to be pursued. What is our primary value discipline? The answer must be embedded in the enterprise business strategy, and then cascaded through all stakeholders and to all levels of the organization. Doing so will prescribe the specific business capabilities required in a way that guides effective IT strategy creation.

Notes

1   See the "Key Terminology" section in Chapter 1.

2   Ibid.

3   Ibid.

4   Ibid.

5   Epiphany Corporation, Customer Spotlight: DHL.
    http://www.epiphany.com/customers/detail_dhl.html.

6   Exploration capabilities include the ability to "sense" and the ability to "respond."
    In Chapter 2, the discussion of exploration emphasizes the ability of IT capital to
    identify opportunities and create options; here we emphasize the ability to respond
    to opportunities.

7   Microsoft Corporation, Southwest Bank of Texas. Bank Streamlines the
    Payment of Online Payment Solution, Microsoft Case Studies. June 24, 2004,
    http://www.microsoft.com/resources/casestudies/CaseStudy.asp?CaseStudyID=15562.

8   "Transforming to Succeed." Network Magazine, 19(7), July, 2004, S7.

9   Girard. K., The Fab Five, CIO Magazine, Nov. 1, 2004,
    http://www.cio.com/archive/110104/office.html.

4

"Superior companies benefit from the appointment of an IT-expert director."

—Heidi Sinclair, Chairwoman of Burson-Marsteller's Global Technology Practices

Governance: Who's in Charge?

In Brief

At a time when business technology has the potential to shape competitive advantage and superior performance, boards and top management teams must remain vigilant.

It is vital that boards appreciate the material risks inherent to the creation and use of business technology and understand the firm's risk-mitigation strategy.

The strategic importance of information and the nature of current business technologies have raised the stakes regarding the privacy, security, and confidentiality of information.

The role of the board is in articulating the vision for business technology, shaping the overall metrics architecture, and in providing oversight regarding strategic risks and compliance.

Although senior management teams have begun devoting attention to strategic Business Technology Management,[1] many boards still adopt an arm's-length attitude. Board-level discussions about technology often tend to be around costs or have been catalyzed by specific events or incidents (for example, Y2K remediation, Internet-based opportunities or threats, or denial-of-service attacks). However, today, boards and top management teams must embrace a more active and systemic perspective on the value and risks of business technology.[2]

Boards and top management must promote a coherent and disciplined approach to BTM for several reasons:

First, business technology offers significant opportunities for competitive advantage and wealth creation. As a strategic resource, business technology facilitates the development and delivery of innovative business models, products, and services, and customer and partner relationship management strategies. At a time when business technology has the potential to shape competitive advantage and superior performance, boards and top management teams must remain vigilant. Their firms must be well positioned to exploit strategic opportunities in which business technology can enable innovation and protect against savvy competitors or start-ups.

Second, business technology provides significant opportunities for productivity enhancement. However, the value in these productivity improvements is not just from the investments in business technology as much as the complementary innovations in business practices (see Figure 4.1).

Figure 4.1 Creating Productivity Enhancements

Managing business and technology together increases productivity.

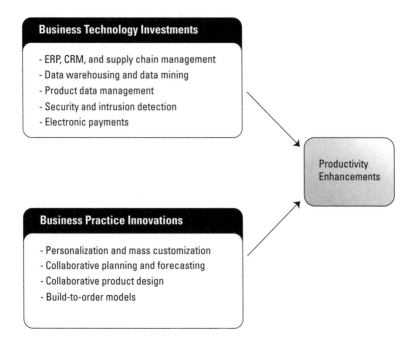

Business Technology Investments

- ERP, CRM, and supply chain management
- Data warehousing and data mining
- Product data management
- Security and intrusion detection
- Electronic payments

Productivity Enhancements

Business Practice Innovations

- Personalization and mass customization
- Collaborative planning and forecasting
- Collaborative product design
- Build-to-order models

The joint attention to business technology and business practice innovation has driven significant productivity improvements in industry leaders such as Wal-Mart and Dell.3 Wal-Mart complemented its investments in information systems, warehouse automation, and collaborative purchasing systems with innovations in supplier relationships, day-to-day store replenishment, and cross-docking. To enhance productivity through business technology, firms must target the right opportunities and appropriately sequence investments in different technologies and organizational innovations (for example, business process, organization, and incentive system redesign). No single business technology investment, business process innovation, or business practice innovation is likely to produce sustained productivity gains as much as a continuing program of synergistic improvement initiatives. An enterprise-wide perspective is required to ensure that specific business technology and organizational change initiatives are being managed as part of an overall program of productivity enhancement. The magnitude of the investments and organizational transformations require commitment and support at the top.

> *The magnitude of the investments and organizational transformations require commitment and support at the top.*

Third, during the late 1990s, high levels of investments in business technology made IT[4] assets one of the most significant areas of capital spending in many firms, particularly for those in the information-intensive sectors (for example, financial services, retail, and hospitality). Maximizing return on capital employed requires an oversight over how well these assets are being deployed to generate shareholder value. Further, even as senior executives acknowledge the strategic role of BTM, business technology spending today is tightly controlled. The question then becomes: How should scarce business technology be deployed toward strategic, high-impact projects? Additionally, as newer technologies continue to emerge at a rapid pace even as firms restrict their IT budgets and R&D allocations, how should firms prioritize their attention toward new technologies and guide strategic experiments?

With new business technology initiatives requiring larger amounts of capital, investment processes must permit a consistent way of evaluating the business value of these projects and investments across the enterprise. These investment processes must be linked with key business metrics so that executives can find it easier to champion critical business technology investments. These metrics must relate to key business processes and operations, such as customer relationship management, procurement, manufacturing, and supply chain management, financial management, and human capital management (see Figure 4.2).

Figure 4.2 Business Value Metrics

Metrics to measure business value vary by process type.

Customer Relationship Management

- Customer acquisition costs
- Share of the customer's wallet
- Customer satisfaction

Financial Management

- Working capital efficiency

Procurement, Manufacturing, and Supply Chain Management

- Manufacturing productivity
- Procurement costs
- Inventory turns
- Warehousing and shipment costs

Human Capital Management

- Recruiting costs
- Training and development productivity
- Retention

For instance, Intel has implemented an approach that categorizes the business value of business technology into 17 categories called value dials that deal with either bottom-line savings or top-line growth. Most of the value dials are based on metrics already used by Intel's business groups to measure business performance. As part of the dials approach, Intel executives first identify a baseline value for the metric that is likely to be impacted by the proposed business technology investment. As a next step, executives specify the likely value of this metric as a result of the successful implementation of the initiative. Finally, the improvement of this metric is monetized on the basis of prior experience with business value management. As an example, if a proposed CRM initiative aims to improve customer satisfaction by two points over the current value, this improvement can be monetized on the basis of an understanding of the relationship between customer satisfaction

Research Insight

Professor F. Warren McFarlan on Governance

F. Warren McFarlan, the Baker Foundation Professor and Albert H. Gordon Professor of Business Administration Emeritus at Harvard Business School, has studied business technology from its infancy—the first of his dozen books dealt with punch card equipment. One change he observes now is the growing interest of boards of directors in technology matters. This is an excerpt from an interview.

A Different Way

"Governance goes higher and deeper than people could possibly have conceived a decade ago. For a series of organizations in which IT is critical, oversight has actually gone on up to the board of directors. Companies like P&G, Home Depot, and Mellon Bank have put together an IT governance committee on the board similar to the other big committees like nominating, audit, and compensation. They have begun to hammer out a set of guidelines and practices for IT. This notion of governance reaching the top of the organization is extremely important. When you drop below the boardroom, over and over again this stuff tends to get sucked up by a CIO, and often there is not enough energy and effort made to get this integrated deeply into the thinking of the business units in a way that they can understand.

"The very viability and success of companies like P&G depend on IT initiatives. We're now in a wonderful process in boards today in the aftermath of Sarbanes-Oxley. The audit committee is meeting three times longer than it used to be. And while all that good inward navel gazing is going on, the stuff that is actually going to determine whether they're going to live, be competitive, be able to operate is being delegated and left elsewhere. For those companies where the technology is adding critical differentiation, in cost or value added services, or where there is just unbelievable operational dependence, the board has to be in the game.

"P&G is a remarkable company. They brought back Scott Cook, who left them as marketing manager and went on to found Intuit. They brought him back three years ago to chair the technology committee of the board, to basically shake up everything from their supply chain to their market research to the next generation of scanners to ensure that they continue to be a world-class competitor.

"There's a steady litany of these stories, and this was largely masked by the Internet bubble and the process of cleaning up after it. There has been all this reinvention going on. It's a ramification of the new potential, the fact that new technologies allow us to do things in a different way."

and future customer revenue. In other cases, the business metrics are more directly monetized (for example, procurement, customer acquisition, or recruiting costs).

These value dials provide Intel's executives with a consistent, enterprise-wide way of evaluating the business value of business technology investments. They allow senior business executives to champion investments as well as prioritize their business technology needs. Therefore, boards and top management teams must direct an enterprise-wide perspective on the organizational value of business technology investments. Such a perspective must identify value metrics that are appropriate for the business of the firm and provide a process for judging the potential impacts of business technology projects and investments on those metrics. Without a coordinated investment philosophy that has the backing of the board, the metrics and the valuation process will lack the needed credibility to guide investments.

Fourth, heightened concerns about risk management, auditing and fraud detection, and corporate governance have sensitized boards and top management teams to adopt an even more active role in the oversight of business strategy and key enterprise activities. Significant regulations including Sarbanes-Oxley, HIPAA, and the Patriot Act have raised the stakes. Failures to meet the required attestations, unintended violations of privacy and confidentiality, or heightened vulnerabilities to identity thefts are likely to invite adverse reactions from regulators and from the stock market. As business technology becomes embedded in core organizational processes, control systems, and decision support systems, it is vital that boards appreciate the material risks due to technology and understand the risk-mitigation strategy.

Further, an enterprise-wide perspective is needed to guide the use of business technology in implementing effective and economical enterprise risk management systems that facilitate both management control and performance auditability. With greater complexity in the processes and structures for managing business technology (for example, outsourcing, offshoring, and applications and website hosting), there is a need for more sophisticated models of enterprise-wide risk assessment that factor in not just the internal risks, but also the risks inherent in sourcing and external partnering. Boards and top management teams must provide active oversight over how business technology risks impact the business, and ensure the effectiveness of the governance systems in mitigating these risks.

> *It is vital that boards appreciate the material risks due to technology and understand the risk-mitigation strategy.*

Boards face significant challenges in overseeing business technology

Although the case for an active board involvement in BTM is clear, creating it is not easy. First, BTM occurs through a distributed process of innovation and collaboration between business and technology executives, as well as with the involvement of external business partners. How should the board maintain oversight and control without restricting autonomy and flexibility? Second, with an overcrowded agenda including competitive, regulatory, shareholder, and financial audit issues, what type of BTM issues should the board address? Third, boards often lack the necessary knowledge to appreciate the complexities and subtleties of BTM. So, for example, how should boards make sense of different current and emerging information technologies? How should they understand the options value of creating next-generation business platforms that tightly integrate an adaptable set of business processes via information technologies? How should they recognize the key value and risk drivers inherent in BTM and provide independent oversight, guidance, and intervention? How do they ensure the continued development of effectual BTM?

BTM provides starting points for effective board oversight and governance of business technology. In particular, two key BTM capabilities[5] are discussed in this chapter: *Strategic and Tactical Governance* and *Compliance and Risk Management*. *Strategic and Tactical Governance* refers to the types of decisions that must be made and who makes those decisions. *Compliance and Risk Management* ensures that government and regulatory conditions are understood and met with regard to business technology initiatives and that appropriate risk-mitigation strategies are in place.

Business technology shapes business strategy in four ways

Determining the organizational role of business technology is a key strategic governance decision that sets the tone for key BTM activities, such as the level of investment, the nature of the applications portfolio, and the type of metrics for evaluating and justifying investments.

Business technology has the potential to shape business strategy through four roles (see Table 4.1):

Automate—This role of business technology is in transaction and work process automation that enable the business goals of higher productivity, low cost, and efficiency. Automation also enables the goal of being easy to do business with, where employees, customers or business partners can access services with speed, convenience, and personalization. Examples include deployment of customer self-service (self-checkouts at retail stores, Internet check-in for airlines), employee self-service (desktop-based self-procurement, self-management of benefits), and online sales. An automate vision signals that the firm's business technology focus will be on seamless enterprise and inter-enterprise services, global process connectivity, and the quest for ever more digitization. Key business value metrics will focus on productivity (for instance, inventory turnover), cycle time (for instance, fulfillment cycle time), and costs (for instance, procurement costs).

Table 4.1	Business Technology Helps Shape Business Strategy

Business technology enables business options through four strategic roles.

Strategic Role	Description	Business Value Metrics
Automate	Target transaction and work process automation to improve the productivity and ease with which the organization conducts its business	- Productivity (e.g., inventory turnover) - Cycle time (e.g., fulfillment cycle time) - Costs (e.g., procurement costs)
Empower	Provide information, decision support, and "best practice" knowledge to the "front end" workers in their interactions with customers, business partners or other external stakeholders	- Partner satisfaction (e.g., customer satisfaction) - Problem resolution productivity (e.g., number of problems resolved, cycle time to resolution) - Resolution costs (e.g., cost per customer call)
Control	Facilitate efficient and real-time monitoring of business operations and business partners	- Completeness, accuracy, validity, and integrity of the firm's transactions and decision-making processes - Accuracy, speed, and economy of financial reporting - Effectiveness of financial audits and fraud detection
Transform	Facilitate the innovation of new business models, new products and services, and new modes of organizing work	- Rate of product, process, or business model innovation -Comprehensiveness and richness of innovation portfolio (number of incremental, architectural and radical innovations)

Empower—This role of business technology is to facilitate fast, effective, and accurate decision making across the enterprise and its partnership network. This is accomplished through investments in decision support tools and technologies (for example, data warehousing, data mining, OLAP), intranets for dissemination of best practices, and extranets for rapid sharing of information with business partners. Empowerment enables the goal of being easy to do business with by providing front-end workers with intelligence and decision support in their interactions with customers, business partners, or other external stakeholders. Many of these interactions (for example, in the customer call center) require problem or dispute resolution. Examples of empowerment include decision support scripts for call centers and customer service agents and visibility tools in supply chain and logistics processes. An empowerment vision signals that the firm's business technology focus will be on decision support and knowledge management. Key business value metrics will focus on partner satisfaction (for example, customer satisfaction), problem resolution productivity (for example, number of problems resolved, cycle time to resolution), and resolution costs (for example, cost per customer call).

Control—This role of business technology is to facilitate efficient and real-time monitoring of business operations and business partners through practices such as daily close, operational alerts, and dashboards with drill-down capabilities. This is accomplished through investments in monitoring tools and technologies (for example, data warehouses, portals) and through the design of enterprise risk-management processes. Control enables the business goals of enhancing transparency of business operations, rapid detection and resolution of management control issues, and accurate reporting of the key metrics of business performance. The emphasis of the control vision is upon strong financial performance management systems. Key business value metrics will include the completeness, accuracy, validity, and integrity of the firm's transactions and decision-making processes; the accuracy, speed, and economy of financial reporting; and the effectiveness of financial audits and fraud detection.

Transform—This role of business technology is to facilitate the innovation of new business models (for example, direct to the customer, multiple-channel integration, whole of the enterprise or "one face" integration, value net integration), new products and services (for example, digital products and services, digitized customer service through online chats), and new modes of organizing work (for example, globally distributed work practices). The focus here is not so much on investment in specific business technologies as much as on the development of digital options, digitization of products and services, and on experimentation with new business technology-enabled business ideas. Transformation enables the business goals of continuous innovation, agility and competitive disruption. Key business value metrics include the rate of product, process, or business model innovation and the

---

Leadership Insight

Barbara Carlini on Communication

When Barbara Carlini arrived at Diageo North America as CIO in 2001, her marching orders were to simplify and cut costs. Today, she is marshalling business technology to drive the company's growth. A critical part of her effort, she said in an interview, has been promoting better communication.

On Speaking Terms

The road to business-technology alignment at Diageo North America, the world's leading premium beverages company, was built on communication, lots of it.

"Communications is huge," CIO Barbara Carlini says. First, it is regular, straightforward discussions with her fellow CXOs on business technology priorities. Next, it is communication from the executive suite to employees on the company's strategies. Then it is communication between her technology troops and their business colleagues. "We do an enormous amount of education and communications training," Carlini says. "For example, how do you speak to a business associate?"

And how do you bring an understanding of the business to technical folks? In that regard, she asked her people to create skits as an attention-focusing exercise. One that was captured on video and drew the attention of the CIO executive board, a working group of senior executive technology professionals, was titled, "Business Eye for an IS Guy." It featured a fictional character named Arnold, a nerd techie transformed into a business savvy person. This was backed up by frequent programs explaining product life cycles, branding strategies, and other business functions to her staff.

Carlini institutionalized the lines of communication in several new organizational structures. Each business technology project now has a steering committee that takes a monthly look at interdependencies, obstacles, architecture, and checkpoints. "These steering committees are just another way we get aligned," Carlini says. "For example, the National Accounts Reporting Program has a steering committee with senior business folks on it. Scope changes and budget changes have to be approved by the steering committee. It's definitely run by business folks, not just IT."

An IS leadership team also meets monthly to review all projects, and a project management office, which Carlini created, coordinates activities. Each of these groups ensures that projects are designed to advance one of the five "pillars" of the company's strategy.

A lot of teeth

She also established an executive-level steering committee. Its members include Carlini, the CFO, the CMO, the head of national accounts, and the head of supply. "So it has a lot of teeth," Carlini says. "This group decides on all projects. I don't like to call them IS projects, but right now, it only reviews projects that have IS components. A business case is put together, and as everyone knows, if an IS person comes in to present, they might as well give up, because we will not accept the project proposal. The business owner from the functional area is required to own the business case and present it to the committee. Not the IS person."

Setting priorities

In her first critical act of communication, Carlini made it clear when she took the job in 2001 that business executives would make business technology decisions. "There really wasn't a lot of strong alignment with the business," she says. "We had about 128 projects, and it was very hard to prioritize. I brought my business colleagues in at one point and they said, Oh, Barb, just go prioritize them yourself. And I said, that's fine. I'll deliver technical upgrades, and that's all I'll work on. And they said, OK, we get your point."

She was able to push through this major procedural change because she first built good relationships with fellow executives. "I think that's absolutely key. If you don't have the respect of your colleagues, you're not going to be able to get this through."

"Once we put the steering group together, the CEO sent out a memo saying this is the group that will make decisions on any project with IS component. Everyone knows you can't get a project approved without going there."

At Diageo, business and technology have moved from alignment toward synchronization—the condition in which the IT function doesn't just follow but takes the lead at times. Because she had experience in it, the company asked Carlini to drive the development of a sales strategy. She sits on the global sales leadership team.

"We started with, what is your vision, and what areas do you want to improve?" she says. "I said, we have to start with your strategy. The system piece is easy. We need to understand where you want to be from a capability standpoint in each region. Once we break that down, I want metrics for each one of these capabilities. Based on those metrics, we'll figure out what the systems are. But are you ready for it? We could put a system in, but if you think a system is going to solve your process, forget it. I'd rather see your process get put in place first and understand what you want to do and what tools you want to give your sales folks before we go down the systems road."

Carlini has never seen the amount of change Diageo has been through, with acquisitions and reorganization, and with new IT structures and processes to match. "If you don't have these things in place, I don't know how you run an organization this size," she says. "I can go in and say, by the way, guys, you just asked for 90 projects. I can't do all this. Now they understand that's crazy, and they ask, why are we doing this? We can sit down together and prioritize the projects."

comprehensiveness and richness of a firm's innovation portfolio (number of incremental, architectural, and radical innovations).

Articulating a strategic vision about the role of business technology is a significant element of strategic governance. Such a strategic vision must capture and reflect three realities:

1. All organizations apply business technology for all four of these strategic roles. Thus, in crafting a strategic vision, the key is to make clear the relative dominance of each role for the enterprise.

2. An organization's various units will likely exhibit differences with regard to the relative importance of these four roles. Thus, in developing processes, organization structures, information requirements and deploying automating technology, such unit differences must be accounted for.

3. Business environments and technology and management teams are always in flux. Thus, while firms might choose a specific vision today, over time, such a vision is likely to change, perhaps dramatically.

Another important decision that must reside at the top is the implementation of an appropriate hierarchy of metrics. At a time when business technology spending is no longer an administrative overhead, but a source of both top-line growth and bottom-line savings, executives must develop an appreciation of how specific investments impact key metrics of firm performance. For instance, Blue Shield of California is a not-for-profit health plan that provides health insurance for 2.7 million members, generating $7 billion in annual revenues. In the perspective of the chief financial officer, technology impacts two key areas: analytics, or the ability to price health-care plan offerings, and services operations such as claims payment, eligibility, and enrollment. This firm views the value of its business technology investments through the lens of operational efficiency, customer service, and pricing effectiveness.[6]

> Business technology spending is no longer an administrative overhead, but a source of both top-line growth and bottom-line savings.

Similarly, as described earlier, Intel's business value dials approach identifies business variables that can be positively impacted by the use of business technology. Each business variable is translated into quantifiable metrics. The business technology value dial approach encourages Intel analysts to examine how certain key business variables are impacted by potential business technology investments. The value dials approach includes the development of a baseline value for the specific dials. Once quantified, the baseline can be compared to the business technology value dials influenced by new initiatives. Further, a process of regular measurement of the value dial improvements against the baseline enables the management of business value throughout the life cycle of that investment.[7]

A metrics hierarchy should consist of three elements that

1. Direct attention toward different types of business technology investments.

2. Identify appropriate business variables.

3. Relate to the management of strategic risk and regulatory compliance.

The first element must direct attention toward different types of business technology investments. In their research, Jeanne Ross and Cynthia Beath[8] discovered four major types:

• Process improvement, where the goal is to enhance business solutions (for example, greater customer personalization, self-checkout in stores)

• Renewal, where the goal is to improve the delivery of business technology services (for example, Web services, intrusion detection)

• Transformation, where the goal is to build a platform for future business capabilities (for example, data mining)

• Experiments, where the goal to engage in R&D and learning about the option value of an emerging technology (for example, RFID)

Each one of these types of investments requires different types of business metrics (see Table 4.2).

Therefore, a second element of the metrics hierarchy is to identify appropriate business variables that will be impacted by each of these types of investments. Collectively, the business variables across the four types of investments should comprise the business technology value dials for the firm. Whereas transformation types of investments must usually be approved by the board, the other three types of investments are funded either out of business budgets (that is, process improvements and experiments) or IT budgets (that is, renewal investments).

A third significant element at the top relates to the management of strategic risk and regulatory compliance. Strategic risk

Table 4.2	Business Technology Investments and Associated Metrics

Metrics vary according to the expected outcomes of business technology investments.

Investment	Description	Appropriate Business Metrics
Process improvement	Enhance business solutions	- Customer satisfaction - Manufacturing productivity
Renewal	Improve delivery of services	- Productivity - Costs - Effectiveness of security - Services availability
Transformation	Build platform for future business capabilities	- New business capability creation - New product, service, or business model innovation
Experiments	Engage in R&D and learning about new technologies	- Knowledge about new technologies - Speed to market in new technology leverage

refers to the risks facing the firm due to poorly envisioned or executed business strategies. In particular, within BTM, the focus is on risks at the intersection of business technology and business strategy. Regulatory compliance refers to corporate adherence to different regulatory expectations related to financial reporting and data management. Poor regulatory compliance invites liabilities of civil or criminal punishment and shareholder lawsuits. As described in Chapter 8, "Considering Risk," there are other forms of risks, including systems and sourcing risks. Although those forms of risk are likely to be managed by business and technology executives, the management of strategic risk and regulatory compliance must reside at the board level.

What strategic risks must be managed at the top? Some of these risks include the following (see Table 4.3):

- Business model risk—This refers to the robustness of the business model and how well it is being executed.

- Competitive risk—This refers to the ability to sustain competitive action and retaliation.

Table 4.3 Strategic Risks

Several categories of strategic risks must be managed.

Strategic Risk	Description

Business model risk	- How robust is the current business model?
	- What are the threats to the execution of the current business model due to
	  · Premature technology
	  · Poor training of employees
	  · Failure to understand the motivations of customers and business partners
	  · Poor project implementation

Competitive risk	- How alert are we to opportunities for IT-based innovation? - Can competitors strategically outmaneuver us with innovative digital products, services or business models? - Are our digital business models sustainable?
Investment risk	From a business technology perspective: - Are we spending the right amount? - Are we spending on the right types, and is our timing right? - Are our investment strategies appropriate to its organizational role? - Are we alert to emerging trends?
Integration risk	- How well are our business processes integrated and enabled with business technology?
Misalignment risk	From a business technology perspective: - Do investments address business priorities? - Do business executives adhere to existing standards for acquisition? - Are data ownership and management policies clearly articulated and understood?
IT governance models risk	- Do business executives champion strategic business technology initiatives? - Is the business case for business technology articulated through the corporate metrics hierarchy? - How well does business technology collaborate in developing strategic initiatives?

- Investment risk—This refers to the ability to manage business technology spending in a business environment where capital is scarce and technologies are volatile, expensive and not easily understood.

- Integration risk—This refers to the risks of inadequate integration between business technology investments and business processes.

- Misalignment risk—This refers to inadequate alignment between business technology spending and business priorities.

- Governance models risk—This refers to the risks of inadequate participation and involvement of business and technology executives on key BTM decisions.

The management of regulatory compliance has always been an area of board oversight. However, the strategic importance of information and the nature of current business technologies have raised the stakes regarding the privacy, security, and confidentiality of information. In particular, there is heightened sensitivity to safeguarding not just sensitive corporate transaction data, but also data about customers, employees, and business partners. The pervasiveness of business technologies has made it far easier for unauthorized pilferage of such information and data. As a result, regulatory agencies, customers and shareholders have become more active in judging and punishing corporations for inadequate attention to the protection of data. In addition, with heightened concerns about terror, regulations increasingly compel organizations to furnish more data than before. The management of compliance requires attention to the following issues:

> *The strategic importance of information and the nature of current business technologies have raised the stakes regarding the privacy, security, and confidentiality of information.*

- Prevailing regulations

  - Maintaining and protecting data about transactions, customers, employees, and business partners

– Alerting stakeholders about incidents of unauthorized access

– Providing the affected stakeholders with assistance

• The potential for economic sanctions and the threats to business continuity due to noncompliance

• Effectiveness with regard to managing data in conformance with the regulations and stakeholder expectations

• The cost of responding to the compliance expectations

Boards need a process for managing technology decisions

Our research suggests that it is appropriate to apply a networked governance model, as shown in Figure 4.3.

The board's role is to articulate a vision for business technology, shaping the overall metrics architecture, and providing oversight for strategic risks and compliance. Business management is primarily responsible for championing innovative applications of business technology, including making the business case for projects. Technology management is responsible for managing business technology services, skill availability, and the technology infrastructure. Finally, external vendors are a key element of the governance network as they increasingly provide access to needed expertise as well as economical and/or world-class services and skills.

Boards usually carry out their governance duties through committees that oversee critical areas such as audit, compensation, and acquisitions. It might be time for firms, particularly those in information-intensive sectors, to consider the setup of a committee responsible for business technology strategy.[9] The charter for this committee would be twofold:

• Active involvement in decisions related to the envisioned role of business technology, the metrics architecture, and strategic risks and compliance

• Monitoring role over other significant BTM decisions, including portfolio (see Chapter 6, "Buy, Hold, or Sell?") and project and sourcing risks (see Chapter 8)

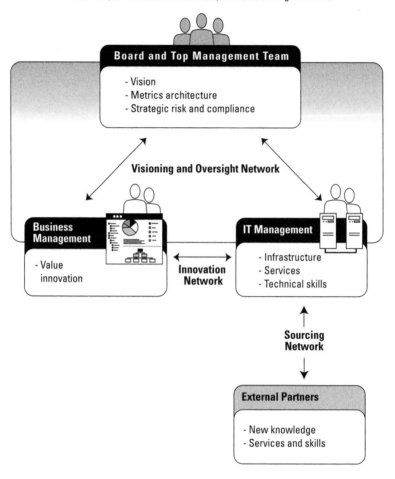

Figure 4.3   **A Networked Governance Model**

A networked governance model includes a visioning and oversight network, an innovation network, and a sourcing network.

Complementary to this board-level committee is an executive committee that has become common in most firms: the business technology executive committee.[10] This committee consists of the CEO, CFO, other senior executives, and the CIO. It is responsible for the following:

• Executing the strategic role of business technology in decisions about investment, applications prioritization, and infrastructure build-ups

- Monitoring the risks of business technology and the effectiveness of the risk-mitigation and control systems

- Communicating policies and standards about the use of business technology assets, data management, and compliance management

- Interacting with the board on key issues

Finally, the office of the CIO has emerged as another important organizational mechanism that complements the effectiveness of the board and the top management team. This consists of all the CIO's direct reports. Key responsibilities of this group include monitoring the business technology portfolio, value metrics, and technology capabilities (staff, infrastructure, services). This group is also responsible for tracking emerging technologies and managing an appropriate R&D posture toward these technologies. It is responsible for vendor relationship management.

Research Insight

Krishna Palepu on Governance

In several programs aimed at corporate board members, Krishna G. Palepu shares his research on how boards can be more effective. He is the Ross Graham Walker Professor of Business Administration and Senior Associate Dean for International Development at the Harvard Business School. This is an excerpt from an interview.

What You Don't Know

"There are two areas that are the responsibility of the board generally, and this applies to technology as well. One is strategic oversight. In thinking about a company's strategy, competitive advantage, and winning in the marketplace, the board has the responsibility to oversee that decision-making process. The other one is risk man-agement. In thinking about things that can really destroy a company, make or break it, the board has a responsibility to make sure that there are plans in place to manage those risks.

"Technology has become very important in both of these areas. The board has to play a role in thinking about how technology is going to be deployed to gain competitive advantage and sustain it over time. And in thinking through the risk-management process of the company, the board has to understand how technology is going to play a role, either in risks that technology can mitigate or when technology itself introduces risks. An example of the latter is privacy issues. That's the kind of the thing the board ought to be learning about and asking questions about—how are we protecting ourselves? Do we have the safeguards we need?

"In the upside, competitive advantage part—as technology becomes fundamental for companies in understanding their customers better, doing one to one marketing, implementing more flexible manufacturing, establishing better supply chain management, creating better internal information to be more responsive —the board has to have at least a framework for what the opportunities are to employ technology in a strategic sense. It must ask, are we doing everything we can in exploiting those opportunities? It does not need to concern itself with the detail of technology choices or implementation.

"But boards don't often do this. They do accept the responsibility at a conceptual level. But usually they only get involved when, for example, an internal audit points out weaknesses in information security. Then the board becomes more active. Similarly, as they see competition taking away market share, the board might respond. In some really very good companies, boards are doing these things on their own. But for many other companies, I think they're still on the learning curve. You don't know what you don't know. When you don't know the possibilities of technology, what it can do, it can be intimidating for the board to actively get in the discussion.

"Right now boards are more focused on the downside, risk management, but they need to focus on the upside as well."

Recent research shows, however, that less than 20 percent of organizations have adopted a business technology governance structure, even though they realize the issues they face could be resolved this way. However, companies that have adopted formal approaches with a strategic perspective are mitigating risks, delivering on the value of their business technology investments, and improving the alignment, synchronization, and even convergence between business and technology.

Business Technology Governance

▶ **Develop** your *Strategic and Tactical Governance* capability, including board oversight. This capability prepares an organization to address questions such as: What decisions must be made? Who are the people responsible for making them? And, what is the process used to decide? Firms must have ready answers that are ingrained and automatic. This relates to the full range of business technology governance issues, investment decisions, standards and principles, and target business and technology architectures.

▶ **Understand** government and regulatory requirements that must be met with regard to business technology initiatives, and appropriate risk-mitigation strategies that must be in place. This starts with the *Compliance and Risk Management* capability supported by the board, and promulgated to everyone involved in enabling required business capabilities through business technology.

▶ **Ensure** that the board has the knowledge and insight it needs regarding BTM. Answer this question for your own organization: How will you increase board-level understanding of these concepts? Consider that some boards have addressed this issue by appointing outside board members, including the CEOs of well-regarded IT companies or well-regarded CIOs, who have a proven track record in BTM. Others have established business technology strategy committees. At a minimum, the delivery of quarterly CIO briefings to the board must be arranged to complement the deliberations of the technology strategy committee.

▶ **Determine** how the organization will configure its infrastructure to facilitate timely access to financial information. What control systems and analytics are needed to detect vulnerabilities and fraud, and how will portals be deployed to provide appropriate dashboards? Devise a strategy to implement a control systems architecture that balances concerns about completeness and timeliness with cost economy.

Notes

1   See the "Key Terminology" section in Chapter 1.

2   Ibid.

3   D. Farrell. "The New Real Economy." *Harvard Business Review*. October 2003, pp 1-10.

4   See the "Key Terminology" section in Chapter 1.

5   Ibid.

6   *IT Moves from Cost Center to Business Contributor: The CFO's View on Measuring IT Value*. CFO Publishing Corporation, September 2004.

7   Curley, M. *Managing Information Technology for Business Value: Practical Strategies for IT and Business Managers*. Intel Press, 2004.

8   Ross, J. and C.M. Beath. "Beyond the Business Case: New Approaches to IT Investment." *Sloan Management Review*, Winter 2002.

9   "Board Briefing on IT Governance." IT Governance Institute, 2003.

10 Carol V. Brown and V. Sambamurthy. *Re-Positioning the IT Organization to Facilitate Business Transformations*. Pinnaflex Press, August 1999. Peter Weill and Jeanne Ross. *IT Governance: How Top Performers Manage IT Decision Rights for Superior Results*. Harvard Business School Press, 2004.

5

chapter

"*One of the things that a digital world allows*

you to do is run your companies in completely

different ways."

—*Jeffrey R. Immelt, Chairman and CEO, GE*

Is Your Organization Ready?

In Brief

Three trends influence organizing for BTM: the need for rapid and innovative use of technology, supply-side pressure to deliver reliable and low-cost services, and new compliance requirements.

Changing business conditions cause alterations to business models and processes. Changing conditions in technology demand also impact how the business should be organized and managed.

It is critical that business and technology stay connected and coordinated. Therefore, BTM capabilities[3] such as *Organization Design and Change Management* become essential.

A company's organizing logic should emphasize relationship networks for visioning, innovation, and sourcing, and it should explicitly manage three categories of value-creating processes.

Firms should adopt a modular organizing logic because it facilitates an efficient and adaptive approach to achieving BTM capabilities.

How an organization is structured—its roles, processes, and coordination mechanisms—can make or break an organization's ability to achieve effective BTM.[1] Peter Weill and Jeanne Ross[2] found that even when firms had similar business strategies, those with well-designed structures reaped at least 20 percent greater returns compared to those with poorly designed structures.

This chapter discusses the logic for creating and evolving organizational structures and examines the organizational models that maximize a company's potential to achieve BTM capabilities. The importance of change management and communication in creating an ideal organization is discussed, and the use of a modular organizing logic in creating the best environment for BTM is explained.

Three significant forces influence how business technology executives think about organization structures for managing business technology[4] today:

Demand-side forces result in the need for rapid, innovative, safe, and cost-effective use of business technology. With technology increasingly embedded into products, services, business processes, and relationships, firms must nurture creative and innovative uses of it. A firm must also encourage initiatives for business technology-based competitive maneuvering, productivity, and cost leverage. Managing these demands requires the blending of business and technology knowledge. When only business executives possess insights about business opportunities and needs, and only technology executives are savvy about how information technologies might support or shape business opportunities, the situation is neither optimal nor sustainable. Instead, demand pressures require organizational structures that facilitate collaboration among business and technology executives so that they can innovate and experiment.

Supply-side forces require delivery of reliable and cost effective business technology. With the horizontal fragmentation of the IT industry and the viability of outsourcing and offshoring options, it is hard to find a firm that doesn't cite "solutions integration" as a major path to added value. That means managing relationships with a diverse number of service providers. It also means rapid delivery of applications by fast-cycle projects, and maintaining a workforce with crucial competencies in the face of rapid obsolescence of business technology skills. Well-designed organizational structures can deliver effective management of external partnerships and human capital.

> *Strategic sourcing and the ability to manage relationships with a diverse number of service providers through multi-sourcing agreements is critical.*

Administrative forces result in the need for better management of business technology. Almost everywhere today, IT assets[5] are a significant proportion of the capital base, and many recent reports have pegged the proportion of this relative to overall capital investments at levels that exceed 50 percent of the total. This fact carries a range of administrative imperatives: greater oversight and management of business technology productivity and risk; appropriate controls and audits as an integral element of enterprise risk management; and continual benchmarking of business technology costs, with transparent costing models for services. Organizational models must explicitly enable the financial management and control of business technology. Similarly, strategic planning for business technology must direct attention toward the timing of investments, anticipating emerging business needs, and developing appropriate infrastructure and services-provisioning capabilities. Organizational models must ensure that this strategic planning is actually carried out with results executed, rather than sitting on a shelf.

Five principles should guide organization design

When designing an appropriate organizational structure for managing business technology, a firm should consider the following five principles:

Organize to foster coordination between business and technology. Chapter 1,"What Is BTM?," discussed the states of alignment, synchronization, and convergence of business and technology management. Key to this discussion was the notion that an organization may operate in one or more of these states simultaneously, and this has significant organizational design ramifications. An organization operating in the state of alignment will find that its organization design must be appropriate for an environment where technology supports, enables, and does not constrain the company's current and evolving business strategies. Operating at a state of synchronization means that sufficient organizational flexibility must exist to allow for business technology that not only enables the execution of current business strategy but also anticipates and shapes future business options. Ultimately, the state of convergence means that an organization's business and technology leaders are able to operate simultaneously in both spaces, and that these areas have merged in both strategic and tactical senses, which brings an entirely different perspective to the design of the organization.

Given that these three states may even occur simultaneously within different sections of an organization, design efforts must consider the current and expected future state of the organization with respect to alignment, synchronization and convergence. These efforts must deliver the right level of coupling between business management and technology management strategies, processes, and activities based on the current operating environment (see Figure 5.1).

Organization design efforts can reflect the current state of an organization and deliver the needed levels of coordination in many ways. For example, in the case of the state of synchronization, organization design should emphasize this organizational vision and related goals about the role of business technology. Therefore, the organization design should encourage business innovation, strategic experiments, and risk-taking with business technology. For organizations operating nearer to convergence, implementing organizational units to catalyze joint attention to business and technology initiatives for innovation and productivity enhancement is an appropriate outcome. One example of such a unit is the corporate Business Technology Council (referred

Figure 5.1 Coordinating Business and Technology

Managing business and technology together maximizes the contributions of each.

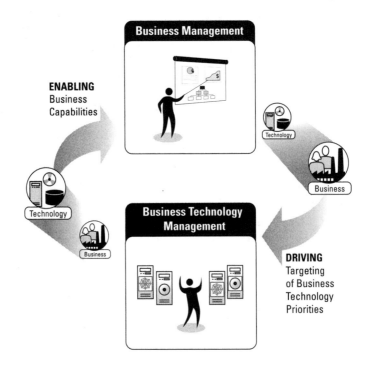

to as the IT Executive Council in many firms). The members of this council include the CEO, CFO, CIO, and other senior business executives. This council promotes organizational awareness of the role of business technology and monitors major enterprise initiatives.

In seeking the right level of coordination, an organization design must weigh the extent to which its business strategy and strategic initiatives help set the priorities for business technology, including investments in infrastructure and services, application portfolios, and sourcing relationships. At the same time, this design must account for the fact that business technology is increasingly shaping future business strategies, processes, and initiatives. For example, with greater data mining and warehousing capabilities in the infrastructure, business strategy could evolve toward greater personalization and customer intimacy, and result in the differentiation of the organization's product or service offerings.

Leadership Insight

Michael Westcott on People

As senior vice president for human resources at Diageo North America, Michael Westcott wants technology executives who will interact with him on business matters and not just be order takers. This kind of interaction, he said in an interview, demands a new level of interpersonal skills. (See Diageo CIO Barbara Carlini's Leadership Insight in Chapter 4.)

The Next Generation of Leaders

From his very different perspective as senior vice president for human resources at Diageo North America, Michael Westcott nevertheless arrives at many of the same conclusions as CIO Barbara Carlini.

As she prepares her technical staff to understand the business, he, as a business customer, demands that understanding. "We want IT people who think and know the HR agenda as well as we do," Westcott says. "It's a basic point. I don't want an IT person I have to second-guess or explain things to. I want someone who has a passion and energy and interest in what we're trying to do. Think HR perspective first, then IT."

He needs strategic creativity from the business technology people assigned to his function. "We can put things out there looking for solutions, and the mode of IT is quite reactive—they're order takers. Rather, I want them asking, why are you doing that? Why haven't you thought of this and thought of that? And kick ideas around with me and actually challenge my thinking in the early stage. Being an order taker is fine, but the real value add is what IT can do from strategic perspective."

The two business technology people dedicated to HR sit with them as an extended part of the team, working with HR on future needs. In a transition to SAP, Westcott says, "We need a lot of IT support at the start rather than coming in at the end."

Westcott also sees the wisdom in the executive steering committee for projects, of which he is a member. "Businesses will come up with their pet projects and say we desperately need this. And of course, everyone's project is massively important. That saps up time and resources. But we're getting into a much better way, a program management way, to manage this. We look at whether things fit against our strategy. It's a way of prioritizing them in terms of benefit."

It's not just a matter of cost, he says, but of scarce resources. "What's the potential waste of what you're doing? It's quite easy to make a business case about how inefficient it is if you don't have

priorities. Are you putting the best people against projects that will deliver biggest return?"

Finally, he would approve of Carlini's efforts to improve the communication skills of her staff. "In my job, I see it time and time again. If you've got great interpersonal style and great intellect and great influence skills, you can pretty much get what you want done in a business. There's never just one thing that creates advantage. It's how it the whole integrated model works together and how sustainable it is, and that means people. That's why I say relationships are critical. We've had smart people who failed on the influencing part and interpersonal side."

As one responsible for finding and training a new generation of leaders, Westcott has several thoughts on developing IT leaders with business acumen.

It starts with the CIO. "The CIO sets the tone and has a huge influence on the IT organization on how important the business piece is. Barbara Carlini does a great job in integrating her function with the business. Any leader can make it happen if they've got the right mindset, and she certainly has."

In supporting these kinds of options, an organizational structure must facilitate true coordination. It must assist firms in exploiting technology-enabled opportunities such as virtual integration, direct access to customers, and cross-divisional or business-unit integration. For example, at Cisco Systems, the executive management team considered customer advocacy and relationships to be the strategic drivers of its business model. Cisco management focused on the coordination of business technology and customer-centric capabilities by having the CIO report to the senior executive responsible for customer advocacy, and by linking business and technology executives' compensation to customer-centric innovation using business technology.

Nurture relationship networks for visioning, innovation, and sourcing.
Chapter 4, "Governance: Who's in Charge?," introduced a networked governance model for business technology management (see Figure 5.2). This model emphasizes that four categories of

Figure 5.2 **A Networked Governance Model**

A networked governance model includes a visioning and oversight network, an innovation network, and a sourcing network.

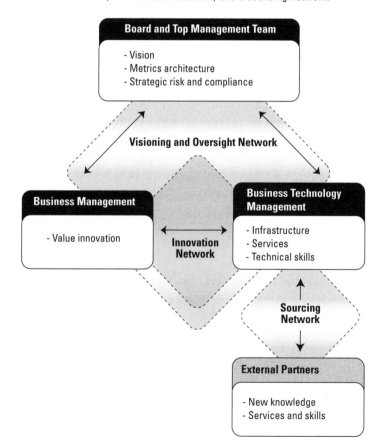

Board and Top Management Team

- Vision
- Metrics architecture
- Strategic risk and compliance

Visioning and Oversight Network

Business Management

- Value innovation

Innovation Network

Business Technology Management

- Infrastructure
- Services
- Technical skills

Sourcing Network

External Partners

- New knowledge
- Services and skills

stakeholders are important: the board and the top management team, business management, technology management, and external vendors. Among these stakeholders, three kinds of relationship networks are important: visioning, innovation, and sourcing.

Visioning networks involve senior business and technology executives and the board. They foster collaboration for creating and articulating a strategic vision about the role and value of business technology. Visioning networks help top management teams describe their perspectives on the role of business technology, their strategic priorities for its use, and the links they see between it and drivers of the business strategy. One of the mechanisms for establishing a visioning network is to have the CIO as a formal member of the top management team. Other mechanisms include the establishment of a Business Technology Management Council and a Business Technology Investment Board.

Innovation networks involve business and technology executives. They foster collaboration for conceptualizing and implementing business technology applications. These applications are often aimed at enhancing the firm's agility and innovation in customer relationships, manufacturing, product development, supply chain management, or enterprise control and governance systems. An example of organizational mechanisms that promote innovation networks is a corporate and divisional project approval committee. Whereas visioning networks engage the board and the top management to shape overall enterprise perspectives about the strategic role and value of business technology, innovation networks focus on specific innovations and strategic applications.

Sourcing networks are relationship networks between business technology executives and external partners. Their purpose is to foster collaboration between these internal and external parties when they are negotiating and managing multi-sourcing arrangements, joint ventures, or strategic alliances. Sourcing networks can help companies not only lower their costs but also augment their capabilities and business thinking about innovative uses of business technology. Attention to sourcing networks must be emphasized in key organizational units that deal with the technical architecture and infrastructure (for example, Office of Architecture and Standards) and the management of technology investments (Enterprise Program Management Office [EPMO]).

Organize to explicitly manage three categories of processes. Successful implementation of BTM capabilities requires not only the design of effective organizational structures, but attention to three categories of processes: *foundation*, *primary*, and *secondary* (see Table 5.1).

Table 5.1	Three Categories of Processes
	Three categories of processes must be addressed by an organizational structure.

Foundation Processes for BTM Supply-Side Management	
Infrastructure management	Activities for building and managing the architectural blueprint for investments in computing, networking, database, object-base, and other key information technologies to deliver a range of communication, collaboration, and productivity-enhancing tools and services. Includes the establishment and management of infrastructure standards.
Human capital management	Acquiring, developing, and retaining talent with an emphasis on managing the portfolio of technology skills needed today and in the future.

Primary Processes for BTM Demand-Side Management	
Value innovation	Strategic analysis of business opportunities for the use of business technology and conceptualization of ways in which it can be used to strengthen business competencies, customer relationships, or partner networks. Developing the business case and investment rationale for the strategic applications and establishing the value metrics.
Solutions delivery	Delivering applications either through internal development, external contracting, or through solutions integration of packaged software.
Services provisioning	The provisioning of utilities, such as data center, and services, such as helpdesk and desktop management, for users across the corporation.

Supporting Processes for BTM Administrative Management	
Business technology strategic planning	Activities aimed at managing the key supply and demand issues for business technology. These issues include the screening of emerging information technologies, IT infrastructure and services planning, human capital planning, and applications portfolio planning.
Business technology financial management	Activities associated with financial management and control, auditing, and risk management. Examples of these activities include the structuring of service level agreements, tracking and benchmarking the cost of services, developing the business case and ROI analyses of infrastructure investment proposals, developing value scorecards for projects, and supporting the monitoring of risks and detection of fraud.

Foundation processes are aimed at managing supply side pressures and relate to the two fundamental competencies of infrastructure and human capital.

Primary processes are aimed at managing demand pressures and relate to the delivery and support of business capabilities through enabling business technology and services. The three *primary* processes are

- Value innovation—Conceptualizing strategic business technology needs and opportunities in the form of applications

- Solutions delivery—Building business technology applications

- Services provisioning—Providing help desk, desktop configuration, and other support services

These *primary* processes are the touch points through which business clients perceive the quality, contributions, and effectiveness of business technology.

Secondary processes are related to administrative needs and requirements. Their contribution is measured by how well they support and enable the *foundation* and *primary* processes. The two *secondary* processes are strategic planning and financial management.

Develop a modular organizing logic.
Experience and research have revealed a number of modular organizational units that should be the building blocks of contemporary organization designs (see Table 5.2).

The effectiveness of these modular organizational units in nurturing visioning and oversight networks, innovation networks, sourcing networks, and in supporting *foundation, primary,* and *secondary* processes varies. Specific modular organizational units have different levels of relevance and impact depending on the type of governance network or value creating process (see Tables 5.3 and 5.4).

Business technology executives must understand how these organizational units should be configured into an overall organizational model for the firm. Also, as business conditions change they must determine the best way of adjusting and improvising specific governance networks or BTM processes. This must be accomplished without disrupting the organization or other networks and processes. The modular organizing logic described in

Leadership Insight

Rob Slagboom on Organization Models

The digitization of Transavia Airlines has brought changes in CIO Rob Slagboom's role. Business technology is no longer a cost center, he said in an interview. It is, instead, a business enabler.

A Business Transformer

As CIO of Transavia Airlines since 2001, Rob Slagboom has seen some big changes. Not the least was that the Amsterdam-based carrier made a major move onto the Web.

"It's the only way to do business with us," he says. "It's how we deal with suppliers, employees, customers. The Web is the business. Transavia Airlines is now transavia.com. We changed the name of the business. It's a new era for us. An old but very creative company declared that it was now a dot.com company."

The nature of his job has changed, as well. "A couple of years ago, IT was managed purely on cost. The change we have made is that we are now being positioned as a business enabler. That was quite new for Transavia. Actually, in our thinking we go beyond being a business enabler. IT is a business transformer."

This new way of thinking is leading to more change. Transavia develops a multiple-year business plan for the whole organization, yearly plans for each department and, from that, IT plans. Business technology program managers use a portfolio system to manage the work that results.

"Now I'm challenging this organizational model and IT governance," Slagboom says. KLM, which owns Transavia and where Slagboom used to work, had a centralized organization, and then decentralized. Then it moved to a federal model. "Now at Transavia, I would like to see business managers who understand IT and who are close to specific businesses. They will align business strategy and IT strategy for the separate departments.

"In the long term, I can see business unit managers understanding the technology better. Technology should be managed under their responsibility."

Given technology's more strategic role, he wants IT people to have different skills, too. "I need people who have a high level view, who can understand longer term approaches, who think strategically about IT. And they have to understand the business."

But where will he and every other CIO find these people?

"Who will be their teachers?" he asks. "It's the classical predicament of a field in development. It has to grow up."

Table 5.2 Modular Organizational Units

Modular organizational units must exist or be created to address specific responsibilities for BTM.

Organization Unit	Members	Responsibilities
Business Technology Investment Board	- **Head of IT Finance** - CIO - CEO - CFO - Business SVPs	- Set corporate budget - High level, exception monitoring of portfolio financials - Set portfolio investment target levels
Business Technology Council	- **Head of IT Strategy** - CIO - Business SVPs - Head of applications - Functional area leads - Client relationship managers	- High level, exception monitoring of portfolio financials, schedule, issues, and risk - "Own" business technology strategies that support business objectives - Review target business architectures - Define major enterprise initiatives to support the strategy - Review decisions by the Project Approval Committee - Ensure business oversight of critical initiatives
Divisional Project Approval Committee	- **Divisional Functional Heads** - Divisional CFO - Divisional PMO and finance representative - Divisional CIO - Divisional CTO - Enterprise functional leads (as needed) - IT directors (as needed)	- Evaluate divisional project requests for divisional and enterprise benefits - Evaluate divisional (and corporate) funding availability for projects - Prioritize project requests - Determine project requests to be submitted to corporate for approval - Review post implementation project benefits versus original business case
Corporate Project Approval Committee	- **Head of Portfolio & Program Management** - Head of enterprise architecture - Head of IT strategy - Business strategy analyst - Finance representative	- Conduct enterprise portfolio review of project requests - Confirm alignment with enterprise strategies - Approve project requests - Prepare reporting for quarterly BTC meetings
Office of Architecture & Standards	- **Head of Enterprise Architecture** - Business architects - Technical architects - CIO - CTO	- Develop architecture strategies - Conduct in-depth EA assessments - Assist project teams - Build "thin layer" of EA models to validate tactical alignment - Review project team EA deliverables - Manage asset portfolios - Develop standards and monitor conformance

Organization Unit	Members	Responsibilities
Office of the CIO	**- CIO** - CTO - Heads of IT security & risk - Heads of IT finance & strategy - Heads of IT HR & partner management - Head of IT application areas - Head of portfolio & program management - Head of enterprise architecture - Head of IT communications	- Manage relationships w/business owners - Coordinate project requests with Office of Portfolio Management - Approval decisions with Corporate Project Approval Committee - Monitor portfolio financials, schedule, issues, and risk - Validate completeness and accuracy of technology architectures - Develop business-driven IT strategies
Enterprise Program Management Office (EPMO)	**- Head of Portfolio & Program Management** - Client relationship managers - Program managers - Program administrators - CIO - CFO of IT	- Define and promote portfolio management approaches - Manage portfolio categories and views/reports - Manage all project requests - Categorize project requests in automated system - Coordinate BTC approval reviews, including portfolio analyses - Initiate formally funded projects - Provide guidance to project teams
Functional Groups	- Functional SMEs - Business analysts	- Provide subject matter expertise to project teams for individual projects - Provide subject matter expertise to BTC in business technology strategy development
BTM Center of Excellence	**- BTM Functional Lead** - Head of portfolio & program management - Head of enterprise architecture - Client relationship managers	- Act as internal BTM SME - Conduct on-going BTM assessments - Track progress and benefits - Identify improvement opportunities - Oversee/lead BTM improvement initiatives
Project Teams	**- Project Managers** - Business analysts - Technical analysts - Developers - Trainers	- Complete EA impact assessments - Plan and execute project work - Participate in stage gate reviews - Provide reporting on status, progress, issues

Tables 5.2, 5.3, and 5.4 best accomplishes these tasks. Using a modular approach, firms choose specific organizational units to address each of the governance networks and to steward process categories (see Table 5.1). Depending on the industry and organizational conditions at any time, specific units might be more appropriate for each network and process. The advantage of the modular logic is that it allows the implementation and adaptation of organizational units for each important governance network and value-creating process. Traditionally, firms have designed their organizational structures using a monolithic organizing logic, by choosing either centralization or decentralization of BTM decisions. However, today's organizing logic requires a much more sophisticated perspective that blends the virtues of centralization and decentralization.[6] The modular logic allows firms to unbundle their implementation of organizational units for different BTM activities.

Develop a strategic sourcing logic.
Building and managing a network of relationships with vendors, systems integrators, third-party applications developers, and business process outsourcing providers is critical. There are at least three reasons why such an extended network is necessary. First, external partners can be used to augment existing proficiencies (for example, solutions delivery, global infrastructure services) in addition to lowering the costs of global services provisioning. Second, external partners can be used to augment existing

Table 5.3	Modular Organizational Units and Governance Network Types
	Necessary organizational units vary by governance network type.

Governance Networks	Recommended Organizational Units
Visioning networks	- Business Technology Council
Innovation networks	- Business Technology Council - Business Technology Investment Board - Corporate Project Approval Committee - Divisional Project Approval Committee
Sourcing networks	- Office of the CIO - Enterprise Program Management Office (EPMO)

business capabilities (for example, online selling or procurement through third-party hosted Web sites) or lower the costs of execution of business processes (for example, call center outsourcing, benefits management). Finally, external partnerships can be leveraged in building new business capabilities, responding to new threats, vulnerabilities, or regulatory demands (for example, SOX attestations and compliance), and conducting strategic business experiments (for example, building business capabilities around RFID technologies).

Sourcing decisions permeate many of the value-creating processes for business technology management. For instance, infrastructure management processes should include leasing of IT assets (for example, desktops), licensing of software, and outsourcing (for example, data centers, network management).

Table 5.4   Modular Organizational Units and Value-Creating Process Types

Organizational unit responsibilities vary by value-creating process type.

Value-Creating Processes	Recommended Organizational Units
Infrastructure management	- Office of Architecture and Standards - Office of the CIO - Corporate Project Approval Committee - Business Technology Investment Board
Human capital management	- BTM Center of Excellence - Office of the CIO
Value innovation	- Business Technology Council - Business Technology Investment Board - Divisional Project Approval Committee - Corporate Project Approval Committee - Functional Groups, Office of the CIO
Solutions delivery	- Enterprise Program Management Office (EPMO) - Office of Architecture and Standards - Project teams
Services provisioning	- Office of the CIO - Business Technology Council
Financial management	- Office of the CIO - Business Technology Investment Board - Business Technology Council

Similarly, with the growing sophistication of outsourcing and off-shore firms, solutions delivery processes include extensive partnering with external firms. As a final example, with the growing tide of interest in enterprise risk management, external auditing firms should become partners in technology risk management and audit.

The following questions should frame decisions about outsourcing and partnering:

What are the core activities of the organization? What activities can be regarded as core—strategic in nature and best managed internally? For example, the development and maintenance of architecture and standards is a core activity and must be managed through the Office of Architecture and Standards. "Context" activities are important but not strategic and can be managed through outsourcing. For example, the procurement and maintenance of desktops, network services, and helpdesk services are appropriately viewed as "context."

What are the comparative capabilities of the external partners? Outsourcing makes sense when external partners possess economies of scale for specific activities (for example, customer call centers, benefits administration) or possess expertise not readily available inside the firm (for example, IT audits or risk assessment).

What are the appropriate monitoring, oversight, and relationship management practices? Service level agreements have traditionally been used to manage outsourcing relationships. Such agreements are appropriate for arm's-length relationships governed through fixed contracts. However, with growth in a number of ongoing and collaborative partnerships with external partners, where the firm engineers shared processes and knowledge with its partners, there is a need for other forms of monitoring and relationship management practices. The creation of a specific role for Partner Relationship Management (PRM) is important. In addition, the establishment of processes for intellectual capital management will be critical. Finally, due diligence processes must be established to monitor the ongoing viability of the business partners and their potential impacts on business and risks.

Leadership Insight

Vincent Stabile on Change

JetBlue is a technology-oriented, fast-growth company, and that has presented unique challenges to Vincent Stabile, vice president for people. In an interview he described how the company is preparing itself to accommodate the change.

Growing Pains

JetBlue expects to add 3,500 employees a year for the next few years, and a second generation of marketing, human resources and technology executives has come on board to prepare the organization for the next stage.

As Vice President for People, the company's title for the HR leader, Vincent Stabile has a front-row seat. "We've got a lot of the right processes started," he says. "Now it's making these a routine part of the way we do business, and not just one-offs."

The company now has around 80 projects underway. "They're not IT projects," Stabile says. "They're business projects with IT components. Each has a business owner."

JetBlue is known for its technology prowess, but it has never pursued technology for its own sake. "There has always been a business-driven IT focus here," Stabile says. "We define what the business needs and then go find the technology to support that. In other places I've worked, it was more the idea that here's this cool technology, now let's figure out how to use it somewhere."

And business needs will change. "One of the terms we use here a lot is scale," Stabile says. "I've never worked at a place that was on this kind of growth trajectory for so long. Anything we want to do, whether it's IT related or not, if it cannot scale to a large magnitude we'll be in trouble."

A more sophisticated logic is needed

Traditional wisdom about organization structures has primarily focused on governance rights for key decisions. Most attention had been on three designs: centralized, decentralized, or federal. In the centralized designs, most decisions are made by the IT function. In the decentralized, most key decisions are made by business. The federal design combines elements of both by dispersing authority for specific decisions to the business units and the IT function. However, as should be evident from the principles described previously, a more sophisticated logic is needed today.

Executive Agenda

Organization Design

▶ **Organize** and manage based on value-creating processes. Do not set up committees for their own sake. Take stock of the value creating processes that these organizational structures will support, as illustrated in Table 5.4. Remember that the level of complexity associated with an organizational unit will vary based on the sophistication of the governance network it supports. Apply a modular organizing logic in designing critical business technology organization structures. Consider explicitly assigning individual executives to each one of these modular organizational units.

▶ **Recognize** that *Organization Design and Change Management* is a critical BTM capability. Organization design changes must be managed with care. Strong relationships need to be built with stakeholders. How can you promote "straight talk" in an environment that values commitment and relationships? How can you lead the your team to accept that difficulties along the way are not failures, but rather a normal part of the change process? How will you resolve these rough spots and build on them to fuel the organizational change effort? Develop "bottom up" change agents—rarely does change result solely from a top-down edict. Lower-level employees must buy in. Cultivating change agents can guarantee their support in selling their peers.

▶ **Develop** your *Communication Strategy and Management* capability, which has significant implications for evolving organization structures. The board, senior management team, business technology executives, and external partners are some of the numerous stakeholders in BTM today. Therefore, *Communications Strategy & Management* is the responsibility of the entire senior management team, and should be supported by expert communications professionals, to ensure the following:

- 1. The communications strategy is based on behavior-based goals/objectives. (Who has to do what for this to be successful?)

- 2. A path is defined to move target audiences from mere awareness to understanding, commitment, and action.

- 3. The plan includes appropriate communications research, channel identification, key messages, timeline, and measurements of success.

Notes

1   See the "Key Terminology" section in Chapter 1.

2   Peter Weill and Jeanne Ross. *IT Governance: How Top Performers Manage IT Decision Rights for Superior Results*. Harvard Business School Press, 2004.

3   See the "Key Terminology" section in Chapter 1.

4   Ibid.

5   Ibid.

6   Agarwal, R. and Sambamurthy, V. *Principles and Models for Organizing the IT Function*. 2002.

II

Leading the Pack

Realizing Critical BTM Capabilities

6

"Portfolio management can serve different purposes at different levels in the organization. Even in an age of rapidly changing technologies and priorities, there is great value in an alignment of efforts, and the avoidance of unnecessary duplication. For the Department of the Navy, we expect IT portfolio management to be the vehicle that allows us to effectively carry out our warfighting mission."

—David Wennergren, CIO, U.S. Navy

Buy, Hold, or Sell?

In Brief

Most companies have not successfully used a portfolio approach to manage business and technology together.

Portfolio and Program Management (PPM) is the enterprise-wide focus on defining, gathering, categorizing, analyzing, and monitoring information on corporate assets and activity.

PPM provides top managers a centralized and balanced view of the payoffs of various business technology[1] projects that lays out the benefits and risks of each.

An effective PPM capability can only be realized through a balanced and thorough focus on organization structures, processes, information, and automation.

The procedure is elemental, and known to anyone hoping to make sense of hundreds of songs or photos on a hard drive, or wanting the basement cleaned out: Discover what you have, sort it into logical piles, and assess the value of the individual items against some larger goal.

In business, this procedure assumes a fancy name, portfolio management, but it is still elemental—in fact, its power is such that it might even be deemed critical. Managers of financial assets would not presume to act without it. It is widely applied in other management functions, including strategic planning and new product development. Most business technology executives know of it, and many practice some form of it, but it has not often been granted the strategic role it deserves.

Many companies do not reap the full rewards because they see it only in financial terms. Or they think of it as a software tool. Or they view it as a tactical approach for managing projects. At its best, however, portfolio management as advanced by the Portfolio and Program

Management (PPM) *capability takes all of a firm's assets and activities into account. It is more a way of doing business that gives the entire company, from the boardroom down, better information to develop strategies, manage risk, and execute more effectively. Contributing authors for this chapter are Michael Fillios, Chief Product Officer, Enamics, Inc.; William Kettinger, Associate Professor and Director of the Center of Information Management and Technology Research at the University of South Carolina; Terry Kirkpatrick, Editor in Chief, Enamics, Inc.; Rajiv Kohli, Associate Professor of Management Information Systems at the College of William and Mary; and James Lebinski, Vice President of Knowledge Products, Enamics.*

Business technology executives are familiar with the general concept of portfolio management. In a recent survey, 89 percent of the 130 Fortune 1000 CIOs polled said they were aware of it. However, most companies have not successfully used it to significantly improve the return on their investment in technology.[2]

Only 17 percent of the companies polled appeared to be realizing its full value. In other companies, key activities such as central oversight of the technology budget and documentation of business technology applications were lacking, and many companies did not properly conduct project evaluation and tracking. The result is that about 68 percent of corporate technology projects run over time or budget and do not deliver the hoped-for business value.[3]

Another survey of 507 business technology executives revealed that only 40 percent practice portfolio management—this despite the fact that, of those who do use it, 92 percent said it led to better decisions. Sixty-seven percent of those with a portfolio approach also said it increased their credibility with business units.[4]

One particularly illuminating finding in the survey: More than half the respondents said that setting priorities on projects in their companies was politically driven. Although this is not surprising, we would argue that by applying the *Portfolio and Program Management (PPM)* capability, organizations can replace political contests with fact-based decision making.

Various terms with various definitions have been used to describe this concept. We use Portfolio and Program Management to convey its holistic nature. We define PPM as the *enterprise-wide* focus on defining, gathering, categorizing, analyzing, and monitoring information on corporate assets and activity to achieve business objectives.

> *More than half the respondents in a survey said that setting priorities on projects in their companies was politically driven.*

PPM elevates decision making

An effective PPM approach can unite an organization's efforts at every level. It is a completely different way of seeing, assessing, and planning the business—analogous, to a degree, to financial portfolio management. For example, in finance, where the concept of portfolio management originated, an investor identifies and categorizes all assets and collects them in a portfolio. This allows the investor to see various aggregated views of individual investments. The investor might see, for instance, that the portfolio is weighted too heavily in one industry, has redundant exposure to one type of security, carries a certain level of risk, and promises a certain level of return. The investor can then set a strategy and construct a new portfolio likely to achieve an appropriate balance of risk-return. In much the same way, IT asset portfolios reveal what a company owns, and business technology project portfolios reveal what its various arms are trying to accomplish. It can thus decide which pieces of all this activity are more likely to support the enterprise business strategy.

PPM plays a strategic role

The bottom line is that effective PPM can help a company better align business technology spending with current and future business needs. PPM creates information and insight to help executives and managers make such decisions as these:

- Defining business improvement options and scenarios
- Analyzing implications/impacts of potential initiatives
- Setting target allocations for investment categories

- Evaluating and making decisions on project requests

- Evaluating the health of IT assets

- Determining appropriate sequencing of major programs

- Managing risk mitigation across the enterprise

- Identifying and resolving critical project-related issues

PPM provides a centralized and balanced view of various projects that lays out the benefits and risks of each one, making it possible to select among them and create an optimal investment portfolio. Through a centralized view of all business technology projects, a good portfolio will make it easy to ensure that investments are well balanced in terms of size, risk, and projected payoff. Used wisely, it will actually increase business technology's value by exposing projects that are redundant or risky, while revealing how to shift funds from low-value investments to high-value, strategic ones.[6]

> *PPM provides top managers a centralized and balanced view of various projects and lays out the benefits and risks of each one, making it possible to select among them and create an optimal investment portfolio.*

PPM leads to smarter decisions, improving the allocation of resources and reducing project failures. For example, in the early days of the Internet, Sun Microsystems decided to move its entire business onto the Web, initiating more than 100 Internet projects that differed significantly in systems, design guidelines, and protocols. Sun eventually realized that this approach made it impossible to balance project risks and optimize its use of resources. So, top management adopted a portfolio approach, and Sun ended up converting its 100 Internet projects into a coordinated, manageable portfolio of about 15 initiatives.[7]

PPM reduces business technology costs by eliminating unnecessary projects and management activities that do not add value. Executives at Guardian Insurance estimated that PPM reduced overall applications expenditures by 20 percent, resulting in a decrease in maintenance costs from 30 percent to 18 percent. The director of enterprise governance at AXA Financial Inc. estimated that PPM saved his company $5 million to $10 million in the first year alone.[8]

PPM improves collaboration between business and technology in several ways: It creates a "single view of the truth" about a firm's operations, and it generates a common vocabulary and set of metrics. It permits a comprehensive set of decisions to be made before action is taken, identifying and resolving conflicts. It allows strategic direction flowing down to meet, in a formal management process, suggested courses of action flowing up. PPM is, in fact, continuous: Strategic planning informs portfolio managers, who reassess programs and projects. Information on the status of IT assets, risks, and financial performance likewise influences subsequent strategic planning.

PPM provides information that links business needs with business technology activities—enabling a converged viewpoint that is simply focused on business outcomes, rather than advancing the interests of one group versus another. PPM allows an organization to get beyond the incomplete approach of computing the

Research Insight

Alan Matula on Portfolio Management

From his experience at another Shell company, Alan Matula intimately knew the many steps involved in balancing technology with the needs of the business. One big step, he said in an interview, was the creation of portfolios.

The Long Journey

When Alan Matula became CIO of Shell Oil Products, where he would oversee a $1.2 billion IT budget and 2,000 employees, he knew what lay ahead, because he had gone through it as CIO of the chemicals division.

The first thing he did was to select members of the non-IT executive team to produce a business architecture. This was a picture of the business—market, process, and organization. It defined the business model and governance, which included structure and decision making. "Without a business architecture you're kind of at the whim of whatever agenda anyone has," Matula says.

The process they used to produce the architecture was homegrown. "You could probably pick up any methodology and use it, but you never want to use a methodology," Matula says. "More than half the battle is to get the business side to own it and be able to describe it in their own words. It's a lot more powerful to give them a blank white board and say draw your business model and how you want to compete. It's an ownership issue. You have to let them create it themselves. Give me half the executive team and four hours a month, and in six months, you'll have a business-driven architecture. As long as the CEO says let's march through this, it works."

Counting things

The business architecture led to a technology architecture, how IT planned to meet the business demand. "The easy part is the business architecture," Matula says. "The next part is laying that supply structure in place. You have to be able to count things. On the supply side, that's people, assets, and money. It's not the easiest thing to do. The first time you actually count things, list things, how many servers you have, sites, employees, it's an emotional event. People will say, 'I had no idea that's what we have.'

"But that's just the first of 10 steps. Next, you start working down the portfolio decisions. A lot of those decisions are long lead time, high investment decisions. I would put us at the early phases of a long journey, a five to seven year journey."

The organization has just concluded what he calls a "pretty ruthless" portfolio prioritization. "It goes from reporting systems to ERP to everything else. It was a painful process because we also capped the spend. We wanted to force a dialog between IT and business around an investment program to drive the journey, and we want the journey to be paced."

Equilibrium cycle

Next comes a natural equilibrium cycle, lasting a year or less, in which supply and demand are tweaked and matched, Matula says. At the same time, the CIO should be optimizing the IT function—for example application rationalization or infrastructure consolidation. Finally, the effort must be sustainable. "It's only sustainable if you build in compliance around some critical IT processes. Demand structure and support structure have to be held hostage to a few functional excellence plays—finance, HR, security, development, support. Those are sacrosanct."

The whole process continues for several years. "Whenever you walk into an organization, supply and demand are usually out of balance," Matula says. "And you've got to put it back into balance, and so you hand it to the business guys. And they start working SLAs and right sizing. My history is they will always go too far. They always turn the crank on costs and staff further than it needs to go, but you can't stop them so you just let it happen. And you coach them, and you eventually get back to equilibrium."

ROI of individual projects. With a portfolio viewpoint, the payback of a project can be evaluated within the context of many projects contributing to a business goal. The merits of individual projects are not seen in isolation but in consideration of their contribution to business capabilities that enable a strategy. In forward-thinking companies, business technology and IT portfolios become inseparable from other portfolios—R&D, new products, and the like—and become just another component of a business initiative.

The anatomy of a portfolio

Portfolios, each with different "views," should be created to support different types of activity at various levels within the organization, as depicted in Figure 6.1.

Figure 6.1 **Sample Portfolio Types**

Different portfolios should be defined for a range of business and technology management purposes, ranging from accurately inventorying IT assets to managing strategic risk.

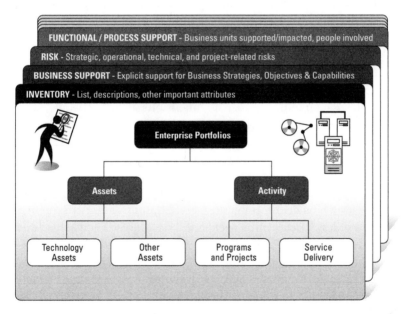

> IT asset portfolios reveal what a company owns, and business technology project portfolios reveal what its various arms are trying to accomplish. It can thus decide which pieces of all this activity are more likely to support the overall business strategy.

Portfolios of assets and activities provide an enterprise-wide perspective for executives and managers to ensure that the organization is deploying resources in such a way that it will meet its business objectives.

Asset-related portfolios, for example, include technology assets and other (nonfinancial) assets:

Technology asset portfolios include business applications and tools, data and infrastructure (that is, hardware, operating systems, systems software, and so on).

Other (nonfinancial) asset portfolios include an organization's people resources, the business processes it performs, and the intellectual property it owns.

Activity-related portfolios consist of discrete projects and programs and efforts related to continuous service delivery:

- *Project-level portfolios* include planned undertakings of related activities, which have a beginning and an end, to reach an objective. Having an enterprise portfolio of projects available to executives and managers enables better monitoring and exception-based management by allowing issues to float to the top. For example, a dashboard providing project-level red/yellow/green indicators across dimensions such as schedule, cost, scope, risk, and governance allows executives to focus on the exceptions, instead of spending their time gathering and reviewing reams of data on all projects.

- *Enterprise project portfolios* also help with a variety of other activities, such as decision making, by helping to identify synergies and redundancies in projects and/or requests; knowledge asset reuse, through identification of opportunities to reuse intellectual property assets produced on related projects; and resource and demand management, by providing accurate and timely information on project-related demand.

- *Program-level portfolios* include groups of related projects that all need to be completed to reach a certain level of benefits, and which are managed in a coordinated way to obtain a level of benefits and control not available from managing them individually. For example, a program to improve customer retention via the Internet might contain such projects as Web site redesign, implementation of a new customer relationship management (CRM) process and tool, and execution of an email marketing campaign. Program managers would ensure that the interdependencies among these projects are well understood, manage risk that cannot be addressed by individual project teams, and deal with other issues such as resource balancing across projects. Having a program view, with linkage to the underlying projects available to executives and managers, enables effective and timely oversight.

Research Insight

Prof. Warren McFarlan on Portfolio Management

His many years of advising companies on managing technology have given F. Warren McFarlan, the Baker Foundation Professor and Albert H. Gordon Professor of Business Administration Emeritus at Harvard Business School, a realistic look at what it takes to implement portfolio management. It means change, and that is hard. This is an excerpt from an interview.

Winners and Losers

"At the base of the portfolio are the "must do's." You don't have any choice whatsoever. You either do them or you're out of business or in front of Eliott Spitzer.

"When you talk about a portfolio, I'm always interested in knowing how I'm doing vis-á-vis my competitors. Am I executing my portfolio from a catch up position? Am I executing it from the position of a leader? Am I just about in the middle of the crowd? Where do I want to be? If I'm in a dominant position, then I may wonder whether I need to add additional features. The portfolio is not done in a corporate vacuum.

"You must look at your portfolio and ask, 'Is this what I really want to do as a company? Do I want to have 95 percent of my money invested in infrastructure? Do I want to have nothing on the customer interface?' There are no right answers to these questions. The question is to be able to tease up the strategic thrust of the portfolio so that you can see if it is aligned to what the company needs to do to compete.

"It's hard to do portfolio management. The portfolio approach cuts across the existing management control systems and allocates scarce resources in a different way. When you're doing that, it creates many political issues, because there are winners and losers and people push back. A good portfolio review process can force dramatic resource allocation shifts.

"It's also hard because in organizations that have an ROI focus, how you think about the portfolio value is complicated. Everybody can think about cost cutting and they can think about generating new revenue. They have more trouble thinking about investments that are primarily revenue protection and what happens if you don't do them. Some people say portfolio management is one more overhead activity and costs too much. Others say, we don't understand it. Finally, another crowd says IT is a commodity. We don't want to look at it in aggregate. Just as we don't look at our electricity budget as a whole. We want it lined up by business unit.

"Remember, in portfolio management, there are winners and there are losers."

• *Service delivery portfolios* include the operational, non-project-related efforts required to support business operations. This is a critical piece of the overall pie when analyzing how well the organization is performing, and whether the company is working on the right things based on business objectives. This information is also critical when examining the enterprise resource portfolio and planning for changes to meet demand.

PPM is a critical enabler of many business activities and BTM capabilities.[9] As illustrated in Figure 6.2, the intelligence and perspectives PPM generates become an integral part of, for example, strategy creation, application management, resource and demand management, project approval and prioritization, and compliance and risk management.

Compliance and risk management. PPM supports the *Compliance and Risk Management* BTM capability by assisting in the definition of enterprise risk types and related portfolio structures, analyzing organizational vulnerabilities and business objectives, developing generic risk mitigation approaches, and gathering enterprise risks and categorizing them into risk portfolios. These portfolios might categorize risks as strategic, operational, technical, or project related. PPM also supports *Compliance and Risk Management* by allowing executives to review an overall enterprise risk map, which provides the ability to analyze and prioritize the risks to be mitigated.

Business-Driven IT Strategy. With regard to the *Business-Driven IT Strategy* capability, PPM aids in gathering information on the enterprise business strategy, its objectives, and desired capabilities. It does so by creating portfolios of current enterprise applications, data and infrastructure assets, and architecture, along with portfolios on current and planned enterprise initiatives. PPM also allows the evaluation of IT assets and business technology initiatives (existing and planned) against business objectives. It identifies business technology enablers to help shape business strategy and guides the development of target architecture vision for applications, data, and infrastructure.

Figure 6.2 **Support for Other Capabilities**

Portfolio and Program Management's impact extends well beyond its core focus.

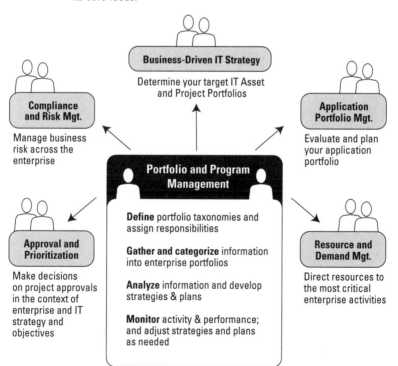

Resource and Demand Management. PPM improves the *Resource and Demand Management* capability through the creation of supply portfolios that identify resources and skills and their availability and allocation. A project demand portfolio should likewise be established for prioritized potential initiatives, planned initiatives, and currently active initiatives. An ongoing operational demand portfolio should be established for problem resolution, minor enhancements (nonproject), service requests, and other maintenance and general support. Using these supply and demand portfolios allows an effective assessment of the balance of risk and reward, as well as performing resource allocation and balancing. This includes assessing utilization and performance, determining a desired target resource portfolio and planning resource portfolio adjustments.

Approval and Prioritization. PPM supports *Approval and Prioritization* by presenting an enterprise perspective on the expected business value of different projects, as well as the potential project risks. In supporting this task, program, project, and risk-assessment portfolios can be built that address evaluation criteria such as[10] project complexity, project uncertainty, the stability and quality of IT development group and ultimately the expected business capabilities that will be enabled.

PPM involves four activities

Many companies are not prepared to adopt a portfolio-level perspective or manage the interdependencies among a large number of initiatives. Often, business technology executives think of portfolio management as strictly a project-based exercise, a province of the IT department with little connection to the rest of the business. An effective PPM capability, however, can be realized only through a balanced and thorough focus on organization structures, processes, information, and automation.

Activity 1. Create structures, define taxonomies, and assign responsibilities. A successful PPM capability requires that the right processes be performed by the right people across the organization at a number of levels.

Ideally, an Enterprise Program Management Office (EPMO) under the CIO will assume responsibility for managing portfolios, programs, and projects. Its responsibilities include educating the company and collaborating with key constituents on PPM processes. This group also ensures that the organization has the appropriate tools and information available to perform portfolio analysis, and it is the source of an accurate inventory of initiatives and assets. The EPMO exercises control in defining and overseeing project justification and prioritization; it is the operational owner of project resources and is responsible for the allocation of scarce resources. This includes defining project management approaches and ultimately offering project-level oversight.

Owners, stakeholders, and customers of the EPMO include the Office of the CIO, Office of Architecture and Standards, and line of business (LOB) executives. The CIO functions as sponsor and reviewer, and in many cases a CFO of IT also participates as a reviewer. Collectively, the owners and stakeholders must execute PPM in a way that ensures that project risks are being managed, process designs meet objectives, applications and requirements support processes, and standards and target architectures are being followed.

The CIO and other CXOs are customers of information provided by the EPMO, although much of their work is done in other bodies. A Business Technology Council (a cross-functional group of senior executives), for example, might be where these executives review the organization's portfolios for strategic fit. This group owns the overall strategy, ensuring that the portfolio of technology investments is in sync with the company's strategy and objectives and that major initiatives are receiving the right level of business sponsorship and attention.

A leadership team in the Office of the CIO should exist to review project requests submitted by divisional project approval committees. It can evaluate project requests against enterprise-wide business objectives, strategies, target architectures, and standards; and it can ensure that the project is appropriately coordinated with other similar initiatives. This leadership team should report its project approval decisions to the Business Technology Council.

Divisional business technology project approval committees can use portfolio information for their slice of the business to evaluate, prioritize, and select business technology investments, annual operating plans, and out-of-cycle projects. Divisional CTOs and CIOs would participate and provide an enterprise perspective to the group's efforts. This group would also identify a business sponsor and a project steering committee.

At the project level, project steering committees, with members from business and IT, would ensure adequate business and IT project resources, provide project-level oversight, participate in stage gate reviews and provide authorization to proceed; resolve critical project issues, and escalate issues as needed to the Business Technology Council.

Activity 2. Gather and categorize information into enterprise portfolios. A discovery needs to take place—involving taking an inventory of company assets and activity. This information-gathering step must be orchestrated effectively because it is no trivial undertaking. Portfolios will support the activities performed by executives and managers in the organization. In creating port-folios, it is critical that these activities be examined in detail so that *customized* portfolios can be created for these users.

A CIO, for example, might have these regular responsibilities (among others): monitoring high-risk projects, collaborating and providing status reports to country business leaders, managing the overall budget, and collaborating with organization's business technology investment board to allocate investment dollars. To perform these tasks, the CIO would need a portfolio categorized by risk level, one categorized by country, one containing all initiatives, and one categorized by investment type (see Figure 6.3). There is no one correct set of portfolios; they should be customized to the strategic needs of the company and the decisions executives must make.

Activity 3. Analyze information and develop strategies and plans. The actual analysis using portfolio information will vary depending on the area of activity. For example, if the Business Technology Council is evaluating out-of-cycle project requests, the aggregate investment portfolio might be analyzed to determine alignment with the company's portfolio investment strategy. If at the outset of the year, the company planned to allocate spending at 50 percent to infrastructure, 20 percent to transaction processing, 20 percent to decision support, and 10 percent to strategic proj-ects, their approval and prioritization decisions should support this distribution.

Another example might be where the company is developing its business-driven IT strategy and is attempting to plan the resources to support the strategy over the next three years. In this case, the resource supply and demand portfolios would be analyzed

Figure 6.3 **Typical CIO Supporting Portfolios**

Portfolios should be created to support various decision makers such as the CIO.

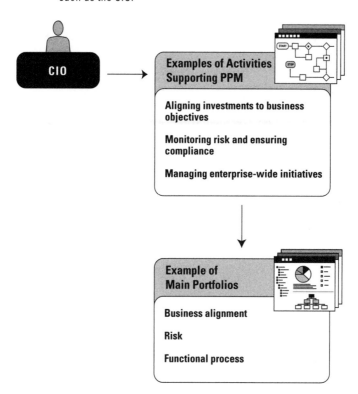

to develop an appropriate balance of risk and reward given the desired business and technology targets.

Activity 4. Monitor operations and performance. PPM analytics should support the automatic roll-up of detailed data (see Figure 6.4), which helps to shift the focus of managers from the administrative task of gathering and summarizing data to analysis and decision making. As in Step 3, the actual monitoring that should be performed will depend on the specific area of activity.

As discussed in Chapter 9, "Measuring Success," defining the appropriate metrics to measure performance is a critical step. After portfolios are created, taxonomies are defined and information is categorized to support decision making, performance metrics should be used to measure the effectiveness of the portfolio. You can use a variety of metrics to measure performance. These metrics typically are organized into categories such as financial—economic cost and benefit; business impact—contribution to business performance; risk—likelihood of success or failure; and architectural fit—compatibility with guidelines.

Ultimately, *Portfolio and Program Management* is a managerial exercise,not a technical one, and certainly not one only for the use of technology executives. When an organization realizes this, PPM will become a strategic tool for top executives to use in setting the company's direction.

Figure 6.4   PPM Data Aggregation

Reporting and scorecards, based on detailed data for tactical decisions, as well as consolidated analysis for strategic oversight, must be automated.

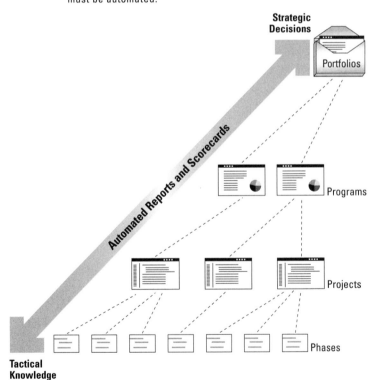

Creating Business Technology Portfolios

▶ **Educate** senior business and technology executives about the benefits of a portfolio approach. Consider developing a PPM capability for a small slice of the business to demonstrate the benefits and build consensus for embarking on an enterprise-wide effort.

▶ **Establish** management commitment and vision. Most of PPM implementation is not technical but managerial, and the commitment and strategic vision of top executives should be established and sustained. PPM involves many different people needing to do things differently within the organization and must be supported by senior management to achieve success.

▶ **Address** new organizational structures early on. Plan the creation of an Enterprise Program Management Office (EPMO), which in most cases owns PPM. The EPMO's responsibilities need to include educating the company on PPM processes and collaborating with key constituents to establish portfolio management approaches. This group will also provide the tools to analyze portfolios and gain access to the inventory of programs, initiatives and assets. Plan, as well, the design of a Business Technology Council, the upper-level strategic decision-making body.

▶ **Design** information management explicitly. PPM will be an outright failure if the information gathering is not performed adequately from the outset and if information is not kept up to date. Specific processes and responsibilities related to the creation, approval, and updating of information are critical.

▶ **Keep** automation in perspective. Do not focus your entire efforts on a PPM tool. The organizational processes and responsibilities to support PPM are far more important. Countless companies have failed in their implementation efforts of PPM tools.

▶ **Sustain** a high degree of focus on PPM end users. PPM requires an intense end-user focus due to the fact that PPM is at its core an enabler of other activity. End users must have access to customized portfolios to support the activities they need to perform daily.

Notes

1   See the "Key Terminology" section in Chapter 1.

2   Jeffery and Leliveld. "Best Practice in IT Portfolio Management." *Sloan Management Review*, Spring 2004, pp. 41–49.

3   Ibid.

4   "Research: Project Management 2004." *CIO Insight*, July 1, 2004.

5   See the "Key Terminology" section in Chapter 1.

6   Berinato, Scott. "Do the Math." *CIO*, October 1, 2001.

7   Tjan. "A Way to Put Your Internet Portfolio in Order." *Harvard Business Review*, February, 2001.

8   Henig, Peter. "The Efficient Frontier: AXA Financial Inc." *CIO Insight*, June 1, 2004.

9   See the "Key Terminology" section in Chapter 1.

10   Lyytinen, K., Mathiassen, L. and Ropponen, J. "Attention Shaping and Software Risk: A Categorical Analysis of Four Classical Risk Management Approaches." *Information Systems Research*, 9(3): 233–255, 1998. McFarlan, F. W. "Portfolio Approach to Information Systems." *Harvard Business Review*. September – October, 1981.

7

"Actual business processes are often way more complex than people think at first. You always write down the straightforward case if everything goes well, but then all the different surprises and error conditions, where it's not just software, but humans calling each other, sending email, faxes, the way you involve them is very tricky."

—Bill Gates, Chairman, Microsoft

The Age of Process

In Brief

The increased demand on firms to sense and respond quickly to changes in their environments requires a Strategic Enterprise Architecture (SEA) to enable business agility.

Developing BTM capabilities[2] in the functional area of SEA will bring a much-needed order to the islands of information in large organizations. SEA can also serve as the basis for a Service-Oriented Architecture (SOA).

Being agile requires sense-and-response capabilities that are shaped by designing and managing business processes and technology enablers together.

Processes in most companies are unmanaged, invisible, and unmeasured, and, consequently, are executed haphazardly and inconsistently. This results in delays, errors, low quality, and high overhead costs.

The Service-Oriented Business Execution Model (SOBEM) is a way of organizing the elements, models, and architecture components that help to design processes for agility.

Recent trends in technology and business have required managers to use business technology[1] to create an agile business. The increased demand on firms to sense and respond quickly to changes in their environments requires the creation of a Strategic Enterprise Architecture (SEA). This chapter first shows how business processes can be improved by redesigning structural arrangements and using contemporary process technologies. It then discusses how business network architectures and SEA can be managed. It also shows how SEA sets the context to determine the services that are required to support business initiatives, and how this can form the basis of a Service-Oriented Architecture (SOA). Finally, a methodology to conceive an overall business process as a collection of lower-level services and to manage them in response to customer needs, called the Service-Oriented Business Execution Model (SOBEM) is discussed.

Contributing authors for this chapter are Michael Fillios, Chief Product Officer,

Enamics, Inc.; James Lebinski, Vice President of Knowledge Products, Enamics, Inc.; Lars Mathiassen, Professor at the Computer Information Systems Department and co-Founder of The Center for Process Innovation at Georgia State University; Arun Rai, the Harkins Chaired Professor, Department of Computer Information Systems from the Robinson College of Business at Georgia State University; and Richard Welke, Director, Center for Process Innovation and Professor, Computer Information Systems, Georgia State University.

An underlying premise of BTM[3] is that business technology enables business processes, which in turn shape the strategic goals a firm can pursue. The BTM Standard directs that technology must be aligned, synchronized or even converged with business processes. This shapes the ability of firms to respond to existing customer demands, as well as shifts in markets, technologies, and government regulations.

Changes in technology and business are dramatically reshaping the process and management capabilities companies require and the means through which they are enabled by business technology. Three trends are significant:

- First, business activities are increasingly connected through global business networks offering new opportunities for horizontal integration and information sharing across firm boundaries. This trend opens new opportunities, but it also makes it difficult to manage effectively from a single center of authority based on one firm's interests.

- Second, business technology is becoming ubiquitous—embedded in activities, machinery, products and services, making it possible to collect data about business processes and outcomes seamlessly. This facilitates the vertical integration of objects and data, and it creates the technological basis for the real-time enterprise.

- Third, models such as the SOBEM make it possible to conceive an overall business process as a collection of lower-level services and to manage them in response to customer needs.

These three trends emphasize the importance of adopting a holistic perspective for horizontal and vertical processes. Only then can senior management follow the interactions between activities end-to-end across firm boundaries, exploit competencies for efficiency, and explore new opportunities.

Rapidly changing environments require firms to adapt quickly. Some changes relate to incremental modifications in customer preferences, technologies and markets; these can typically be predicted and planned for. Others, such as technological breakthroughs (for example, the Internet), terrorist attacks (for example, as they impact security), government interventions (for example, Sarbanes-Oxley), and mergers between firms (for example, as they impact infrastructure integration), require firms to reconfigure processes and IT infrastructures in unpredictable ways. The increased demand on firms to be able to sense and respond quickly requires firms to create a Strategic Enterprise Architecture (SEA). A SEA is a robust description of a firm's business strategy and the technology that supports it. SEA is one of the four functional areas of BTM.

How firms develop business agility

Success requires innovation in services and products. It also requires the continuous improvement of business processes within and across firm boundaries. These two mandates are mirror images. Innovation of services and products cannot occur without well-defined and aligned processes; nor can business processes be improved without attention to changes in customer needs.

The BTM functional area of Strategic Enterprise Architecture (SEA) includes the capabilities necessary to design the enterprise from business, process, application, data and infrastructure perspectives. These are the *Business Architecture* (business strategies, operating models, and processes) and *Technology Architecture* (applications, data, and infrastructure) capabilities. These BTM capabilities will bring order to the islands of information that exist typically in large organizations (see Figure 7.1).

Organizations have used a variety of resources to document bits and pieces of the way they operate over time, yet much of this information is disjointed, incomplete and of little value. This is often the result of not using commonly agreed-on standards and terminology, or of architectures that are not complete. This makes it difficult to formulate a cohesive picture of the business and technology architectures.

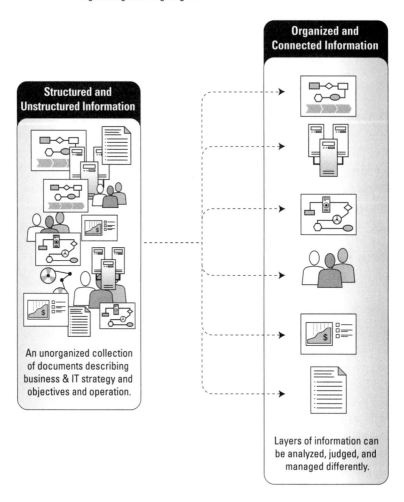

Figure 7.1   **Strategic Enterprise Architecture**

SEA transforms structured and unstructured information by organizing and aligning it.

Organized and Connected Information

Structured and Unstructured Information

An unorganized collection of documents describing business & IT strategy and objectives and operation.

Layers of information can be analyzed, judged, and managed differently.

Agility introduces new challenges

Agility is a new paradigm for the production and distribution of services and products. It achieves economies of scope rather than economies of scale. To be agile, firms must serve ever-smaller niche markets and individual customers without the high cost traditionally associated with customization. Being agile requires sense-and-respond capabilities that are shaped by designing and managing business processes and technology enablers together. Three requirements express the challenges managers face:

Sense-and-respond capability. To respond to changes in their environment, firms must facilitate learning from various processes. This learning must operate at different levels and within different areas of the firm and should be based on recurrent sense-and-respond cycles.[4] Business technology can facilitate these learning processes by supporting (1) collection, distribution, analysis, and interpretation of data associated with business processes; and (2) generation of response alternatives, decisions on appropriate courses of action, and orchestration of selected responses.

Improvement and innovation emphasis. Business agility combines improvement and innovation responses (see Figure 7.2). Opportunistic firms emphasize improvements, but often fail to foster innovations. They follow best practices, listen to the customer, and are good at improving current capabilities. Innovative firms, by contrast, are focused on innovating processes through new technologies, services, and strategies. They generate "next" practices but have a limited focus on fine-tuning current operations. Fragile firms lack both the ability to identify and explore opportunities, as well as the ability to innovate. When market pressures are high and the environment is turbulent, the ideal is an agile firm that combines improvement and innovation initiatives to constantly reposition itself.

Distributed and coordinated authority. Agile firms must adopt radically different forms of governance and translate their mission and objectives into information that can easily be interpreted by constituents.[6] These firms must replace traditional command and control approaches with mechanisms that facilitate coordination within and across locales. These mechanisms must provide individuals, groups and units the autonomy to improvise and act on local knowledge, while orchestrating coherent behavior across the firm. Also, processes ("who or what does what to what and with what") must be supplemented with personal accountability ("who owes what to whom and by when").

Regardless of where one begins the journey toward agility, one quickly encounters the issue of having to align processes of business networks and the information service architecture that supports them.

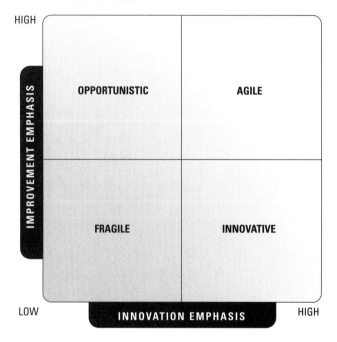

Figure 7.2 **Response-Ability States[5]**
Agile firms are able to improve existing practices and innovate new ones.

How process perspectives have evolved

Organizational processes have been an object of improvement for as long as formalized management studies have existed. A short list of key ideas associated with this evolution is provided in Table 7.1. These are but a sampling of ideas that have influenced how business processes can be managed.

Despite this multi-decade focus, business technology processes in many companies are unmanaged, invisible, and unmeasured, and, consequently, are executed haphazardly and inconsistently. This results in delays, errors, low quality, and high overhead costs. Such unmanaged processes cannot detect and adapt to changing market conditions—which in today's business environment can be fatal. There are countless reasons for this continuing malaise.[7] Chief among them is that processes cross both internal and external firm boundaries as part of business networks. They therefore become the province of no one. In most cases, there are no single-point-of-responsibility process owners. Although there are some recent exceptions to this in best practice companies (for example, supply chain management), few firms currently have managers for their key processes.

Table 7.1 **History of Process Improvement**
Key ideas associated with the evolution of the process perspective.

Decade	Idea	Focus
1900	Scientific management	Arrangement of processes and their content to simplify work
1940	Operations research	Optimal resource and location allocations
1940	Systems thinking	Holistic view of interactions among processes and their environment, including feedback and control
1950	Quality management	Outcome variance reduction and defect elimination
1950	Socio-technical work design	Co-improvement of worker QWL and process outcomes in technology-induced process changes
1960	Data processing	Process digitization of routine transactional processing
1970	Office automation	Computer support of office work
1980	Information systems	Computer support of non-routine activities and processes
1990	Process re-engineering	Cycle-time reduction through aggressive re-thinking of a process thread
1990	e-commerce	End-to-end, seamless customer process interactions across multiple channels
1990	Supply chain management	Inter-organizational coordination of vendors along a chain that extends from the customer to the initial suppliers
2000	Sarbanes-Oxley, BASEL II, and HIPAA	Documentation and control evaluation of processes for regulatory compliance
2000	Process outsourcing and off-shoring	Transferring the execution of selected business processes to external service providers
2000	Service-Oriented Architectures	Interconnecting separate process execution sequences into a virtual single process
2000	Business Technology Management (BTM)	Aligning, synchronizing, and even converging IT and business management

Building on previous work, a new perspective on business processes and their technology enablement has emerged. This perspective is based on new business technology capabilities, the increasing need for real-time metrics, and adoption of an external orientation that is customer focused and interorganizational. It has been variously termed "the real-time enterprise," "the on-demand organization," "business process fusion," or the "service-oriented enterprise," among others. The basics of this perspective are as follows:

Service and customer emphasis. All processes have a customer for what they produce. This includes internal (employee) and external (market) customers. Seen from a customer perspective, the delivery end of a process chain is a service. To view a process as a service is to ask what solution it provides or what problem it solves, rather than how it does it (a process viewpoint).

Rule-based business process management. A rules-based approach establishes guidelines that coordinate the relationship among activities and tasks along an entire process chain. A rules-based approach helps to prevent the processes that collectively produce customer services from becoming fragmented. These processes are typically a mixture of digitized and manual activities spanning many functional areas and their associated automated (sometimes legacy) applications. Moreover, the processes that deliver value to the end customer will generally extend beyond the firm into the business network. An earlier approach to connecting separate (automated) process islands was enterprise application integration. However, this primarily dealt with the digitized process subset of the broader picture, which includes manual and semi-automated actions as well. The current view is that one should describe digitized applications (for example, ERP, SCM, CRM, HRM systems) as a set of services and invoke them as needed, along with manual or semi-automated tasks, in a broader control framework called business process management. We'll adopt the term process orchestration to denote a rules-based mechanism used to coordinate processing tasks along an entire process chain.

Event-spawned metrics. Process orchestration makes it possible to monitor event data across the entire process chain. With this potential for fine-grained event and status visibility comes a new set of issues to be reconciled, including what metrics are appropriate, at what level of aggregation, to whom they are delivered and in what form. At the same time, compliance issues (for example, Sarbanes-Oxley) are increasingly focused on, if not demanding, the reporting of non-compliant events and deviations from prescribed operating rules. Finally, real-time, end-to-end process status information permits continuous business optimization.

From a BTM perspective, a service and customer emphasis, rules-based business process management, and event-spawned metrics are enabled by SEA capabilities. Building these capabilities and delivering support for these processes relies on components ranging from enterprise-level architecture standards to other more tactical methodologies and concepts. The tactical methodologies that support an organization's overall management approach must be recognized as being components that form just one part of a larger improvement effort. This larger effort is guided by BTM, which sits above and encompasses these tactical methodologies and assembles them into a comprehensive

Leadership Insight

Steven Sheinheit on Processes

At MetLife, innovations in business processes are common, but CIO Steven Sheinheit says he often doesn't know whether they come from the business or technology people. That close coupling, he said in an interview, is as it should be for an information-based company.

Chicken or Egg

Financial services being an information-based business, information technology resides at the heart of everything MetLife, Inc., does.

"Many of our businesses today view their business as IT—it's one and the same," says CIO Steven Sheinheit. "Nothing can be done or changed in the business without IT."

As a result, Sheinheit can identify many instances when a new technology opened up a new business opportunity. What he can't always do is say whether the new idea originated in the business or technology staffs. "It's always hard to know which comes first, the chicken or the egg," he says.

"In some cases, it's brought forth by technologists who understand the business opportunities, but it could be business folk who understand the opportunities for technology. I don't know which comes first. Actually, I know I'm successful when I hear a 'big new idea' from one of the businesses, and they're telling me about an idea that IT had begun talking about months before."

Business technology is critical in three ways. It delivers the ability to handle huge amounts of data and create information to make decisions. It provides the capability for customer service and self-service. And it handles voluminous transactions in a cost effective way. "All these things mean that the business and IT really integrate at very close level," Sheinheit says.

Several things are necessary for this close alignment:

Support at the top. "Our chairman is into it," Sheinheit says. "He is a tremendous supporter, and he understands the importance of technology to the future of the company. It starts there."

The right structure. "As long as you think about business and IT separately, you're going to get separate results," Sheinheit says. "Here it's an inclusive process, jointly owned. We govern IT at the highest level through an IT governance board, which I chair. The board is focused on the strategy of IT." While the line of business CIOs report to Sheinheit, they are focused on their businesses. They sit on the businesses' planning boards and IT governance boards.

Good communication. "It starts with communication, constant, frequent communication," Sheinheit says. "It's getting the message communicated in business terms and creating an understanding of where the joint responsibilities lie. We spend a lot of time on knowledge transfer and understanding and communications."

A blurring of roles. Because they have to design a system to make a business process work, technologists often understand the process better than most, he says. "It's the role of the technologist to understand the business at a level of detail and understanding that probably no one else has," Sheinheit says. "And then it's the role of the businesses to understand what the technology can provide so they can make good decisions about the their investments."

After ensuring the reliability of MetLife's technology and its cost effectiveness, Sheinheit is now focused on how technology can differentiate the company in the marketplace. "It's a growth model. What I've defined as the vision for IT is that it is recognized as a competitive differentiator. That's the test I put to the investments we make today. Will it differentiate us or not, give us a leg up in the marketplace, or is it technology for technology's sake? That's the lens. We are investing to support growth and innovation. We've got to know that we are keeping up with the latest technologies that our customers and the marketplace will be using. And the technology that will allow us to support the growth we envision."

His "deal" with business executives is that he will ensure that their money is being spent wisely and that they get the service and support they need. In return, he says, "It's their responsibility to direct the next dollar of discretionary IT spending for their business. They should take over that responsibility, and we will help them understand the technology. This changes the view of whether technology is doing something to them or for them. You have to get the businesses to understand that just as they are engaged in finance or marketing, they have to be engaged in technology."

approach to managing business technology. In the case of SEA, one such methodology is that of the Service-Oriented Business Execution Model (SOBEM).

The term Service-Oriented Business Execution Model represents frameworks, models, and architectures that reflect the fundamental aspects of a business process perspective. The need for improved business agility can be achieved, in part, through a SOBEM perspective. One can explicitly elect to design agile or less-agile processes through choices regarding process architecture and governance. The SOBEM model can help executives implement the *Business Architecture* and *Technical Architecture* capabilities by aiding in analyzing design questions such as: Where and what kind of information is being sensed? How quickly and by whom? Where is the sensory information responded to? and How and with what authority? SOBEM provides the ability to capture sensory intelligence in real time and develop appropriate responses to events in business processes. Similarly, the flexibility offered in process orchestration allows firms to greatly improve their ability to change how basic processes behave.

SOBEM offers the opportunity for creating both innovations and improvements, as products and services can be framed as responses that are "rented" by a customer to solve, as completely as possible, a problem.[8] From this perspective, if the deliverable of a process is the solution, what then is the problem, and is it the appropriate problem from the perspective of the target customer? One can think in terms of improving the solution relative to a better understanding of the problem (that is, an incremental improvement), or to identify new customer problems to which innovative process-based services can be directed (that is, a disruptive innovation).

The practical implementation of SOBEM requires a modeling approach to discover, diagnose, and redesign business processes. BTM provides this modeling approach and the SOBEM methodology can be integrated into and harmonized by BTM to elevate its transaction-level design toward enterprise-wide integration and BTM maturity. Ultimately, however, the business process model must first define the necessary levels of integration between this methodology and BTM. Firms can choose between descriptive or normative models.

Descriptive models provide guidance on the type of process information to be captured and on the form and level of detail. Because the emphasis is on the particulars of processes without general norms for how processes are structured, the analyst must discover the actual processes and represent them within the modeling framework.

Normative models, on the other hand, prescribe generic types of processes, such as multi-echelon supply chains. The analyst must find and map existing activities to those that are prescribed in the model. Many normative models are in use. For supply chains, the Supply Chain Operations Reference (SCOR) model is widely used. The group behind this effort, The Supply Chain Council is also developing models for product development and customer demand chains. Similar models exist for other domains, including telecommunications and HR. A special, but common set of normative models is the embedded process models found in application software suites such as ERP, CRM, and SCM. Here, the software suite assumes a "best practices" operating model and the firm essentially adheres to it, although the underlying process model itself may or may not be made available to the user.

Normative models enforce a common vocabulary across different firms and industries. This permits the sharing of common approaches, metrics, best practices and benchmarks. They also provide visibility into external upstream and downstream processes without having to directly investigate and document them. And, given a broad adoption community, they give rise to third-party tools for modeling, score-carding, and simulation of current and alternative business networks. Descriptive models, by contrast, are open ended and, as such, do not enforce any common structure and naming conventions. Their key strength is that they help emphasize the problems specific to a particular business. They are more attuned to developing next practices than adopting best practices.

Processes enable real-time business networks

To enable agility, process improvement and innovation initiatives must span a firm's business network, which includes its customers, suppliers, and regulators. Traditionally siloed, technological devel-

---

Leadership Insight

William Allen on Process

Process improvement at Maersk, Inc., could not be accomplished with technology alone, says William Allen, senior vice president of human resources and corporate communications. A critical ingredient is people.

People, Process, Technology

Handling tens of thousands of shipping containers around the globe and getting them to the right place on time is an intricate dance of ships, terminals, trucks, and warehouses. For A.P. Moller-Maersk Group, the global terminal operator, technology is critical.

William Allen, senior vice president of human resources and corporate communications for Maersk, Inc., the North American unit, simplifies it as a matter of people, process, and technology coming together to get work done. "Many companies don't have either the people or the process or the technology right," he says. "If one of the three doesn't work, then you have a suboptimized business."

Allen is using business technology to maximize HR's strategic contribution to the business. His director of HRIS is his link to IT. "He is strategically probably the most important person on my team in terms of improving the capability of the HR function," Allen says.

In a study of his department, Allen discovered that it spent 85 percent of its time on transactions, record keeping, and providing services. He wants to reverse that: 85 percent of HR's time on consulting with the organization to improve performance. A survey of business leaders in the company indicated that HR did well on transactions but poorly on succession planning, recruiting talent and leadership development. "We absolutely have to get out of this idea of HR being a transactional function," Allen says. "The one thing that justifies the existence of HR is improving performance in the organization. All these HR systems are useless unless they enable our leaders to improve performance."

Technology is stepping up to the challenge in two ways. With business technology, basic transaction functions went online. Now, for example, managers considering pay increases can visit a portal to make their decisions, instead of working on spreadsheets. It takes a tenth of the time.

"And what I need and what I will get on the strategic side," Allen says, "is a talent management system so that we know who is where, with what skills, and we're in a position to say we're going to have a job for a terminal manager on the West Coast—what is the slate of candidates for that? Right now it's a scavenger hunt."

The ultimate goal, he says, is to design the organization "so that our customers are absolutely delighted, our colleagues are incredibly engaged and invigorated by the working environment, our shareholders are getting a great return on their investment and our competitors were scratching their heads, saying how do we keep up with these guys. If we can marry technology and process and people, we will have accomplished something few companies ever do."

opments have enabled business networks to coordinate predictable activities. For instance, many companies share their forecasts and plans with suppliers and distributors to extract networkwide efficiencies. Going further, some firms, such as retailers, have relinquished their decision rights on when and how much to replenish to their suppliers, assuming that creates even greater efficiencies for all concerned.

Although efficiencies can be extracted through the coordination of predictable activities across a business network, such processes impose significant constraints on the sensing of and responding to unpredictable events.[9] Simply put, these disciplined business networks perform well in a predictable world but are not robust in an uncertain world. Agility requires the dynamic configuration of processes across a business network based on changes in customer requirements. This shift toward real-time business networks requires five key enablers that are summarized in Table 7.2.

First, managers must focus on process enablement of customer requirements. Agility requires that customer requests be sensed and interpreted so they can be negotiated and translated into specifications of production and distributed across the business network.

Second, managers must ensure process enablement of business network intelligence. Business network intelligence requires the aggregation of disparate information, and the filtering and distribution of this information to points of relevance. Processes must be established to not only share information between two partners but to aggregate information across the network and create intelligence for agile behavior. It is critical to not overload nodes in the network with information. This requires the constraints of governance arrangements. It is also critical to safeguard sensitive information from inappropriate access or use.

Third, managers must emphasize partnering agility. Agile partnering requires that firms initiate, reconfigure, or sever ties with

Table 7.2 Enablers of Real-Time Business Networks

Firms must create processes that enable five needs.

Process Enablers	Real-Time Business Network Capability
Customer Requirements	- Determine specifications for products and services - Identify production and distribution activities
Business Network Intelligence	- Integrate information across partners - Filter and distribute information to partners for leverage
Partnering Agility	- Safeguard intellectual property based on the relationship - Tailor collaboration processes based on the relationship
Activity Management	- Re-allocate activities to contracts and spot markets - Use business rules to coordinate distributed activities
Relationship Governance	- Negotiate expectations and roles through business and process modeling - Monitor performance and investigate initiatives for improvement and innovation

others. Both core and noncore activities can be distributed across business partners. While core activities are typically distributed only to long-term, trusted partners, noncore activities are typically distributed across long-term partners that excel in commodity provisioning or, alternatively, across spot markets. Both the nature of the partnership and the type of activities should shape process requirements for partner interactions. Processes supporting the exchange of limited information must be tailored for spot market interactions, while processes supporting exchange of private and idiosyncratic information will be required for the long term.

Fourth, managers must focus on process enablement of activity allocation and coordination across the business network. The distribution of activities for real-time configuration of products and services requires visibility of contracted resources and capacities, and service levels with which these activities can be completed. The coordination of these distributed activities requires a rule-based architecture for the enforcement of their interdependencies. The rules depend on the granularity with which activities are traced. Granular tracking and high levels of awareness provide superior control capabilities in that exceptions can be detected, alerts cascaded, and corrective actions initiated.

Fifth, managers must emphasize process enablement of relationship governance. This requires negotiation of outcomes and approaches to achieve them, and on learning for continuous improvement. Negotiation of contracts, including service level agreements, can be facilitated by business and process models. These models can be used to establish a shared understanding of approaches and outcomes, including incentives under different conditions. Once negotiated, service level goals must be monitored against performance.

Business networks must be managed

A business architecture allows an organization to express its key business strategies and their impact on business functions and processes. Typically, the business architecture is comprised of both current and future state models that define how the organization maintains its competitive advantage. Business architectures are then linked to technology architectures that include applications, data, and infrastructure elements. The joining of these architectures comprises the SEA.

SEA is important in achieving a real-time business network, but not sufficient in itself. In addition, an architecture that represents the various business processes and sub processes as manageable

Figure 7.3   The Linkage Between SEA and SOA

BTM capabilities enable the existence of SEA, which can drive a SOA implementation.

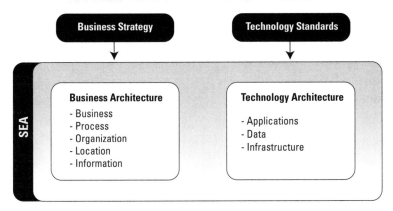

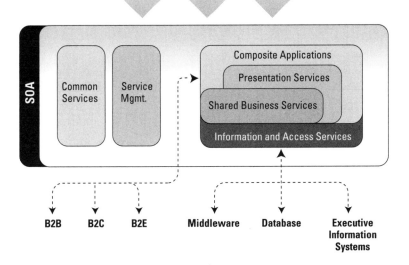

components used to create an overall business process is also needed. SEA sets the context to determine the various services that are required to support the business initiatives. These services form the basis of a Service-Oriented Architecture (SOA) (see Figure 7.3).

A service is a business functionality (for example, "check credit") with an interface that interacts with other services via a loosely coupled, message-based communication model. Services can consist of coarse or fine-grained components, encapsulated business functions within existing application suites, or actions taken by people. At the highest level, service orchestration is the operational realization of process descriptions.

> *A service is a business functionality (for example, "check credit") with an interface that interacts with other services via a loosely coupled, message-based communication model.*

Business process models capture the overall business process logic down to the level of a services orchestration language specification. Ideally, this is done in a way that business rules are separated from the execution syntax to allow the overall business process to be dynamically reconfigured.

Below the level of services, we find preexisting components, objects, and application suites that comprise a firm's current application portfolio. These must be encapsulated and given service abstractions that, in turn, allow their orchestration. New process functionality is added directly as services are intentionally designed to work in an SOA.

At the interface between the layers and within the layers themselves we find a variety of standardized but evolving protocols that aim to increase interoperability across platforms and firms. Standards exist for everything from defining and locating a service description to requesting a web service invocation, to various aspects of orchestration, and additional protocols for security, quality of service, and monitoring.

Beyond service orchestration, however, there is also a mediation component to service inter-operability: the task of translating between information models and data models, and the translation of documents and messages into the correct format for interaction with existing applications and infrastructure. Of course, many other issues need to be addressed, including service quality, security, data consistency, and integrity, to name a few.

The issues of orchestration, mediation, and network-wide management become more complicated when one leaves the confines of a specific firm. For this, a more comprehensive SOA model is needed. Some of the major issues to be dealt with in contemplating the interaction of services across business networks include (1) coupling among partners—different degree of tightness of integration and duration in networks; (2) heterogeneity—differences in hardware, software, structural, at the business process layer, and data within the business network; (3) autonomy—the degree of partner compliance to global control rules; (4) external manageability—the degree of external visibility and manageability of partners' processes; (5) adaptability—the degree to which processes are able to adapt to changes in an environment with dynamic orchestration; (6) security—the degree to which transactions can be executed securely; and (7) scalability—the ability to extend the architecture due to growth in volume of data, transactions, or services. [10]

Strategic Enterprise Architecture

▶ **Understand** the appropriate level of business agility for your firm. Chapter 2, "Strategic Positions," contrasted the requirement of agility based on the need for firms to (1) refine and exploit competencies required to operate competitively in strategic positions and (2) strategically reposition itself into new product-market spaces through exploration. Understanding the appropriate level of agility has vast implications for how processes are modeled, configured across business networks, and then enabled by SOA.

▶ **Select** modeling approaches for your business processes. New information technologies and architectures (for example, SOA), coupled with SEA and BTM capabilities or a mandate for agile design, require senior management to reconsider the firm's core processes.

▶ **Create** the appropriate level of agility for a business network. Processes must first be established to sense and capture customer requirements and translate them into specifications of outcomes. Second, processes are required to integrate information from the business network and add to the base of public and market information. Third, processes must enable tailoring of interactions, information sharing, and intellectual property protection. Fourth, processes are required for the management of activities associated with production and distribution of products and services as they must be re-allocated and coordinated based on changing conditions. Fifth, governance of relationships must be implemented to enable negotiation and monitoring across activities in business processes and networks. Given the process enablers that are required for the real-time enterprise, it is critical to establish the information services platform required by these processes.

▶ **Develop** your BTM capabilities in the SEA functional area. This is necessary to be an agile organization. Business technology capabilities must be synchronized with the process requirements of real-time business networks. This synchronization requires senior executives to think primarily in terms of the services they provide and the key business processes and networks that enable, and are enabled by, these services. Senior executives must define the necessary leadership roles, structures, and processes.

Notes

1   See the "Key Terminology" section in Chapter 1.

2   Ibid.

3   Ibid.

4   Haeckel, S. H. *Adaptive Enterprise: Creating and Leading Sense-and-Respond Organizations*. Boston: Harvard Business School Press, 1999.

5   These response-ability states are adapted from Dove, R. *Response Ability—The Language, Structure, and Culture of the Agile Enterprise*. New York: Wiley, 2001.

6   Haeckel, 1999.

7   Hammer, M. Chief Process Officer? *Optimize*, Issue 29, March 2004.

8   Christensen, C. and M. Raynor. *The Innovator's Solution*. Cambridge, MA: Harvard Business Press, 2004.

9   Lee, H. The Tripple-A-Supply Chain. *Harvard Business Review*, October 2004, pp.102–112.

10 Medjahed, B., B. Benatallah, A. Bouguettaya, A. H. H. Ngu, and A. Elmagarmid. Business-to-Business Interactions: Issues and Enabling Technologies. *The VLDB Journal*, Vol. 12 (2003), No. 1, pp. 59–85.

8

"In these matters, the only certainty

is that nothing is certain."

—Pliny the Elder

Considering Risk

In Brief

Significant changes in business technology have created a compelling need to expand the focus of risk management from the micro project view to a broader enterprise perspective.

Risks are classified into three broad categories: systems, sourcing, and strategy, based on where they originate. Some risks are predominantly intra-enterprise in nature, such as systems and strategy, whereas others, notably sourcing, reflect interorganizational challenges.

Project risks fall into six major categories: organizational environment, user, requirements, project complexity, planning and control, and team.

The risks of outsourcing in general and offshoring in particular can be classified into five major categories: vendor selection, location, technical, people, and legal.

Business technology is fraught with risk. Successfully conceptualizing, implementing, and deploying business technology to achieve operational excellence and strategic advantage leaves a firm open to much vulnerability. It may arise from a variety of sources that can range from choosing to invest in the wrong system, to selecting partners who are unable to deliver, to implementing a system that is not used to its fullest potential.

Unless executives are vigilant about these risks and execute mitigation strategies, the potential value of business technology may never be realized. In other words, Compliance and Risk Management *is a core BTM capability*[1] *that cuts across all the BTM functional areas.*

This chapter discusses the nature of risks in the context of business technology and offers broad risk mitigation strategies. Because business technology touches all aspects of an enterprise and affects strategies, tactics, and operations in every functional area, executive involvement across the entire enterprise is essential for the effective curtailment of risks.

Contributing authors for this chapter are Ritu Agarwal, Professor and Robert H. Smith Dean's Chair of Information Systems at the University of Maryland; Anandhi Bharadwaj, Associate Professor of Decision & Information Analysis at Emory University; and Mark Minevich, Chief Strategy Officer at Enamics, Inc.

I n the fall of 2003, a major customer relationship management (CRM) system at AT&T Wireless crashed. Many customers were unable to get through to overworked customer service reps, who were unable to process new accounts, and many customers deserted the carrier for its competitors. The company lost not only thousands of potential new customers but also an estimated $100 million in revenue. Some analysts believe this system failure encouraged an early sale of AT&T Wireless to Cingular—at $15 per share, or just less than half their value when the company went public in April 2000.[2]

Just before midnight on May 4, 2003, an F-4 category tornado ripped through Jackson, Tennessee, leveling houses and downtown buildings—including the one-story office of Aeneas Internet and Telephone. The company, which served 2,500 telephone and 10,000 Internet customers lost nearly $1 million in hardware and software, and it was shut down for 72 hours.[3]

What do these examples vividly demonstrate?

One, that the source of business risks can be both internal to the firm, such as rolling out an inadequately tested system, as well as environmental, in the form of an unanticipated natural disaster. That creates a challenge for business and technology executives in that while the former type of risk is somewhat more recurring, predictable, and perhaps controllable, and, therefore, the business case for investment in risk management is often easier to justify, the latter type of risk is unanticipated and episodic, and the typical firm questions the outlay of resources to protect against such rare occurrences. Yet, the consequences of not doing adequate business continuity planning can be potentially disastrous.

Two, the experiences of these firms establish that the outcomes of inadequate risk management span the gamut from financial losses, which can potentially be overcome, to a loss of customer goodwill that may well threaten the long-term viability and survival of a firm. Today, with an increasingly unforgiving regulatory environment and legislation such as Sarbanes-Oxley that requires business technology systems to function without error, executives need to be concerned about risk management more than ever before. At its essence, risk management involves three steps: (1) identifying the nature of risks inherent in the situation, (2) assessing the likelihood of the risks manifesting themselves, and (3) taking preventive and corrective action to reduce the firm's level of exposure to the risk.

The outcomes of inadequate risk management span the gamut from financial losses, which can potentially be overcome, to a loss of customer goodwill that may well threaten the survival of a firm.

The nature of risks in technology is broad

The past three decades of business computing have contributed much to our understanding of risk in the technology context.[4,5] Unfortunately, a dominant focus in this prior work has been narrow—on controlling and managing projects—rather than on the broader risks that executives face in firms where technology is deeply and fundamentally embedded within the business. Indeed, the turn of the century has heralded significant changes in the business technology milieu that have created a compelling need to expand the focus of risk management from the micro project view to a broader enterprise perspective. These changes include an increasing emphasis on (1) buying and customizing packaged solutions rather than building systems in-house (that is, on solutions integration rather than software development); (2) partnering with a wide array of providers to acquire needed technical competencies and skills, including taking advantage of offshore resources; (3) using business technology for systems that span organizational boundaries and help link customers, through electronic commerce and CRM systems, suppliers, through fully integrated electronic supply chains, and other business partners

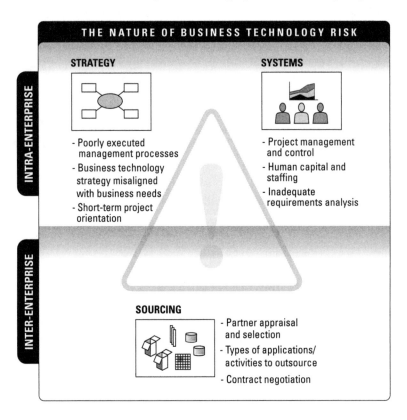

Figure 8.1 **Three Risk Categories**

Risks can be categorized in strategy, systems, and sourcing categories.

THE NATURE OF BUSINESS TECHNOLOGY RISK

INTRA-ENTERPRISE

INTER-ENTERPRISE

STRATEGY

- Poorly executed management processes
- Business technology strategy misaligned with business needs
- Short-term project orientation

SYSTEMS

- Project management and control
- Human capital and staffing
- Inadequate requirements analysis

SOURCING

- Partner appraisal and selection
- Types of applications/ activities to outsource
- Contract negotiation

together; and (4) deploying business technology as the platform on which the entire business is run.

In this environment where business technology is pervasive, what is the nature of risks? In Figure 8.1, these risks are classified into three broad categories: systems, sourcing, and strategy, based on where they originate. Some risks are predominantly intra-enterprise in nature, such as systems and strategy, whereas others, notably sourcing, reflect the challenges that arise in interorgani-zational settings. Note that although these categories are some-what overlapping and not mutually exclusive, they nonetheless provide a conceptually simple framework that can be populated through conversations and interactions among executives from both technology and business.

Risks originating from systems are typically intra-organizational, although in some instances when external partners are used for system development and integration, they may be interorganizational in nature. The risks emanate from all aspects of systems deployment, including project planning and control; human capital and staffing; inadequate user requirements; changes in technology; the complexity, scope, and structure of systems; and inadequate support from senior management. BTM capabilities such as *Strategic & Tactical Governance* and *Project Analysis & Design* explicitly address these issues. But when these risks are not managed, the firm leaves itself open to dissatisfied users and failed implementations, to cost and budget overruns, and to not being able to achieve the strategic objectives originally envisioned when

Leadership Insight

Lester Diamond on Risk

Lester Diamond has an unusual perspective on managing technology. As an assistant director of the U.S. Government Accountability Office, he has been studying the governance of business technology in corporations to develop a set of best practices for government CIOs. As he related in an interview, he has seen clearly the risks in business technology.

Organizational Fault Lines

"We're finding a great deal of diversity in how the private sector goes at it," Lester Diamond, assistant director of the U.S. Government Accountability Office, says of corporate technology governance. "In government, we tend to be more structured in our approaches, and we tend to be more formal in our mechanisms. From what I've seen, the private sector often does not have as many formal processes as we do. They tend to be more collaborative and more flexible in how they approach problems."

Although there are clear differences, government agencies and corporations face some of the same issues. Projects fail for many of the same reasons, for example. "In some cases, they fail because they have a problem as early as the development of requirements for the project," Diamond says. "There's no real sponsorship. The requirements are not adequately being described. Or they evolved and the project doesn't keep up with them. Or the users never really buy in, so you get to the end of the project and you approach acceptance testing and you find that this thing doesn't actually do what the top executives expected it to do or the users expected it to do. And so that leads to a failure.

"Also, these things are just huge; they are very complicated. Sometimes, they begin to spin out of control, and the right incentives aren't in place for identifying that and bringing them back under control."

Organizational failures

Managing complicated technology projects would be difficult in the best circumstances, but they have a tendency to identify the weakest elements in an organization, Diamond says. "Managing IT is big and complicated, and it seems to reflect all the complexities that the organization encounters in any of its other dimensions. When I see IT management fail in a broad way, I usually look to the organization. IT doesn't often fail by itself. I believe IT more often fails as a result of other organizational problems. As you approach IT management, to think of it as simply managing technology is short sighted and probably won't lead you where you want to go."

A case in point is implementing an ERP system. "You need to pull together components of an organization that are much broader

and create much broader change than may have been demanded in the past. Organizations need to get very good at driving change, but I'm not sure that kind of change management skill is in place. And even if it were it would still be a tremendous challenge."

An often-cited example is information sharing among agencies charged with national security. There is a technical aspect to it—systems that can't talk to each other. But a greater issue is people who won't talk with each other. "It's a cultural and organizational issue," Diamond says. "Just getting people to share information within the organization or across organizations, getting Homeland Security and the FBI and intelligence together in identifying risks and sharing information about them. That's an organizational management issue, not a technology issue. But if the organization fails, the technology would be useless."

Equally at issue is the mindset of the various agencies grouped under a department. "They may have distinct missions, but they need to accept that it is not a sign of weakness to receive services from a central organization. They need to consider giving up responsibility and authority in certain areas in order to achieve efficiencies and become more effective in achieving their missions."

A maturity model

Diamond has helped develop a five-stage maturity model for agencies. Each stage might take two years to complete. So it is a real problem that the average tenure of a government CIO is 23 months. The answer is governance processes that outlive any one individual.

All would benefit from a broad framework for business technology management. "A framework, a way of understanding, a way of bringing together information and evaluating it and from that understanding what configuration is most appropriate could evolve. And it makes sense that it be integrative, because these things don't stand independently. Enterprise architecture and investment management and strategic planning are not independent.

"And understanding the implications on one when making decisions about another is very important. It would be a huge advantage to have a framework that would help organizations achieve that understanding."

the system need was identified and the project approved. In addition to these immediate negative consequences, a longer-term undesirable outcome of inadequate attention to systems risks is an increasing lack of credibility for the IT function and growing distrust between IT staff and users. Particularly, given the scope and complexity of enterprise systems, the magnitude of change they entail in work processes, and the need to align business processes and system logic together, effectively managing the implementation process and actively controlling risks poses a considerable challenge.

Today, with the burgeoning growth in the business technology service provider market, firms are actively seeking external partners and vendors to assist with all types of activities, including data center operations, application service provisioning, help desk support, and systems customization and implementation. The rationale behind this movement is the simple logic that for many firms frequently the purely technical aspects of business technology are not a core competency, and external providers offer the necessary skills and capabilities that the firm may not desire to develop and nurture internally.[6] Sourcing risks, which are interorganizational in nature, are inherent in the partnerships and relationships that firms develop with outsourcers and span the gamut from deciding what to outsource, to selecting the right partner, to crafting and negotiating the right contract. Further, as the vendor marketplace matures in offshore locations that offer relative cost advantages, senior executives have the additional option of using partners that are not located within the same country. Although the value proposition of offshoring can be quite compelling, managing off-shore relationships escalates the level of sourcing risk.

Finally, risks and threats emanating from strategy represent the dangers a firm faces when its management of business technology is poorly executed. Such systemic risks are manifest, for example, when business technology strategy is developed without the involvement of key business stakeholders, when project portfolios are constructed with a short-term orientation and with little or no consideration of strategic goals and priorities, and when sourcing decisions are made in a vacuum without sufficient understanding of the hazards of a lean in-house capability. The net negative result of not managing strategy risks is twofold. One, the firm is unable to extract the maximum value from its IT assets[7] and business technology capabilities, and over time the ability of the firm to deploy business technology effectively declines. Two, there is a potential for business suboptimization due to either insufficient or inappropriate investment in business technology or BTM.[8]

> *Although the value proposition of off-shoring can be quite compelling, managing offshore relationships escalates the level of sourcing risk.*

The following discussion elaborates upon the two risk domains of systems and sourcing.

The environment for managing project risk is becoming more dynamic

The landscape for business technology project management today is characterized by a strange paradox: On the one hand, very few firms develop large multiyear software applications in-house, as was the practice in the past. Rather, they seek to leverage the speed with which packaged applications can be acquired and implemented. Thus, the typical project involves system *integration* rather than system *development*. On the other, the growing complexity and scope of today's enterprise applications often results in implementations that last for two to three years. These applications typically necessitate significant changes to business processes, reporting relationships, and decision-making structures, thereby contributing to further lengthening the implementation cycle. Yet, competitive pressures and increasing business velocity demand that application provisioning be accomplished in a speedy manner. Additionally, as discussed previously, service providers and vendors are used increasingly to assist in system integration, leading to project teams comprised of a mix of internal employees and multiple external partners. All of these factors collectively create an extremely dynamic and complex project management environment. It has been estimated that at least 50 percent, and perhaps as much as 80 percent, of all business technology projects fail.[9] What are the risks embedded in such fast-cycle multifunctional projects?

For the past two decades, scholars have examined the major sources of risk in technology projects,[10] and multiple classifications have been proposed. In Figure 8.2, based on a recent synthesis of this research, project risks are summarized into six major

Figure 8.2 Six Sources of Risk

There are six fundamental sources of risk to be addressed in managing business and technology together.

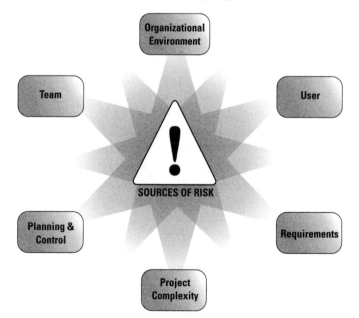

categories:[11] organizational environment, user, requirements, project complexity, planning and control, and team.

The organizational environment refers to the broader context within which the target system will be integrated and implemented. Frequently, the culture, the politics, other simultaneous change initiatives, and the support of top management affect the likelihood of project success. In general, where the culture is not accepting of technological change, where vested interests have different perspectives on the need for and importance of the system, where there are other significant organizational changes occurring, and where top management does not send strong signals endorsing the project, environments have been found to be more risky.

> *Not surprisingly, user involvement in every phase of a project is critical for success —user risk occurs when users are "disenfranchised."*

Information systems are developed for use by organizational personnel in accomplishing operational, strategic, and tactical goals. Not surprisingly, therefore, user involvement in every phase of the project is critical for success. User risk occurs when users are "disenfranchised" and their input is not sought in every aspect of system conceptualization, selection, design, and customization. Research has consistently shown that in situations where users are not involved, negative attitudes are formed, ultimately leading to implementation failure.

A related risk that increases in intensity when user involvement is low is the peril of inadequate requirements determination. Systems embody functionality that reflects the needs of users— needs that they are frequently unable to articulate in a precise manner. Ambiguous or poorly stated requirements lead to systems and processes that are incongruent with the users' desires, and such systems often get relegated to "shelfware." Performing a thorough and complete requirements analysis helps ensure that the outcomes of the project are aligned with users' goals (for example, performance improvements, better information, speedier transactions) and increases their willingness to accept and use the system.

Projects can be situated along a continuum of complexity. In general, more complex projects are also more risky. Project complexity is an outcome of a number of factors, including—for example, the "newness" of the technology, the number and complexity of the business processes and applications involved, and the number of organizational units and individuals who are likely to be affected by the project.

Planning and control risks can occur in the typical project management activities associated with any complex project. These include risks associated with developing a project schedule and milestones, monitoring project progress, and estimating resource requirements. Arguably, project management is one of the most important capabilities an IT organization needs to possess—regardless of the scope and size of its operations. An inability to successfully execute any or all of these activities

Research Insight

Leslie Willcocks on Risk

Dr. Leslie Willcocks, professor of technology, work, and globalization, London School of Economics, London, England, observes many companies, and it has given him a deep understanding of the risks firms face and how they succeed or fail in managing them. This is an excerpt from an interview.

You Still Need Imagination

"Organizations incur different risks. The four most prevalent I encounter are, first, security. That might be blindingly obvious, but I don't think it's going to go away. It's a function of having an interconnectivity level that we've never seen before. We're in a networked economy enabled by technology, and everyone praises the interconnectivity. The downside is that security issues are massively magnified, and I don't think we've caught up with the size of that issue yet.

"Equally, I see organizations still mismanaging outsourcing. They believe that they should focus on the core and use outsourcing to reduce costs on things they don't see as core. But I don't think organizations are good at outsourcing.

"Thirdly, and somewhat surprisingly, few organizations create a project-led culture. They still tend to be quite hierarchical and function based, including the IT department, and until they get a project management culture they can't move swiftly or well on new technology and institutionalize it.

"Fourth, organizations have a focus on technology that is too technical, as opposed to seeing it in its social and organizational dimensions and how it fits with the business. That's still prevalent in a lot of organizations, and it creates unnecessary risks.

Competitive advantage

"Technology by itself is not the key to competitive advantage. It's also about business imagination, business vision, business organization. Technology can amplify your success, but also the technologies coming through now in terms of the Internet provide a bigger scope for what you can do, especially the level of interconnectivity that is allowed.

"So technology makes more things possible, but you still have to have imagination, and you still have to have the business management understand where IT can do a critical thing for you. I see it more as an amplifier and accelerator of good business practice, good business imagination, good business ideas and models, rather than the key in itself. In fact, it can disable organizations if they get it wrong. You can spend hundreds of millions on IT, and if you haven't got the connection between what the business model is and what you're trying to achieve as a business, you can lose a lot of money and a lot of time and competitive positioning.

"A frequent problem I see is that the business doesn't understand how IT can be used. They don't have an IT view of their business. People very often accuse IT people of not being business focused. But I think there's an alternative accusation: Business managers and business strategists don't really have a technology view of their business, and yet this stuff is absolutely in the skeleton of the operation. And as a result they don't optimize it and they tend to push it over into a functional silo that is IT, and they don't get the people in IT involved in their own businesses enough. It's a two-way thing, and quite frequently IT gets blamed for things that business people are not actually doing themselves.

Clear business strategy

"What distinguishes companies that manage technology well is that they do a number of things, not just one. The most obvious is that they have a clear business strategy. If you haven't got that then what you do in IT makes little difference. They do think strategically about the use of IT, and they do allocate people who are responsible for what I would call information systems strategy, which is about business applications, as opposed to IT strategy, which is about the IT supply, the technology hardware and software. They make a distinction between those two, and they start the IT strategy thinking with business people. And also they've sorted out the governance of their IT in a way that they know who is responsible for what and who is going to be able to make what decisions and where the funding goes. They are also well sorted on getting things delivered and getting IT imbedded into how work is accomplished through social relations and business processes.

Successful companies

"Among the successful companies are the obvious ones like Wal-Mart in its supply chain logistics, and UPS for its ability to expand their offerings in logistics services. Walgreen's is an interesting one. It was sort of a traditional drug store in the United States, but moved into satellite communications and network computing around 2001 to gain competitive advantage when they saw how it fit into their business model on how they operated drug stores. Tesco in the United Kingdom, originally a supermarket chain, has some 15 percent of the total U.K. retail market and is hugely IT-enabled, and also runs a profitable online business. One company I've tracked very carefully is British Petroleum. They went from being not a very successful organization in 1989 to being one of the world's leading oil companies. What is interesting is how they've been willing to experiment. They were the first into outsourcing the accounting function in 1992. They were one of the first to go into multiple-supplier IT outsourcing in 1993. They were one of the first to experiment with IT-enabled outsourcing of the human resource function in 2000. None of those have been seamless, but they all eventually achieved a certain business advantage. So I've admired their ability to take controlled risks."

increases the likelihood of implementation failure. Even if the system is eventually delivered "successfully," inadequate attention to planning and control risks often results in schedule and budget overruns and reduces the overall value of the project.

Finally, team risk reflects the people element of projects. Project teams are generally composed of members from a wide variety of backgrounds and functional areas, and may include professionals from partner firms, too. The first challenge arises in assembling the project team such that the right mix and level of skills and knowledge is present to accomplish the target project. Consider, for example, Enterprise Resource Planning (ERP) implementation project teams. Not only do such teams need to understand the nuances of the software, they have to possess a deep understanding of the business processes that will be affected by the software. A second major challenge is the communication barriers between business technology professionals and users and between internal employees and external consultants. Developing the right *esprit de corps* in the team is a key prerequisite for system success.

It is important to note that the risk categories described previously affect each other and interact in multiple and sometimes unanticipated ways. For instance, requirements risk and user risk are interrelated. To the extent that the organizational environment is unstable because of current business imperatives, organizational environment risk contributes to requirements risk. Likewise, project complexity risk and team risk are related—the more complex the project, the greater the requirement for high levels of knowledge and skills, and therefore, the possibility for higher team risk is amplified. Finally, most types of project risks are amplified when projects span large geographical distances, time zones, and cultures, as in the case of projects that are sourced offshore.

Effectively managing project risk requires that a structured process and organizational responsibilities be implemented at both the project and program levels. A formal risk management plan should be developed to clarify risk management roles and responsibilities; risk management processes, procedures, standards, training and tools; the method and frequency of risk progress reporting; and what should be monitored to determine whether risks are occurring. A project should attempt to manage only the risks it can handle. Other risks should be elevated to the program level. Determination of whether to elevate should be made based on examination of whether the mitigation action steps are within the control of the project team.

> *Effectively managing project risk requires that a structured process and organizational responsibilities be implemented at both the project and program levels.*

Managing risk at a program level involves a review of project risks and program risks by an Enterprise Program Management Office (EPMO). The EPMO should analyze project risk across the entire program to determine whether the same risk occurs in different projects and requires concerted action. The EPMO should document the inventory of risks, their assessment and mitigation plans in a database. If after analyzing program risk the overall program risk level is deemed to be higher than originally documented in the cost/benefit plan (that is, the business case), the business case should be updated—reflecting the adjustment in the range of costs and/or benefits or a lower confidence measure. It is important that the EPMO collaborate with an Enterprise Risk Management (ERM) group to ensure that the business impacts of project-related risks are well understood, and that a periodic evaluation can be made concerning the impact of other enterprise risks on the project.

Leadership Insight

Leon Schumacher on Uncertainty

Aligning business technology to Mittal Steel's business strategy of growth through acquisitions and of serving customers with a worldwide presence has presented CIO Leon V. Schumacher with a unique set of challenges.

What a New Day Brings

Many of the acquisitions that have made Mittal Steel the largest steel producer in the world have been in far-flung places—Trinidad, France, South Africa, Romania, Bosnia, Macedonia, Kazakhstan, and Algeria, for example—and often were state-owned operations. "The business strategy is to grow and manage the resources we have," Schumacher says. "We can do a lot to help manage the business, but many of our sites are undeveloped from an IT point of view. A lot of what they do is manual, paper driven. A consequence is that those units are not familiar nor trained in advanced tools."

Many of the facilities were run down or shut down when they were acquired. Some facilities had been bombed, other had not paid their employees for months prior to the acquisition. "In one example, anything not bolted or chained 'walked out,'" Schumacher says. "We might find only a small percentage of the PCs that were supposed to be in a company. What you face in places such as Algeria, Bosnia, or Macedonia, is quite a challenge—in many cases, you basically start from zero. But it becomes a process that gets easier every time that you execute it."

Legacy systems
When he joined in 2003, there was no corporate IT function; it had not been filled for three or four years. But the company saw the need because it was getting so large. "The environment we have has

advantages and disadvantages," Schumacher says. "In many places, we have nothing or very little when it comes to IT systems. We are free to do the right thing from the start. But there are legacy systems in many other locations, and it's more difficult to replace a legacy system people are used to. However, in places where they don't have anything, any system will bring a benefit. The first thing I said was that we need to standardize at all levels—email, software on PCs, ERP systems, manufacturing systems. We will pick one and this will be the solution for anyone in the group. But we will not force you to change a system that works."

Best practices

A key company strategy is spreading best practices among its mills, and IT mirrors this. "Most units are not highly trained in advanced tools, so although we have a small staff I make sure that we have specialists who can work with the local people."

In the company's decentralized model, local units scope a project, price it and get local approval, followed by corporate approval. Requests should generally come from the business side and must meet corporate guidelines and standards. A member of Schumacher's staff is usually involved in the process. "Our model would not work in some other companies. It's a decentralized operation with independent business units and a centralized corporate governance that has been developed over the years,

and it actually works well."

Policies that are developed by groups of people from the different units, and different areas, such as infrastructure or manufacturing, are guided by someone on Schumacher's staff. "We have said this is how it should look and what should be replicated through all the plants and units. We'll only do new things if the old isn't delivering the value they need."

One of his recent initiatives involves purchase reporting, the development of a business intelligence tool to manage purchases and pricing. Data from every unit will go into this tool and be accessible by everyone, replacing spreadsheets. "It's less a control mechanism than a way everyone can see what others are doing, the prices they're getting. Everyone knows prices for the top 20 items we purchase, but the real potential is in the hundreds that come after that. It's too much to handle unless it's automated."

Moving fast

Schumacher needs to move as fast as he can on all fronts. "Because we have so many needs, we want to do as many projects as we can. Some of our inherited systems are so bad we can't continue with them, and we need new systems tomorrow. We have currently five SAP implementation projects running, for example. We're trying to teach people new skills, get more project management skills out there."

At the same time, he is working on a portfolio-management tool that can track resources and projects. "Everybody can use it, but they will have to put all the information in one place so we can get a complete picture."

But he never knows what a new day will bring. It took six months to get servers through customs into one country. "When we wanted to run a VPN into another country, the secret service wanted to house the firewall with the encryption in their location. Where does this come from? What's the benefit? You run into plenty of surprising things when you deal with further-out countries."

Partnerships increase the risk

It is widely accepted that outsourcing expands the capabilities of the firm and allows it to exploit the vendor's economies of scale and scope. In addition to the resources and productivity gains it provides, there is another compelling reason for using external providers to fulfill business technology needs. For activities that are undifferentiated and not core to the business of the company, such as managing and running a data center, and, therefore, do not contribute to strategic advantage or a unique product-market position, the decision to outsource makes eminent business sense. However, it is important to note that this decision must be based on a careful and thorough strategic assessment that takes into account the level of in-house technical capability needed to effectively manage the IT function and its relationships into the future. In other words, business technology executives must determine the optimal level and volume of outsourcing so as to protect against losing all internal expertise. This optimal level will vary depending on the unique context and needs of the firm, and must be determined collectively by all concerned stakeholders.

Consider, for example, the case of Procter & Gamble (P&G).[12] More than 25 years ago, the company developed an in-house e-mail application that was used extensively for R&D activities and for exchanging information about new product development. In the 1980s, this was viewed as a strategic application—today, it is no longer seen as a source of competitive advantage and has therefore been outsourced to Hewlett-Packard as one component of a multiyear outsourcing arrangement. The same philosophy drives other outsourcing decisions at P&G: Today, the company outsources most of its operational systems and infrastructure services. At the same time, the company has determined what skills are important to develop and maintain in-house, and it invests in staff to retain these capabilities.

For the firm that chooses to outsource, managing partnerships is not easy and requires considerable managerial expertise and foresight. To the degree that the outsourcer does not understand the unique internal requirements, culture, and constraints of the firm, solutions integration and implementation may not be successful. Often, firms choose partners without conducting due diligence and may find themselves locked into a relationship with a vendor whose viability is in question or into a contract that does not deliver the cost economies sought.

The risks of outsourcing in general and offshoring in particular can be classified into five major categories:[13,14] vendor selection, location, technical, people, and legal (see Figure 8.3). Some of

Figure 8.3 **Five Outsourcing Risks**

Outsourcing, especially offshoring, brings five fundamental sources of risk to be addressed in managing business and technology together.

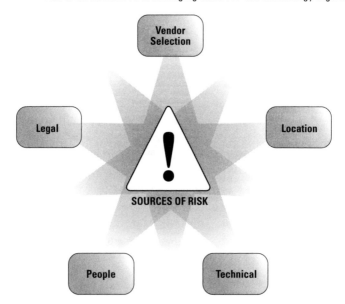

these risks are applicable to both domestic and offshore outsourcing, such as vendor selection, whereas others are unique to the offshore context, such as location.

Technology service providers can be differentiated along multiple dimensions including size, the portfolio of services provided, the vendor's experience with different technologies and systems, process maturity, reputation, and longevity. The fallout from selecting the wrong vendor can be significant—from delays in system implementation to a complete shutdown of business operations in the case of an outsourced data center. A systematic and thorough vendor evaluation and selection process can help reduce the likelihood of experiencing such adverse outcomes. Questions for executives to ask in this context include: What should our overall vendor selection strategy be? Should we use multiple providers for different activities, or should we select a few strategic vendors to provide the whole range of desired services? What is the vendor's capability for delivering the services desired?

> *Given the effort it takes to learn the nuances of doing business in a new country and to develop a relationship with a vendor in an offshore location, there is considerable lock-in after a location decision is made.*

The number of offshore destinations for business technology services has expanded considerably.[15] Along with the traditional destinations such as India, Ireland, and China, a variety of boutique locations including Eastern Europe and Southeast Asia are emerging. The location decision is fraught with risk and can create significant vulnerability for a firm if not carefully managed. Location-related risks include political instability, language barriers, cultural differences, and difficulties in communication and coordination due to time-zone differences. Given the amount of time and effort it takes for managers and IT staff to learn the nuances of doing business in a new country and to develop a relationship with a vendor in an offshore location, there is considerable lock-in after a location decision is made. Therefore, choosing the right location is all the more important from the very beginning of the outsourcing journey.

Technical risks in the outsourcing context relate to standards, methodologies, infrastructure, and tools. From an IT architecture perspective, it is critical that the outsourcing partner and client adhere to the same set of standard architectural principles and target business and technology architectures that need to drive design decisions. This means a fair degree of collaboration among a client's Enterprise Business and Technology Architecture groups and the outsourcing partner. An additional challenge arises when the vendor's process maturity is "out of sync" with that of the firm. For instance, several offshore providers in India are CMM-Level 5 certified—this requires a certain level of process sophistication on the part of the client firm as well. Alternatively, if the firm has a high level of process maturity, there is a clear risk in partnering with a vendor who is unable to conform to the requirements of repeatable, standardized approaches to system construction. With regard to infrastructure, because offshore sourcing, and, indeed, any outsourced project, requires constant communication between the parties involved, it is imperative that the vendor have access to adequate bandwidth and communication capability, in addition to any collaboration tools that might be necessary. Finally, the development tools and methodologies used by the vendor must conform to the standards and specifications of those used internally so that future integration problems can be obviated.

> It is critical that the outsourcing partner and client adhere to the same standard architectural principles and target business and technology architectures to drive design decisions. This means a fair degree of collaboration.

The construction and management of business technology systems is a human-capital intensive activity and, as such, people risks are inevitably present in any project. For offshore sourcing, people risks are likely to be present in three forms: (1) the capability and expertise level of the vendor's staff; (2) communication bottlenecks caused by differences in culture, language, value systems, and the like; and (3) the ability of the vendor to retain business technology professionals for the desired length of time. Frequently, although a vendor may claim to have the capability to deliver on specific projects, in the offshore context it is difficult to assess precisely at what level the vendor's staff performs. A lack of expertise on the part of the vendor may quickly destroy any productivity or cost-related benefits the firm was seeking to achieve—particularly when contracts are structured as time and materials rather than fixed price. In any outsourcing relationship, because of the need to develop considerable relationship-specific assets where the vendor learns about the business processes and unique requirements of the firm, and the firm learns how to work with the vendor's staff, high turnover is undesirable as it inhibits the firm's ability to capitalize on this mutual learning. Communication bottlenecks can frequently derail a project or lead to unanticipated delays if they are not addressed.

Outsourcing, whether domestic or offshore, opens up a wealth of possibilities, but without adequate risk assessment and management, any type of outsourcing can spell disaster—with the challenge becoming particularly acute in the case of offshoring.

The final set of risks in outsourcing are those that may arise as a result of the legal and regulatory environment in the nation where the vendor is located. Examples of such risks are when there are import and export limitations and other trade barriers on data that can cross national boundaries, when intellectual property protection is not available, or even if it is available not enforced to the extent it is domestically, and when institutions such as the judicial system that aids in contract enforcement are not well developed. These risks are particularly acute for firms in regulated sectors such as financial services and healthcare that need to keep a closer watch over data and software development than firms in other industries such as manufacturing.

In summary, outsourcing, whether domestic or offshore opens up a wealth of possibilities for all senior business technology executives, including the CIO, to obtain world-class services at relatively lower levels of investment. However, without adequate risk assessment and management, any type of outsourcing can spell disaster—with the challenge becoming particularly acute in the case of offshoring.

Risk mitigation approaches

Business technology executives must seek a mature *Compliance and Risk Management* capability to ensure that the firm's investments in technology are protected. Doing so requires increasing the organizations level of BTM maturity and selecting appropriate techniques based on the nature of the perceived risk (see Figure 8.4).

Although numerous risk mitigation prescriptions and control strategies are commonly discussed, a few recurring meta-themes emerge. Integrating these practices, as a part of developing the organization's *Compliance and Risk Management* capability, will reduce the likelihood of exposure to risks and improve the chances of obtaining value from business technology.

Figure 8.4   **Risk Mitigation Approaches**

Six meta-themes for mitigating risk exist and can be applied to internal and external risk.

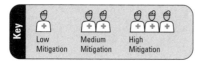

Mitigation Approach	Project Risks	Partnership Risks
IT-User Partnerships	High Mitigation	Medium Mitigation
User Education	Medium Mitigation	Medium Mitigation
Comprehensive Sourcing Strategy	Medium Mitigation	High Mitigation
Vendor Management Capabilities	Low Mitigation	High Mitigation
Project Management Culture	High Mitigation	High Mitigation
Metrics Programs	High Mitigation	High Mitigation

Key: Low Mitigation, Medium Mitigation, High Mitigation

Managing Business Technology Risk

▶ **Develop** strong partnerships between IT and users and increase the level of trust and understanding by providing forums for frequent interactions. Strong partnerships promote user involvement, permit requirements to be defined in a more cooperative climate, ensure that business technology investments are aligned with business priorities, and facilitate user ownership of projects.

▶ **Educate** executives and knowledge workers about the unique challenges of business technology. In many firms, users have a limited understanding of the complex technologies and the effort is takes to implement complex systems. As a result, their expectations are not realistic.

▶ **Craft** a comprehensive sourcing strategy that articulates the desired mix of in-sourcing, domestic outsourcing, and offshoring, and that recognizes the long-term capability necessary to meet strategic objectives. Too lean an IT organization that is highly outsourced may inhibit the development of strategic applications, while too large an organization is likely to not deliver desired business value in the form of cost economy.

▶ **Develop** vendor management expertise that includes knowledge about location constraints, vendor performance and vendor abilities. Such capabilities will facilitate careful vendor selection and help mitigate the multiple risks associated with outsourcing. Using pilot projects related to non-mission critical applications is a low-risk tactic for learning the strengths and weaknesses of offshore locations.

▶ **Instill** a project management culture and imbue the IT organization with project management expertise. Project management is both a science and an art and needs to be formally learned and practiced on the job. Poor project management is one of the most significant risks that IT organizations face, and can frequently spell the difference between firms that are able to exploit business technology for business value and those that are not.

Notes

1   See the "Key Terminology" section in Chapter 1.

2   Koch, Christopher. "AT&T Wireless Self-Destructs." *CIO*, April 15, 2004.

3   Villano, Matt. "Twisters, Hurricanes, Floods (oh my)." *CIO*, Sept. 1, 2003.

4   Keil, Mark, Tiwana, Amrit, and Bush, Ashley. "Reconciling User and Project Manager Perceptions of IT Project Risk: A Delphi Sudy." *Information Systems Journal*, Vol. 12, 2002, 103–119.

5   Wallace, Linda, Keil, Mark, and Rai, Arun. "Understanding Software Project Risk: A Cluster Analysis." *Information and Management*, Vol. 42, 2004, 115–125.

6   Prahalad, C.K. and Hamel, G. "The Core Competence of the Corporation." *Harvard Business Review*, Vol. 68, 1990, 79–91.

7   See the "Key Terminology" section in Chapter 1.

8   Ibid.

9   Zhen, J. "Why IT Projects Fail." *Computerworld*, February 7, 2005.

10 Brooks, F.P. "No silver bullet: Essence and Accidents of Software Engineering." *Computer*, April 1987, 10–19. Wallace, et al, 2004.

11 Wallace, Keil and Rai. 2004.

12 Smith. G. "You Can't Outsource Everything." *CIO Magazine*, Nov. 1, 2005.

13 Rottman, J.W. and Lacity. "Twenty Practices for Offshore Sourcing." *MISQ Executive*, Vol. 3, 2004, 117–130.

14 Kliem, R.L. "Managing the Risks of Offshore IT Development Projects." *Information Systems Management*, Vol. 21, 2004, 22–27.

15 Carmel, Erran and Agarwal, Ritu. "The Maturation of Offshore Sourcing of Information Technology Work." *MISQ Executive*, Vol. 1, 2002, 65–77.

9

"If you can't measure it, you can't manage it."

—*Anonymous*

Measuring Success

In Brief

The objective of business technology must be clearly understood before the legitimacy of its business value can be established.

Metrics for business technology benefits must keep up with the changing nature of the business and the technology.

Before technology alignment can be effective, the business strategy must be converted into specific activities.

Business technology investments do not occur in isolation. They are among several investments on the way to accomplishing a business strategy.

A process approach provides a roadmap for business technology impact and value creation, and statistical methods provide the tools to capture, isolate, and measure such impacts.

Senior executives increasingly demand an understanding of how business technology[1] can lead to improvement in operations, enhance managers' decision making, and place the organization in better shape to compete. They want practical ways to decide when to invest, how to channel investments toward appropriate problem solving, and how to ensure that this leads to value.

Most importantly, executives want evidence of a positive relationship between business technology investment and a firm's performance. This chapter explores various methodologies that can be used, how metrics can be created to measure value, and how the value of business technology investments is enhanced by complementary investments elsewhere. Contributing authors for this chapter are Rajiv Kohli, associate professor of management information systems at the College of William & Mary, School of Business; Michael Fillios, Chief Product Officer at Enamics, Inc.; William Kettinger, associate professor and director of the Center of Information Management and Technology

Research at the University of South Carolina, Moore School of Business; and James Lebinski, Vice President of Knowledge Products, at Enamics, Inc.

Most CEOs and board members accept that investing in business technology is necessary and beneficial—the evidence is in their budgets. Where they have difficulty is in determining whether this spending is returning genuine value. To find their way through this fog, they need a framework for making decisions. Benchmarking against other firms may offer some insight, but better is a system of measurement specific to their own unique business needs.

Top executives can be forgiven for their skepticism about the huge sums they are plowing into technology. Two decades ago, they were alerted to the "productivity paradox," a phenomenon based in part on an observation by the Nobel laureate Robert Solow: "We see computers everywhere, except in productivity statistics." This led to a string of research projects to examine whether and why such was the case. After all, it was counterintuitive that computers would not improve productivity. But if that were the case, should organizations large and small continue to invest in technology?

Subsequent studies attributed the apparent paradox to weaknesses in data and the measurement of business technology value.[2,3] We learned that as technology and business processes change, so must the metrics. This critical insight has yet to be embraced in many executive suites, even today.

This is especially the case for metrics for intangible benefits. For example, it has been reported that since the 1970s productivity in banks is down; however, the metrics capturing this change were based on the number of transactions per bank teller. We know that business technology has played a significant role in enabling online banking and automated teller machines (ATMs), so tellers are handling relatively more complicated transactions. Therefore, the metrics must be updated to capture the changing nature of value enabled by business technology investments.

More recently, the widely quoted article by Nick Carr, "IT Doesn't Matter," in the *Harvard Business Review*, gave ambivalent executives even more reason to wonder about the role of IT[4] in improving business performance and their support for IT funding.

How should executives make sense of the business value of business technology?

Leaders must clearly understand the objective of business technology in their firms before its business value can be established. Although we use business technology as a generic term, it has various and diverse purposes. Attempts to paint all technologies with the same brush can lead to misplaced applications and subsequent disappointment with payoffs.

Such asymmetry in the types of business technology and the implications for value is evident in Carr's argument that technology is a necessary commodity that adds no significant strategic value.[5] One can argue this, if business technology is defined narrowly as a tool to improve back-office operations such as payroll or billing. Using Carr's logic, as long as business technology delivers timely paychecks and accurate invoices, there is no compelling reason to invest further in these nonstrategic applications.

There are other types of business technology investments. Some are meant to ensure compliance, such as with the Sarbanes-Oxley Act of 2002 or the Health Insurance Portability and Accountability Act (HIPAA) for health-care organizations, the value for which is hardly strategic. Other types of investments are focused on improved decision making and competitiveness such as Wal-Mart's purchasing system or Dell's online sales. These are truly strategic, and anything but a commodity. Still others prevent security breaches and downtime; although not strategic, these investments have indirect payoffs through risk mitigation.

Therefore, an understanding of the objective and capabilities of business technology is the first step in setting goals for expected value.

How are metrics to assess business value derived?

Once business technology objectives are established, metrics can be developed to monitor their value. The suitability of the metrics depends on what is of interest to the business managers—value is in the eye of the beholder.[6] Establishing metrics and agreeing on their validity is to view business technology through the beholders' eyes.[7] It is also important to understand that metrics will vary depending on the nature of the BTM capability.[8] For example, BTM capabilities such as *Approval and Prioritization* require metrics that analyze the implications and impact of potential business technology investments. Others such as *Consolidation and Standardization* are used to measure the effectiveness of potential acquisitions or adoption of certain technology standards, (for example, databases, and application servers). Thus, business technology managers should identify key stakeholders and their orientation toward business technology.[9] An understanding of the roles and needs of these users will lead to mutually acceptable metrics that accurately measure business value.

> *Establishing metrics and agreeing on their validity is to view business technology through the beholders' eyes. Business technology managers should identify key stakeholders and their orientation toward business technology.*

For example, Citigroup, the global financial services company, lacked standard processes following the mergers and acquisitions that created its Global Corporate and Investment Banking (GCIB) group. A system called Mystic, designed to respond to such issues, provides Citicorp with the capability to track projects, align them with business strategy, and communicate the value to internal customers.[10] Mystic allows these customers to prioritize projects and track their status. Upon completion of a project, both developers and customers rate their satisfaction with each other. This orients business technology projects to solving business needs. Consistent with the steps in the previous examples, an alignment, involvement, analysis, communication (AIAC) framework has been proposed so that firms can create a process in which the measurement of business technology value is the responsibility of the entire organization.[11]

An information system such as Mystic also enables the transfer of learning among business functions that can help future projects. It provides time and cost estimates so that the business can align strategy with the technological capability. It provides actionable steps on how to extract business value from business technology and sidestep potential landmines.

Once established, however, metrics must change as the business and technology change. As mentioned previously, productivity metrics in banking must reflect changing customer preferences and technological developments that enable online loan processing and electronic funds transfers, as opposed to old metrics that tracked number of customers served by a bank teller.

How does one derive appropriate metrics? First, the business mission and profitability model must be well understood. Everyone in the organization must understand how a firm generates revenue and profits, not just those in finance. Metrics established with such an understanding will most likely provide a clear link from business technology investment to business value (see Figure 9.1).

Metrics fall into three broad categories: productivity, profitability, and consumer value.[12] Business technology's ability to reduce operational costs and improve internal coordination can lead to higher productivity. Improved productivity can lead to higher profitability, but factors such as increased competition and substitute products can mitigate this contribution. A likely

Figure 9.1 **Selecting Appropriate Metrics**

An organization's mission and operating models determine the relevant business metrics.

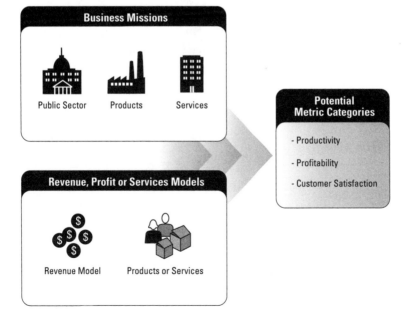

outcome of improved productivity is passing on the gains to consumers through richer features, better service, and improved interaction. Therefore, for each of these categories of metrics, executives must take a holistic approach, understanding all contributors to business value.

What are the various roles of business technology?

Business technology contributes business value in several ways, and metrics must be fashioned to capture these contributions. For example, in addition to the enabling agility and market alertness, business technology creates "digital options," such as new ways to build enterprise processes and knowledge systems.[13] Assessing the business value will require metrics revealing how organizations create agility, sense-and-respond capabilities, and digital options.[14]

Business technology investment is also crucial in integrating products with services and products with other products. Schwab.com, the financial services company, for example, provides trading facilities via phone, the Internet, and cell phone. Integration of services that allow customers to access their accounts through a variety of systems requires a significant effort in programming and adaptation to various media.

Assessing business value will require metrics revealing how organizations create agility, sense-and-respond capabilities, and digital options.

Otis, through its Remote Elevator Monitoring (REM) application, continuously monitors customer elevators and reports problems to technicians, who sometimes respond even before the customer realizes that there was a problem. As another example of knowledge systems and processes that create new digital options,[15] Otis offers a Web-based system that enables customers to view information about elevators such as traffic patterns, security status, maintenance data, and floor accessibility. , this goes beyond maintenance and repair. The services allow the building owner, (for example, a hospital) to understand the origin and destination of visitors. It can then plan on locating other services such as cafeteria and security around high traffic areas or vice versa. It can also improve response times by locating physicians and nurse stations closer to elevators. The electronics in the elevators can be integrated with the hospital's on-call system such that in a medical emergency, as the clinical team's beepers or cell phones ring, the elevators move to where members of the team are expected to be.

Another role stems from corporate privacy transgressions and misconduct, which led to regulations such as HIPAA, the Sarbanes-Oxley Act, and even Graham-Leach-Bliley, which regulates the sharing of personal information about individuals who obtain financial products or services from financial institutions and attempts to inform individuals about the privacy policies and practices of the institutions. Each new regulation has contributed to a redefinition of the role of business technology in supporting processes and ensuring compliance.

Research Insight

Kees Jans on Convergence

In the fast-moving world at Schiphol Airport, technology is at the heart of innovation, and CIO Kees Jans recognizes his department's responsibility to not just support business innovation, but also to help create it. In his tenure there, he related in an interview, he has watched as the importance of technology has caused business managers and technology managers to think more alike.

Intertwined with Technology

Business and technology are said to be synchronized when they share the lead in moving the company forward. That would seem to be the case at Amsterdam's Schiphol Airport, which is managed by the Schiphol Group.

"One of our main business objectives is to be known as a very innovative airport," says Kees Jans, CIO and General Manager, Information/Communication Technology. "We want to be an innovative company that drives the airport business not only at Schiphol, but everywhere we do business. IT is part of that innovative strategy."

All of his projects are designed to fulfill the business strategy, and his architecture conforms tightly to the business architecture. But more and more he sees a pattern of synchronization. "We have a five-year plan, and all business and IT developments are in it. You can see that the business has plans for which technology doesn't exist. The technology is not mature. At the same time, we saw new technology coming along, and there were no business initiatives to take advantage of it. Like biometrics. We were able to identify large advantages in using it."

Schiphol developed an iris-scan system that allows certain passengers to speed through long lines at the airport, and several other countries are now studying the system. The airport also built a new flight-information system that processes two million transactions a day, providing data to 2,500 screens around the airport used by more than 50,000 employees and more than 50 external companies serving the airport.

Because technology is at the heart of what Schiphol is trying to do, "our senior management has to know why technology is important to them," Jans says. "Some are already picking up the view that it's not something I can leave to the tech guys, because my business goals are so intertwined with technology that I have to understand the business impact of it myself. As more innovative areas of Schiphol

are managed by someone with a real feel for the impact of technology, the employees of the IT department can act more as partners than as people dropping by to say, hey, you can use this."

The HR department is developing competencies in senior management so that new executive managers will have a good sense of what technology can do. As this progresses, Jans says, business and technology management will increasingly fall under the same person. The role now played by the CIO will be split among business managers. "The role of senior management will change. It's too risky for them to rely on someone telling them what to do."

There will be changes in the IT staff, as well, he says. Commodity services will be outsourced, and IT staff will have to become more business savvy. And there's no reason to automatically assume that they couldn't become business managers. "In the end," Jans says, "there will be some people running business operations with a good knowledge of technology. I also think it will be the other way around."

Business technology's role in managing the risk from privacy and confidentiality violations is now at the center of its return on investment (ROI), prompting one author to refer to it as "risk of incarceration." Section 404 of the Sarbanes-Oxley Act, which requires companies and third-party auditors to document procedures for ensuring the accuracy of their financial statements, is estimated to cost $4.36 million for an average public company.[16] The Web site ITfactsbiz.com reports that 40 percent of all spending on Sarbanes-Oxley is for improving IT and security infrastructure, and 30 percent for document and records management systems. Can we place a value on business technology investment in mitigating risk? With investments of such magnitude, metrics for the value of business technology must be reinvented.

How do we develop the capability to monitor and use business technology?

As the speed of change has accelerated, so have firms' reaction times. As fast reaction times become common, so are consumer expectations increasing. A bank can no longer take three weeks to process an application for a home mortgage loan; neither can an airline wait two weeks to reexamine fares when a competitor has lowered its rates. When one credit card company offers variable interest rates, other companies have to follow suit in offering flexible payment plans to retain customers. In each example, the firm must possess capabilities to quickly gather information (sense) and to take action (respond). Business technology has a unique role in delivering both sense and respond capabilities, (for example, through processing large amounts of data quickly and testing and formulating counter strategies). Interestingly, in many cases, the new products are created by changing the accounting and tracking rules. For instance, online home mortgages approvals require replicating loan officers' expertise in a set of knowledge-based rules; the credit card variable interest rates require revising the program that calculates interest; revised fares for an airline require similar change in the origin-destination rate table. Most of these changes are enabled by business technology applications (see Figure 9.2).

Firms continuously gather information to examine changes in the external or internal environment. The changes must then be evaluated for their potential impact on operations. These capabilities require analytical skills to establish the link between business imperatives and business technology initiatives. This requires a deep understanding of the business environment and how strategic changes in the firm's response will address the challenges. Often the response requires real-time adjustments in operations and strategy, thus placing greater onus on the IT function to have a well-oiled system to gather accurate information and present efficient business alternatives. The following two examples of business technology's role in monitoring changes in the external

Figure 9.2   The Sense and Respond Cycle

Business options are enabled by a business technology-enabled sense and respond cycle.

Sense

- Gather data
- Analyze results
- Process feedback

Deliver

- New processes
- New business models
- New products
- New pricing plans

Decide

- Efficiency and effectiveness improvements
- New business capability requirements

Respond

- Create business technology enabled capabilities
- Create business technology enabled product offerings

and internal environments demonstrate the importance of creating business capabilities to respond to customer needs.

During the last economic downturn, banks began offering creative home mortgages to keep revenues flowing. The mortgages included products such as low interest in the first five years and adjustable-rate mortgages so that more first-time homebuyers could afford a home. One successful bank continued to operate conservatively and carried the traditional 30-year home mortgages. As home owners asked for greater choice and flexibility, the bank's customers —that is, the mortgage companies—warned the bank that they would take their business elsewhere if the bank did not provide flexible new mortgage products within 45 days. The bank struggled to bring such products to market because it lacked the technical resources to modify mortgage applications and test them in the 45-day deadline.

Its competitors, on the other hand, were able to modify their programs and continued to bring new mortgage products to the market by combining their technical prowess with attention to the customers' needs. The ability to mesh the business expertise with business technology capabilities proved to be a winning proposition for these banks. Prior investment in infrastructure set the stage, and a keen sense of the customers' changing preferences helped in bringing new products to market. As they sensed change in the marketplace, these banks exploited their expertise to analyze various financial products to meet the new demand. They examined the costs of the business technology investment in developing new programs to offer Internet-based products and the expected increase in revenue and profitability. Following the decision to proceed, they built real-time metrics modules to analyze the performance of new mortgage products, thus creating a loop for continuous sense-and-respond activities.

After understanding the needs of the customers, the firm must turn its attention to exploiting business technology to create competencies and the infrastructure for efficiency and cost effectiveness. On any given day, every IT department has many projects underway, each of which has a relationship to efficiency, improved quality, or better control. In large organizations, however, such projects can become monsters that at best delay the delivery of business value and at worst actually destroy value.

How can firms increase the value of business technology investment?

Companies can ensure in several ways that their business technology investments contribute real value. One is to identify appropriate complementary investments. It is estimated that for every dollar of technology investment, firms will spend between $5 and $9 in complementary investments.[17] Examples are process innovation and (re)design, governance, reward mechanisms, and training.

Business technology investments are among several investments on the way to accomplishing a business strategy.

For instance, when United Parcel Service (UPS) wanted to achieve total supply chain transparency, it looked to several functions, including IT, for help. Transparency required integration of various systems—"customer powership," storage and tran-shipment warehouses, sorting conveyers, and delivery trucks. The information system serves as the integrating link; however, processes among each system must be streamlined with training and established policies about who, when, and how to input business activity into the information system. UPS deployed an information system that not only provided transparency in the supply chain but, because complementary investments were made, expanded the scope to extract logistical efficiencies and compliance with stricter post 9-11 federal customs regulations.

Process innovation and (re)design are key complementary investments without which one runs the risk of doing unnecessary things faster. Many organizations now require evidence of process evaluation or redesign with requests for new business technology funding. The return on investment (ROI) can be significantly enhanced when processes are optimized and business technology is targeted to activities or tasks that otherwise take too long, are error-prone, or cost too much.

Three other familiar kinds of complementary investments—training, operational acceptance, and reward mechanisms—are related in that they can be seen to both flow from, and be dependent upon, one another. A variety of training types, focused at users, managers, and executives must be made available in support of a new system. Training is critical to ensure that change occurs smoothly, and training efforts must be customized to directly address the change brought about by business technology. Building on this training, communication about and sponsorship of the change must be comprehensive. Efforts made to gain end-user consensus and support of a new system or initiative aids in fostering operational acceptance (actual productive use) of the new system. Establishing reward mechanisms helps to ensure that sponsors and users commit themselves to training, communication, and the swift acceptance of any new system.

Another kind of complementary investment is in the creation of systems that continue to reinforce the objectives of senior executives with managers and decision makers.[18] By ensuring the continued use of a system, its very existence can inform and influence day-to-day decisions and even create peer influence to reinforce the demand for its use.

Companies can also ensure value by communicating with employees. Although business technology is deployed with the

Leadership Insight

Jean Holley on Governance

As it emerged from the telecom meltdown, Tellabs recognized the need for better governance of its technology. When Jean Holley became the CIO, she helped establish a formal governance structure, and, as she described in an interview, this gave the company a decided advantage when it underwent a major acquisition.

"Plain Old Simple Business"

"Elevator phobia" is one sign that a company's IT governance could be better.

"When your IT staff is afraid to get in the elevator, because they fear they'll get five more projects, that is evidence that your governance needs improvement," says Jean K. Holley, executive vice president and CIO at Tellabs Inc., a supplier of equipment to the telecom industry. Business executives were frustrated, as well, because they did not have enough insight into how projects were prioritized.

That is what Holley found when she arrived in April 2004. It was a result of the many challenges Tellabs faced following the telecom meltdown. After listening to her staff and the people on the business side, she proposed a formal structure for managing technology, and it was adopted in two months. "This basic model works for us," Holley says. "Simplicity is an important part of it. When you review some governance programs such as the federated model, your eyes glaze over. Do we really have to do all that?"

The Tellabs structure has two basic tiers. A steering council of all the direct reports to the CEO meets two to four times a year to make strategic decisions on technology. A business council of a dozen vice presidents and directors from key functional areas meets monthly "and really rolls up its sleeves to evaluate the business cases for specific investments," Holley says. Both of these groups review the IT strategic plan.

Seat at the table
Holley also restructured the Global Information Services staff, putting in place a Business Relationship Management group dedicated to working directly with business leaders. "We've pulled them out of the classic development environment and given them a seat at the business table to understand business challenges and work with the leaders to develop solutions."

This governance structure made it a lot easier when Tellabs acquired Advanced Fibre Communications, a company half its size, last year. The steering committee agreed that the combined companies should have only one enterprise resource planning (ERP) system. The business council analyzed that decision to understand the implications. And it set unify-

ing ERP as the top priority, because it offered the biggest bang for the buck. That focus meant the work could be done faster, and savings could begin sooner.

One key step was giving ownership of the integration effort to a strong business leader, one who had been involved with the business council. "We have clear business ownership for this integration at a senior level," Holley says. "You start with the right people in place, then you look at the processes, then you look at the technology. In each functional area, we have named business leaders, and then we align IT people under this. I can't emphasize this enough. It's business people first, and then IT people."

To make governance work, Holley in effect ceded her potential authority to make decisions to the business side. "I only have one vote," she says. "There are 12 other votes that determine where our priorities will be and where the project investments should be. It's not me making that determination, it's the business leaders.

"You have to trust the business leaders. But you have to help lead them to make the right decisions. You can do that by saying, look, if we don't consolidate, we will be running two ERPs, and we're going to have double maintenance and support costs. And every time we have to make a change we're going to have to do it in two places, so it's going to take twice as long. So you give them logical, plain old simple business reasons for consolidating ERP. You approach it from a businessperson's perspective."

And she sought to get strong business leaders with strong opinions on the business council. "Some of your business leaders are really going to challenge IT, and it's better to have them in the council asking questions up front versus firing their bullets at you after the fact. They have proven to be some of our most active business council members, and it's been great."

Out of the hot box
Setting priorities is now much easier. "Previously we'd say, let's inventory all our projects, and people would say, 'Oh that would take weeks.' That means you're working on too many things. You're trying to move 100 projects forward, and you can only move them one inch. We could really feel that problem inside GIS." Now, with the councils setting priorities, "it takes IT out of the hot box of saying no.

You're prioritizing projects for business purposes, not for IT purposes, and that's how it should be."

The company is also making more global decisions. For example, a new email and calendar system was implemented globally rather than region by region. Productivity soared. "It's great," Holley says, "because when we bought the company last year, we knew exactly what to do."

Now Holley is adding one more piece: post project reviews to determine and measure if they are producing the value that was expected.

"We've become much closer to the business," she says, "and that is one of our key goals, to build a very strong relationship with the business. Not one in which we wait until we're called and someone says I need help with my machine, but one in which we are really at the table discussing the business challenges and adding value."

objective of improving corporate efficiency and profitability, any new deployment causes disruption and change in work routines. It is natural for people to resist. Without a buy-in and organizational commitment from top to bottom, it is unlikely that the expected payoff will occur.

Sustaining momentum in business technology projects is directly related to finding new ways to improve work and business activities. Typically, creative uses of information from a data warehouse or a business insight resulting from a business intelligence query originate from a few end users who were seeking answers to a problem. However, dissemination of such insights can benefit the entire organization. It is important for executives to communicate areas of opportunity where business technology can add value. As described previously (with regard to complementary investments), to be effective, these areas of opportunity must be illustrated so that people can relate them to their work activities. This requires that managers understand the business context and frame the insights in the form of customized actionable steps for the business managers.

Visualize, communicate, orient is the new mantra. Managers should relate specific examples of how business technology made a difference or can make a difference. In this, the CIO must partner with other senior executives to raise the "information orientation" of all the people who make up the organization.[19] Companies that have information-oriented cultures emphasize constant improvement in IT practices, information management practices, and the most often overlooked value creating information capability, employees' information behaviors and values. (See Figure 9.3.)

When a company has a high information orientation, senior managers perceive that their organization can improve business performance through business technology. BTM capabilities become catalysts for improvement as they define the information (data, metrics, and so on) required to support business technology decision making. In the following example, BTM capabilities such as *Business-Driven IT Strategy*, *Business Architecture*, and *Technical Architecture* would provide the necessary information to determine improvements to products and services.

Companies in such diverse industries as cement (for example, Holcim) and banking (for example, Citigroup) recognize that raising the information orientation of their senior executives will pay great dividends. These companies focus their resources on information capabilities that make them distinctive. They leverage business technology to create new products and services and improve management decision making. They outsource the rest. In contrast, companies with low information orientation dissipate their best resources. Such companies never seem to have enough time or people to devote to what is important, because the pressures to do what is necessary seem to be forever urgent.

A good way to determine a company's information orientation is to benchmark its performance across the three critical dimensions. An organization must focus on all of these dimensions

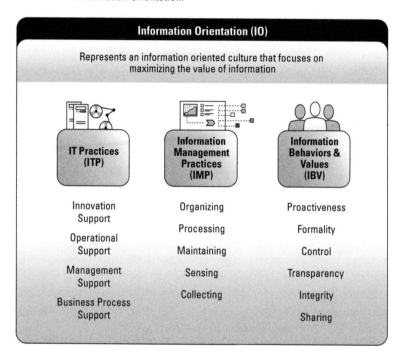

Figure 9.3 **Dimensions of Information Orientation**

Organizations display multiple characteristics with regard to their Information Orientation.

if they want to achieve high business performance. Conducting an information orientation assessment helps establish an enterprise-wide common language or mindset that is crucial to setting the right path for future value improvement.

Methods, mechanisms, and tactics to measure business technology's contribution

What are the steps in the business technology investment process that provide an opportunity to measure its impact? What BTM capabilities can be used to support this process? Several methods and mechanisms have been suggested, and a number of these are discussed here from a high-level perspective.

A process approach to business technology investment can better explain how it creates value for the firm.[20] The process approach involves an assessment (1) if proper IT assets were created, (2) if the assets led to business technology impacts, and (3) if the business technology impacts led to firm-level impacts. IT assets and corresponding business technology must be aligned with the firm's market position and the competitive environment to see a measurable impact of organizational performance. The process approach has several implications for measuring business technology's contribution to business value. The first is that business technology investment must be viewed in the business context. Second, this investment must be aligned with business processes that make a difference to the operation of business activities. Finally, business technology must support business activities that take advantage of the competitive position or create a niche position to which the competition must react.

Whereas the process approach provides a roadmap for business technology impact and value creation, statistical methods provide the tools to measure such impacts. Some statistical methods can also provide analytical support for future investment based on historical data or managerial assumption. Such methods can also be used in conjunction with a BTM capability (see Table 9.1).

Cost-benefit analysis measures the difference between the investment and returns from such investment. The challenge is to identify and agree on the intangible costs and intangible benefits, which often are a source of discord among the stakeholders. For instance, an analysis of the payoff from investment in customer relationship management (CRM) may reveal in higher sales from better tracking of customer leads but overlook the costs of data acquisition or analysis and system maintenance. In another instance, higher sales may be accounted for in the performance of the sales function instead of being attributed to business technology, thus leading to incomplete analysis. For this reason, firms are considering total cost of ownership (TCO) as an approach to quantifying the value of business technology. TCO takes into account all costs over the life of the system when comparing with the total benefits. TCO can be time-consuming and makes certain assumptions about the future.

Net present value (NPV) is a commonly used approach to measure the future value of a current investment by discounting the investment by a given rate. The rationale for using NPV is that every dollar invested today will be worth less in the future. The reason is that it costs to borrow capital, called the cost of capital, incurred as interest and other costs. In other words, future benefits of today's investment must be discounted by at least the cost of capital, also called weighted average cost of capital (WACC). WACC is commonly at 12 percent to 15 percent, implying that the business technology investment must yield more than the WACC to return value to the firm. NPV is an effective tool to compare the relative returns of two or more projects and is often used by managers to prioritize opportunities for investment.

Measuring the business value of future business technology investment, particularly in emerging technologies, can be difficult and risky. Because little historical information is available and

Table 9.1 Statistical Measurement Methods

A number of statistical methods support investment analysis.

Method	Characteristics	Use When	Supporting BTM Capability
Cost-Benefit Analysis	Seeks to find the surplus of benefits after accounting for costs. Does not consider the strategic value of the investment.	Investments have mostly tangible costs and tangible benefits	Approval and Prioritization
Total Cost of Ownership (TCO)	Accounts for all costs – present and future, direct and indirect TCO can be used as an input into cost-benefit analysis.	Investments have longer life span and recurring support expenses, e.g., software licences, process skills	Technology Architecture
Net Present Value (NPV)	Measures the contribution of a project after discounting the borrowing costs.	Comparing the financial contribution of two or more investments	Portfolio and Program Management
Real Options	Measures benefits or opportunities for benefits beyond the direct benefits. Costs of the option are known but the benefits are contingent upon future conditions.	Investment can be staggered; opportunities have uncertain outcomes; investments are for emerging technologies	Consolidation and Standardization

the payoff depends upon the accuracy of the predictions, the risks as well as opportunities must be accounted for. Given that the potential benefits of business technology are harder to define than costs, *real options* methodology proposes that business technology investment can be made in stages such that preliminary investment provides a stake as well as a choice to reverse the investment decision. Drawn from options theory, the *real options* approach suggests that an initial investment creates future opportunities for the firm.[21] Given favorable market conditions, the firm can exercise the option to make a secondary investment and take advantage of the business opportunity. However, market conditions may remain unfavorable and the option may not be exercisable. Because the value of the investment in the option is known, firms can choose or decline to bear the risk. Real options methodology is a useful tool when business technology is being considered in emerging areas such as electronic commerce and other innovative areas of business.[22]

Research Insight

Jerry Luftman on Alignment

Jerry N. Luftman is a Distinguished Professor at the Howe School of Technology Management, Stevens Institute of Technology. He conducts research on the maturity of business-technology alignment efforts in major corporations. In this excerpt from an interview, he discusses the strategic importance of managing business technology.

No Silver Bullet

"With the large corporations, alignment is only getting better in those organizations that are really focusing their attention on it. In other words, it's not going to get better by itself. I measure maturity with a one to five scale, and over the years the average company has been between two and three. It has not gotten much higher than that. It's really frozen in the high two level. These are global 1000 companies, and these are companies who requested to be assessed—companies that you would'd think are a little bit more concerned about alignment and paying more attention to enhancing it. So the companies that didn't take part would, I think, bring the average down.

"Given that for more than 20 years IT-business alignment has received top ranking in surveys (done by academics, consulting firms, and research organizations) identifying key IT management concerns, this now pervasive problem/opportunity continues to live on. The reason is likely to be that everyone is looking for the silver bullet, which just does not exist. The alignment assessment tool has identified six important criteria, all of which need to be addressed."

Focus on governance

"The six major areas in the assessment are effective communication, value measurement, governance, partnership, human resources, and technology itself. Governance seems to be the thing that people believe is most important. They believe that's the area they need to focus on. However, if you don't do any one of those things well, it could impact the overall effectiveness of alignment.

"No one industry appears better than others. It's relatively consistent. There are some industries that show slightly higher numbers, but nothing statistically significant.

"It's clearly the case that companies that do this right create a competitive advantage that may be hard to close. The ones that have seen the opportunity and impact IT can have on the bottom line and the difficulty it might place on their competitors say we need to ensure that we have the IT execu-

tive sitting at the table; and they try to identify opportunities to leverage the technology. These are companies such aslike FedEx, Wal-Mart, and Cisco."

The winners

"Some companies understand that they need alignment not just between IT and the business but alignment across all parts of the business, as well as across their suppliers and their customers. If an organization could see what the opportunities are to improve the interactions that take place across their business, partners, and customers, and then say, let's focus on how we can improve the harmony across all these groups—these are the companies that are winners.

"BTM is fundamental in mapping this out, taking a look at the business elements—the processes both internally and externally—with your strategic partners and customers to make that happen.

"Too many people, leading practitioners, some academics, and some consulting firms, put too much focus on infrastructure and compliance issues. Not that we can avoid them, but they put too much focus on that and not enough on the strategic way we can leverage technology.

"I have to have an infrastructure; I have to comply with government regulations; and I could do those things better than anyone in the world. However, if I don't have the leading applications and the business taking advantage of those systems in a unique way, who cares?

"Why don't more CIOs report to the CEO? If you focus on IT infrastructure or IT being needed for compliance, if you focus on project failures, why the heck would the CEOs want IT to report to them anyway? However, if you focus on the strategic impact that IT is having, could be having, should be having, on the business, now you've got a better rationale for reporting to the CEO. But IT budgets are so large, with the largest expense going to infrastructure; that's no reason to report to the CEO. All the CEO wants to know in that case is are we able to pay the bills, rather than how we are leveraging IT for strategic advantage?"

Getting the payoff

For many companies, the link between business technology investment and business performance remains elusive. However, high information-oriented companies know how to break out of the cycle of spending more on technology and getting less. These companies use business technology and BTM capabilities to leverage information across their business processes and with customers and suppliers to gain knowledge for developing new products, spotting emergent customer needs, forming strategy, and analyzing risk. Such companies understand that the payoff demands moving the conversation beyond "smokescreen" technical infrastructure issues to the more difficult job of delivering the right information to the right person at the right time. However, even delivering the right information does not guarantee effective use. To ensure that good information delivery results in a good business outcomes, companies must push to instill in their employees precisely those behaviors and values that affect how the company best uses information for customer, supplier, and partner relationships. With this, an information-oriented culture flourishes, and business technology payoff is achieved.

Measuring Success

▶ **Establish** the business purpose of each investment in technology: Is it to enable growth, maintain the infrastructure, manage risk?

▶ **Determine** whether the metrics you use have changed along with changes in business processes and technology.

▶ **Agree** on new metrics that show how your organization creates agility, sense-and-respond capabilities, and digital options. This agreement will ultimately lead to metrics that accurately measure business value.

▶ **Understand** the business environment and how the firm adjusts its strategy to changes in the environment. This often requires real-time adjustments in operations, placing a greater onus on business technology executives to have a well-oiled system to gather information and present business alternatives.

▶ **Leverage** BTM capabilities such as *Approval and Prioritization* and *Consolidation and Standardization* to manage and define the information requirements to support a high information-orientation culture.

▶ **Translate** the business strategy into tactical plans for which information and communication technologies can be deployed. It is increasingly the role of the technology executives to make this connection. Executives must take the lead in communicating areas where business technology can add value. Employees must be made aware of how these opportunities relate to their jobs.

▶ **Identify** complementary investments necessary to get full value out of technology investments.

▶ **Instill** in employees the behaviors and values that will lead to the best use of information for customer, supplier and partner relationships.

Notes

1   See the "Key Terminology" section in Chapter 1.

2   Brynjolfsson, E., and Hitt, L. "Beyond the productivity paradox." *Communications of the ACM* (41:8) 1998, pp. 49–55.

3   Kohli, R., and Devaraj, S. "Measuring Information Technology Payoff: A Meta-Analysis of Structural Variables in Firm Level Empirical Research." *Information Systems Research* (14:2) 2003, pp. 127–145.

4   See the "Key Terminology" section in Chapter 1.

5   Carr, N.G. "IT Doesn't Matter." *Harvard Business Review* (81:5), May 2003, pp. 41.

6   Marchand, D.A., Kettinger, W.J. and Rollins. "Information Orientation: People, Technology, and the Bottom Line." *Sloan Management Review.* Vol. 41. N. 4, pp. 69–80, 2000.

7   Sawhney, M. "Damn the ROI, Full Speed Ahead; "Show me the money" may not be the right demand for e-business projects." CIO (15:19), July 15, 2002, p. 1.

8   See the "Key Terminology" section in Chapter 1.

9   Marchand, D. A., Kettinger, W. J. and Rollins. *Information Orientation: The Link to Business Performance,* Second Edition. Oxford UK: Oxford University Press, 2002.

10   Low, 2004.Low, L. "How Citigroup Measures Up." *CIO,* April 24, 2004.

11   Kohli, R., and Devaraj, S. "Realizing the Business Value of Information Technology Investments: An Organizational Process." *MIS Quarterly Executive* (3:1) 2004, pp. 55–70.

12   Hitt, L. M., and Brynjolfsson, E. "Productivity, business profitability, and consumer surplus: Three different measures of information technology value." *MIS Quarterly* (20:2) 1996, pp. 121–142.

13   Sambamurthy, V., Bharadwaj, A., and Grover, V. "Shaping Agility Through Digital Options: Reconceptualizing the Role of Information Technology in Contemporary Firms." *MIS Quarterly* (27:2) 2003, pp. 237–263.

14   Bradley, S. P., and Nolan, R. L. *Sense & respond: capturing value in the network era* Harvard Business School Press, Boston, 1998, pp. xi, 339.

15   Sambamurthy, V., Bharadwaj, A., and Grover, V. "Shaping Agility Through Digital Options: Reconceptualizing the Role of Information Technology in Contemporary Firms." *MIS Quarterly* (27:2) 2003, pp. 237–263.

16   Jenny Strasburg. *San Francisco Chronicle,* March 23, 2005.

17   Brynjolfsson, E., and Hitt, L. "Beyond the productivity paradox." *Communications of the ACM* (41:8) 1998, pp. 49–55.

18   Kohli, R., and Kettinger, W. J. "Informating the Clan: Controlling Physicians' Costs and Outcomes." *MIS Quarterly* (28:3) 2004, pp. 363–394.

19   Marchand, D. A., Kettinger, W. J. and Rollins. *Making the Invisible Visible: How Companies Win with the Right Information, People and IT,* with Donald A. Marchand and John D. Rollins. Chichester & NY: John Wiley & Sons Ltd., 2001.

20   Soh, C., and Markus, M. "How IT Creates Business Value: A Process Theory Synthesis." Proceedings of the Sixteenth International Conference on Information Systems, Amsterdam, The Netherlands, 1995, pp. 29–41.

21   Benarock, M. "Managing information technology investment risk: A real options perspective." *Journal of Management Information Systems* (19:2), Fall 2002, pp. 43–84.

22   Fichman, R. "Going Beyond the Dominant Paradigm for Information Technology Innovation Research: Emerging Concepts and Methods." *Journal of Association for Information Systems* (5:8) 2004, pp. 314–355.

By **Tom Trainer**

Senior Vice President and Global CIO
PepsiCo, Inc.
Co-Chair
BTM Global Leadership Council
BTM Institute

PLANO, TEXAS

Peering Into the Future

When I began my career in information technology, it was still the era of the "glass house," the room that held our only computer. It was enclosed for climate control and located somewhere in the back of the building or the basement. It was there because when computing came along it was just tacked on to a business already in progress. We who labored in the glass house mostly used the computer to process transactions.

When we think back on those days, we usually remark that our smallest laptop today has more computing power than the machine, an IBM 360, that occupied the glass house.

More important, however, is the symbolism of the glass house: We in information technology were isolated, set apart, somewhat odd and mysterious in our "cage." People would walk by the glass house and peer in curiously. No one on the business side was quite sure what we were doing in there.

Today, the glass wall that once separated business and technology is coming down. I expend most of my energy as a CIO on my relationships with business executives, sitting with them to make business decisions. For example, I co-own with a top business executive our program to redesign business processes across PepsiCo. I'm not just the "techie" observer.

As the examples in this book vividly demonstrate, the leading companies—those that are winning in the marketplace—do not choose sides any longer. Their "business" executives are conversant in technology. Their "technology" executives can talk the business. They are all in the glass house together. This is a critical point and worth repeating: To succeed today, companies must manage business and technology together.

Have you experienced this epiphany yet? If you take nothing else away from this book, grapple with the significance of this new mindset for your business.

I have had CIO-level responsibilities for more than 20 years, and in that time, I've watched as the management of technology became more important than the technology itself. Because we can all buy the same machines, the only differentiator is how we use them. And as technology has become embedded in every nook and cranny of the organization, the firms that have pulled ahead are those that manage business and technology as one. They design business processes and the enabling technology together.

What are the characteristics of the leaders who can do this? For one thing, understanding technology, although important, is not the most important. What will be increasingly vital is the human side of things. A leader must know how to communicate across organizational boundaries. He or she needs to do this to develop and manage relationships. A leader must understand the political network as well as the official organizational structure. Where are the power bases? How do they work? When things change, can the leader adjust to and align with the new power structure? This has nothing to do with technology. It has everything to do with the ability to think and act at an organizational level to get the right deployment of resources, human and otherwise, to deliver the value the organization needs from technology.

As I reflect on those who will follow in my footsteps, I realize that they will need a different set of skills and perspectives. I'm convinced that leaders of the future must:

- *Come out of the glass house for good.* They must understand that business technology is strategic. Executives of the future will know that merely looking over their shoulders at what the competition is doing with technology will only strengthen the competition. They will know that the appropriate level and mix of investment in technology is a function of what their own firms are trying to achieve strategically.

- *Know that managing technology is as important as the technology itself.* The next generation of leaders will understand, or should if they want to succeed, that they must invest in the management of technology as well as in the technology itself. If there is any remaining doubt today, there will not be in the future: Technology per se is an equalizer. Only in the management of it can firms eke out advantage. As Professor John Henderson of Boston University noted in Chapter 3, "Making the Right Investments," "Leadership is a differentiator of companies. Technology is not a differentiator."

- *Understand what technology does.* Unless they appreciate that business technology often plays a critical role in establishing or maintaining a strategic position, future leaders may well spend inappropriately. But appreciation must evolve to an understanding of how the various types of technology—those that enable transactions, for example, or decisions or relationships—contribute to a firm's strategic actions. More often than not in the first half century of business technology, it was thought about only tactically.

- *Follow the money.* They must focus on the business and understand how it earns a profit. Leaders must understand the business strategy: With regard to each product-market, is the firm in an exploratory or exploitative posture? This assumes that the firm *has* a strategy that is well articulated and supported by appropriate structures, processes, and information.

- *See through walls.* Tomorrow's leaders will, I suspect, be far more comfortable than my generation with deriving value through partnerships and other types of engagements with other firms. They must understand the role technology plays in enabling these partnerships. They must learn to manage the technology that stretches across internal firm boundaries as well. BTM will break down many existing silos.

- *Manage business and technology as one.* The moments of dissension, the pointing of fingers for failures, will, I hope, disappear as executives come to see that business technology failure is often due to a weak or nonexistent business strategy or a failure to create a business-driven IT strategy. Alignment will increasingly be seen as only the first step; it will occur to all that the design and management of business cannot be done apart from the design and management of technology.

- *Scrap the org chart.* We are already seeing the blending of corporate roles, and I predict that it will be commonplace in the future. The CIOs at Schneider National, for example, who moved into business positions, are harbingers of what is to come. Most of the executives interviewed for this book talked of the need for people who are comfortable in both the business and technology realms. This re-identity is underway in many firms.

- *Get underneath the hood.* Executives of the next generation must be able to discern the business processes, below the overarching posture of a firm, that advance the strategy. Moreover, they must see technology as part and parcel of these processes; the two are inseparable. This is going to require untying the functional straitjackets in which many firms have existed.

- *Get comfortable with speed.* Is it too much of a cliché to say that everything will move faster and faster, that interconnectivity makes the whole world our playing field, and that we must give up command and control so that our people on the edges of the organization can react to events in real time? And that this is an entirely new way of thinking about management and leadership? And that even if we pay lip service to it today, it will be very hard to accomplish?

- *Wake up each day and be ready.* Expect unimaginable change. Leaders of the future may well look back on the years of my career as somewhat curious. Perhaps they will look back on these days of business and technology wrestling toward alignment and wonder what in the world we were thinking. Why didn't we get it? Well, I do hope that this book will some day be outdated, quaint, and amusing.

In his interview for this book, Rob Slagboom, vice president of information and communications technology at Transavia Airlines, said he needs "people who have a high-level view, who can understand longer-term approaches, who think strategically about IT. And they have to understand the business. But who will be their teachers? It's the classical predicament of a field in development. It has to grow up."

I want this book to be a step in that direction.

Let me step back now to the generation before me to illustrate an important point about our future.

When I was growing up in Scotland in the 1950s, one of the more remarkable stories of business technology was unfolding in London.

It seems that the very first use of a computer for a routine business process occurred in 1951 at a bakery in London. J. Lyons & Co., with 33,000 employees, was a huge supplier of cakes, pastries, teas, and other foods to hundreds of teashops and other outlets around the country.

Lyons was an innovative company. It built its own delivery vans and baking equipment, and it was an early adopter of such technologies as microwave and microfilm. So, as bold as it sounds today, it is not surprising that the firm's executives, hearing of the new "electronic brains" at work in the military and science, would decide to build their own. They named their machine LEO, for Lyons Electronic Office. And they created software to run it before the word software even existed.[1]

What is of interest to us here is that the people at Lyons, alongside their derring-do with hardware and software, also understood many of the principles espoused in this book. Many years earlier, the company had established a Systems Research Office to study its operations and look for ways to make them better.

Lyons executives understood that business processes and technology were intricately linked. David Caminer, who headed the Systems Research Office and was asked to create software for the LEO, has written:

> It was a cardinal principle at Lyons that new machinery should not be introduced without the system as a whole being reexamined. There was no question of leaving the system as it stood and merely mechanizing those aspects that most readily presented themselves. It was now the turn of the computer to be considered in the same ambience.[2]

The LEO found its way into every corner of the business. It ran the payroll, cranking out a paycheck in 1.5 seconds, compared to 8 minutes by hand. It charted the international supply chain of the tea business, providing managers with information they never had before. It automated operations, issuing instructions on which type of cartons to use for baked goods for each order and directing trolley loadings.

It was deployed to manage shipments of up to 250 items to some 180 teashops. This business process was altered because of the LEO. Managers discovered that most shops' orders did not change that much. It would be simpler to calculate deviations from the basic order as they were phoned in. It was management by exception. The LEO also made it possible for management to have a nearly real-time view of the operation.

It is fun to think about working in such an innovative, greenfield environment, but Lyons offers two serious lessons. One is that its success was due not just to building a computer, but to the way it managed its business and technology together. The second is that computers were only introduced into business a scant half century ago.

We have learned a lot since then, but 50 years is not a long time, and there is still much to discover about managing business technology. Only now is what we know being codified in a standard. By contrast, consider the discipline of accounting. Nearly 100 years before the LEO, the Institute of Accountants in Glasgow petitioned the queen for a royal charter.[3] Soon, use of the term chartered accountant would be widespread. More than 450 years before the LEO, Luca Pacioli, a Franciscan friar, published a book summing up what was known about double-entry book-keeping "in order that the subjects of the most gracious Duke of Urbino may have complete instructions in the conduct of business." That sounds to me like an attempt to create a standard.

Pacioli could draw on centuries of insight. Some 5,500 years before the LEO, accounting was being practiced in Mesopotamia. And, as we know, the accountants are still trying to get it right. So we who seek to manage business technology today might be forgiven our occasional bewilderment—we've only been at it for 50 years!

The BTM Standard—toward which this book is an important step—will be significant, not in and of itself, but for what it makes possible. The companies and organizations we have talked with for this book bring us food and medicine. They offer investments and insurance. They make the steel for our cars and the gasoline to power them. They deliver our packages and fly us around the world.

Increasingly, they depend on information technology to do all this. If we help them do it quicker, cheaper, better, if they discover through technology entirely new products and services, if they can move this remarkable computing power we have forever out of the glass house and into the heart of their businesses, then they will win—and so will we all.

Notes

1 Hayes, Brian. "Study: J. Lyons & Co." *CIO Insight*, Nov. 1, 2001.

2 Caminer, David. "LEO and its Applications: The Beginning of Business Computing." *The Computer Journal*, Nov.7, 1997.

3 Alexander, John R. "History of Accounting." Association of Chartered Accountants in the United States.

About the Authors
and Contributors

Faisal Hoque
Chairman and CEO, Enamics, Inc.
Founder and Chair, BTM Institute

Faisal Hoque created the concept of Business Technology Management. In 1999, he founded Enamics, Inc., a winner of the 2004 Deloitte Technology Fast 500 and Connecticut Fast 50 awards. He has nearly two decades of experience helping organizations secure value from their technology investments, including American Express, Chase, CompUSA, Dun and Bradstreet, General Electric, Great American Insurance, JP Morgan, MasterCard, Pitney Bowes, Paccar, and PepsiCo. A seasoned entrepreneur and operating executive, he was recruited by GE Capital in 1994 to launch a B2B electronic commerce spin-off. He is the author of *The Alignment Effect*, which is used in more than a dozen universities. He founded two other award-winning companies prior to Enamics, and over the years, he has personally led more than $200M in private equity and venture capital transactions. In 2003, he founded the BTM Institute, The Michael Nobel Harriet Fulbright Institute of Business Technology Management.

V. Sambamurthy
Eli Broad Professor of IT, Michigan State University
Co-Chair, BTM Global Research Council, BTM Institute

V. Sambamurthy is a recognized researcher on business-IT alignment. His expertise is in how firms leverage information technologies in their business strategies, products, services, and organizational processes. His research explores the impact of CIO and top management team characteristics on a firm's success with IT assimilation; the impacts of institutional forces on organizational IT assimilation; and the organization designs and capabilities associated with the strategic use of IT. He sits on the editorial board of a half-dozen leading IS journals, is a frequent speaker and commentator for CIO-related forums, and has received funding from the National Science Foundation, Financial Executives Research Foundation, and the Advanced Practice Council to work with Fortune 500 companies on research intended to provide insight on leveraging IT value. He actively consults with companies on issues related to Business Technology Management.

Robert Zmud
Michael F. Price Chair in MIS, University of Oklahoma
Co-Chair, BTM Global Research Council, BTM Institute

Robert Zmud has written eight books and more than 70 articles in scholarly journals on topics pertaining to IT, has served as editor-in-chief of *MIS Quarterly*, and has been elected a fellow of both the Decision Science Institute and the Association for Information Systems. He served for 12 years (1992–2004) as the research director for the Advanced Practices Council of the Society for Information Management, International. He teaches in the areas of information systems, information systems management, and technology management, with research interests focusing on the impact of information technology in facilitating a variety of organizational behaviors and on organizational efforts involved with planning, managing, and diffusing information technology.

Tom Trainer
Senior Vice President and Global CIO, PepsiCo, Inc.
Co-Chair, BTM Global Leadership Council, BTM Institute

In his 36-year career, Tom Trainer has helped companies such as Citigroup, Eli Lilly and Company, Reebok International, and Joseph E. Seagram and Sons rise to the forefront of their industries. At PepsiCo since 2003, he is transforming IT into a world-class organization while enabling a business transformation/process harmonization initiative globally. He has been *Information Week's* "CIO of the Year" and was termed the "Quintessential CIO" by *CIO* magazine. He lectures internationally on business and technology issues.

Carl Wilson
Executive Vice President and CIO, Marriott International, Inc.
Co-Chair, BTM Global Leadership Council, BTM Institute

Carl Wilson has global accountability for all business information technology resources at Marriott. He joined Marriott from Georgia-Pacific Corporation in 1997, where he had served as their CIO and vice president of information resources. During his career, Mr. Wilson has been the senior vice president of management information services for the Food and International Retailing Sectors of Grand Metropolitan Plc. and vice president of information management for The Pillsbury Company, Inc. He serves on various boards, including the AT&T Executive Customer Advisory Council; American University, Kogod School of Business' IT Executive Board; and the Board of Directors of both Global eXchange Services, Inc., and Software Architects, Inc. He was named to *CIO* magazine's "CIO 100" list.

Contributing Authors

Ritu Agarwal
Professor and Robert H. Smith Dean's Chair of Information Systems University of Maryland

Ritu Agarwal is also director of the Center for Health Information and Decision Systems at the Robert H. Smith School of Business. Her widely published research is currently focused on how organizations derive value from IT through adoption, diffusion, and creative use and the transformation of the health-care industry through IT. She has worked extensively with Fortune 500 companies on research, consulting, and speaking engagements; is active in executive education in the Smith School's Executive MBA Program; serves several editorial appointments; and is a member of AIS, INFORMS, and the Academy of Management, as well as a vice president on the INFORMS Board.

Anandhi Bharadwaj
Associate Professor of Decision and Information Analysis, Emory University

Anandhi Bharadwaj is a visiting associate professor of information systems in the School of Information Systems at Singapore Management University. Her research focuses on the organizational impacts of information technology, IT, and business agility, business value of IT, IT and business process outsourcing, and knowledge management. Her work has been widely presented in academic conferences and practitioner forums and has been sponsored by the Society for Information Management. She currently serves as associate editor of information systems research and is on the editorial board of *The Journal of the Association for Information Systems* (JAIS). She has served as the associate editor of *MIS Quarterly*. Prior to her doctoral studies, she worked as a consultant and trainer at a worldwide IT consulting firm.

Michael Fillios
Chief Product Officer, Enamics, Inc.
Executive Director, BTM Global Research Council, BTM Institute

Michael Fillios is responsible for research, development, marketing, and commercialization of Enamics knowledge and software products. He has more than 15 years of experience in corporate and product strategy, research, management consulting, business development, and finance and has co-authored several management papers on BTM. He is the executive director of the BTM Institute's Global Research Council. He came to Enamics from Grant Thornton, where he managed strategic partnerships and business development for the Northeast Enterprise Solutions Group. Previously, he was director of finance for Penwest Pharmaceuticals where he managed financial and information technology functions. He began his career as a senior auditor for Ernst & Young where he performed financial and systems audits for companies across the manufacturing, service, and financial industries.

Varun Grover
William S. Lee Distinguished Professor of Information Systems
Department of Management, Clemson University

Varun Grover's research interests are in a variety of topics pertaining to business value creation through IT, including strategic information management, IT governance, knowledge management, and e-business, and he is currently co-editing his third book on business process transformation. He has authored more than 130 articles and has been frequently ranked among the top five researchers based on publications in top IS journals over the past decade. He is a senior editor or the associate editor of a number of prestigious IS journals and has received recognitions for his research from the Decision Sciences Institute, PriceWaterhouse Coopers, AIS, and Anbar Intelligence. His primary teaching interests are in the management of IS at the MBA level and IS research at the doctoral level.

William Kettinger
Associate Professor of Information Systems, Moore School of Business
University of South Carolina

William Kettinger focuses on strategic information management, process management, and IS service quality. He also regularly teaches in MBA programs in Switzerland, Austria, and Mexico. He is a highly sought conference speaker and leads executive development programs both domestically and abroad. He is the co-author of four books, including the highly acclaimed *Making the Invisible Visible: How Companies Win with the Right Information, People and IT*. He routinely publishes his research in the top IS journals and is the recipient of numerous awards and grants.

Terry Kirkpatrick
Editor in Chief, Enamics, Inc.

Terry Kirkpatrick has been a contributing editor of Booz Allen Hamilton's *strategy+business* and contributing and deputy editor of *CIO Insight* magazine. He has also written and edited for McKinsey & Co. and Gartner, Inc. He was editorial director at the Peppers and Rogers Group, where he launched *1to1 Quarterly*, a thought leadership journal. At IBM, he launched the award-winning *Think Leadership* Web site for CEOs, as well as an internal site for the company's scientists and technologists. He had been a managing editor at *The Reader's Digest* and a business writer for The Associated Press.

Rajiv Kohli
Associate Professor of Management Information Systems
College of William & Mary

Rajiv Kohli's research interests include information technology payoff, enhanced decision support systems, process innovation, and the role of information technologies as enablers of competitive advantage. He has worked and consulted with major global companies, has received several awards, and is widely published, including his most recent and popular book, *The IT Payoff: Measuring Business Value of Information Technology Investment.*

James Lebinski
Vice President, Knowledge Products, Enamics, Inc.

James Lebinski leads the research, analysis, design, and implementation of the full range Enamics knowledge products, including the Enamics BTM Framework™. He regularly contributes to Enamics publications. Previously, as vice president and research director of Gartner, Inc.'s Decision Tools business unit, he was responsible for a research agenda covering more than 20 technology areas. His 15-year track record of working with Fortune 100/Global 2000 clients includes leading more than 100 business technology vendor selection and Total Cost of Ownership (TCO) analysis projects. Clients with which he has worked include IBM, SAP AG, The Tennessee Valley Authority (TVA), Hillenbrand Industries, Lockheed Martin, The United Nations (UNHCR), and Cap Gemini. His domain and functional expertise encompasses vendor selection, needs analysis, standards definition, product implementation, and support.

Lars Mathiassen

Professor of Computer Information Systems, Center for Process Innovation and Department of Computer Information Systems, Georgia State University

Lars Mathiassen's research interests are focused on business process innovation and engineering and management of IT services. He is a co-author of *Professional Systems Development-Experiences, Ideas and Action, Computers in Context—The Philosophy and Practice of Systems Design, Object-Oriented Analysis & Design,* and *Improving Software Organizations: From Principles to Practice.* His research has been published in several international journals, including *MIS Quarterly, Information Systems Journal,* and *Information Systems Research,* among others. His research is based on extensive collaboration with many small- to medium-size enterprises and leading organizations, including Ericsson, Astra Zeneca, Volvo, Danske Bank, and Gartner, Inc.

Mark Minevich

Chief Strategy Officer, Enamics, Inc.
Executive Director, BTM Global Leadership Council, BTM Institute

Mark Minevich is responsible for corporate strategy, investment initiatives, and strategic alliances at Enamics, Inc. He was the author of *The CTO Handbook: The Indispensable Technology Leadership Resource.* Recognized as an authority on CIO/CTO community, globalization, innovation, and strategic outsourcing, he serves on the advisory boards of USC Globalization Institute, Global Capital Associates, Ziff Davis/CIO Insight, Global Equations, Mirador Capital, and Hypha Holdings (Singapore). Previously, he was CTO and senior strategist of the IBM Next Generation Group. He founded and acted as a chairman of The Technology Leadership Council, Global Innovation Network, and is a senior member of CIO Collective.

Frank Ovaitt

President and CEO, Institute for Public Relations
Fellow, Enamics, Inc.

Frank Ovaitt helped launch Enamics in 1999 and continues to serve as an executive advisor to help drive the company's global expansion. He leads the Communication Strategy and Management Practice and drives many strategic initiatives in the areas of media, public relations, and editorial content for the publications programs of Enamics and the Business Technology Management Institute. His 35 years of professional experience include serving as vice president of corporate affairs for MCI.

He held executive positions with AT&T, including public relations vice president-International, and he was customer communications director for Bell Laboratories. In 1995 he founded Crossover International, Inc., an independent firm providing communications management services to leading multinationals and young entrepreneurial companies.

Arun Rai

Harkins Professor, Center for Process Innovation and Department of Computer Information Systems, Georgia State University

Arun Rai's research interests are focused on digitally enabled supply chain management, diffusion and impacts of information technology, and management of systems delivery. He has published more than 50 journal articles in leading scholarly and practitioner journals on these subjects. He serves on the editorial boards for *IEEE Transactions on Engineering Management, Information Systems Research, MIS Quarterly, Journal of Strategic Information Systems,* and other journals. His research has been sponsored by leading organizations, including A.T. Kearney, Bozell Worldwide, Daimler-Chrysler, Comdisco, SAP, IBM, and the Advanced Practices Council for the Society for Information Management, among others.

Richard J. Welke

Professor and Director, Center for Process Innovation & Department of Computer Information Systems, Georgia State University
Cor Wit Professor, TBM Faculty, Technical University Delft

Richard Welke holds the Cor Wit research professorship at TU-Delft and is a professor at Georgia State University and director of the Center for Process Innovation. His current research interests are centered on ICT-enabled service innovation and delivery, with continuing work as well on meta-modeling and methodology engineering. Current research projects include BAM frameworks and cases, BPM/SOA implementations, and comparative methodologies for business service discovery, composition, and development. He is presently spearheading the formation of a multi-university Institute on Services Sciences and Innovation in The Netherlands. He has published more than 50 papers in conferences, journals, or books. He is a founding member of the principle IS academic organizations including ICIS and IFIP WG82 and has served in numerous capacities in these organizations, including chairman. Professionally, he was primary owner and CEO of two CASE software companies, and CIO for several large engineering companies based in Atlanta.

A

activity-related portfolios, 124-126
administrative forces, organization
    structures, 96
Advance Transformer, 66
Aeneas Internet and Telephone, 158
agility
    challenges of, 138-139
    developing business agility, 137
AIAC (alignment, involvement,
    analysis, communication), 184
alignment, 6-7
    Luftman, Jerry N., 200-202
    Poussereau, Alain, 66-67
The Alignment Effect, XVIII
Allen, William (processes),
    147-148
analyzing information and
    development strategies
    and plans, 130
Application Portfolio
    Management, 21
Approval and Prioritization, 17
    PPM, 128
architecture, business architecture
    Henderson, John, 37-39
    managing, 150, 152-153
assessing business value with
    metrics, 183-185
Asset Rationalization, 21
assigning responsibilities, PPM,
    128-130
AT&T Wireless, 158
authority, distributed and coordi-
    nated authority, 139
automation, business technology
    shaping business strategy, 78

B

Beath, Cynthia, 85
Berdowski, P.A.M. (synchronization),
    13-15
Blue Shield of California, 84
blurring of roles, 144
boards
    challenges in overseeing busi-
        ness technology, 77
    processes for managing technol-
        ogy decisions, 89-91

BTM (Business Technology
    Management), XXIII, XXV,
    5, 7
    dimensions of, 9, 11-12
    Governance & Organization,
        XXIV
    implementing, 24-25
    Managing Technology
        Investments, XXIV
    role of, 8
    step-by-step approach to, 26
    Strategic Enterprise Architecture,
        XXIV
    Strategy & Planning, XXIV
BTM capability, 5, 13
BTM Framework, XVIII, 8
BTM Institute, XVIII
BTM Maturity Model, 3, 21-24
BTM Standard, 3, 8
business agility. *See* agility
Business Architecture. *See*
    architecture
    Henderson, John, 37-39
    managing, 150, 152-153
business model risk, 86
business network intelligence, 149
business networks, SEA, 151
business strategy, 54
business technology, 5
    challenges in overseeing busi-
        ness technology, 77
    concerns about, 77
    decision-focused investments, 36
    enterprise-wide perspective, 77
    increasing value of, 192-196
    intellectual capital-focused
        investments, 36
    making sense of business
        value, 183
    measuring contributions, 197-199
    monitoring, 189, 191
    productivity enhancements,
        72-73
    relationship-focused invest-
        ments, 37
    roles of, 186, 188
    shaping business strategy, 78-81
    spending, 73-74
    strategic risks, 86
    transaction-focused invest-
        ments, 36

trends, 136-137
value dials, 76
business technology
investments, 186
changes with strategic
positioning, 47
enabling strategic actions, 35-40
four steps of decisions, 56
strategic positioning, 48
Business Technology Management
Framework, XVII
Business Technology Management.
See BTM
business technology portfolios.
See portfolios
business technology processes.
See processes
business value metrics, 74-75
Business-Driven IT Strategy, 19,
54, 69
PPM, 127

C

Caminer, David, 209
capabilities
exploitative capabilities, leveraging stable platform
resources, 62, 64-65
explorative capabilities and
dynamic leverage options,
65-66
identifying required business
capabilities, 54-56
required business capabilities,
strategic positioning, 57, 59
Capability Maturity Model
(CMM), 8
Carlini, Barbara (communication),
81-83
Carr, Nick, 182
categories of metrics, 185
categories of processes, organization structures, 103
categories of three processes,
principles of organization
design, 103-104
categorizing information into
enterprise portfolios, 130
centralized designs, 111
challenges
of agility, 138-139

in overseeing business
technology, 77
changes in technology and
business, 136
characteristics of leaders, 206-208
CIOs, Daniel Hartert, 57-58
Citicorp, 184
Citigroup, 184
CMM (Capability Maturity
Model), 8
communication, 144, 195
Carlini, Barbara, 81-83
outsourcing, 177
Communication Strategy
Management, 16
competitive risk, 86
compliance
managing, 88
regulatory compliance, 86, 88
Compliance and Risk
Management, 16
PPM, 126
conflict between business and
technology, XXII
Consolidation and
Standardization, 20
control, business technology shaping business strategy, 80
convergence, 7, 18
Jans, Kees, 187-188
Matheys, Steve, 60, 62-63
cooperating firms, 32
coordinated authority, 139
coordination, principles of organization design, 97-99, 101
cost-benefit analysis, measuring
business technology's contribution, 198
CRM (customer relationship
management), 198
culture, Christopher Wrenn, 43-45
customer intimacy, 58
customers, business technology
processes, 142

D

data, 11
decentralized designs, 111
decision making, PPM, 119
decision-focused investments, 36
decoupling points, 43, 45

demand-side forces, organization structures, 96
descriptive models, 146
DHL, 64
Diamond, Lester (risk), 161-163
dimensions of BTM, 9, 11-12
distributed authority, 139
double-loop learning, 41
Duke of Urbino, 210

E

EA (Enterprise Architecture), 17
effective technology, 12
empowerment, business technology shaping business strategy, 80
Enamics, Inc., XVI
Enterprise Architecture (EA), 17
Enterprise Architecture (EA) Standards, 21
Enterprise Business Strategy, 54
Enterprise IT Strategy, 55
enterprise portfolios, gathering and categorizing information, 130
Enterprise Program Management Office. See EPMO
enterprise project portfolios, 124
enterprise-wide perspective, of business technology, 77
EPMO (Enterprise Program Management Office), 11, 16, 128, 170
equilibrium cycles, 122
ERM (Enterprise Risk Management), 171
ERP (Enterprise Resoucre Planning), 169
executives, making sense of business value of business technology, 183
experiments, 85
exploitation, 33-34
exploitative actions, 32
exploitative capabilities, leveraging stable platform resources, 62, 64-65
exploration, 34
explorative capabilities and dynamic leverage options, 65-66
exploratory actions, 33

F-G

failure, 4-5
federal design, 111
formal risk management plans, 170
The Fulbright Center, XVIII
GCIB (Global Corporate and Investment Banking), 184
"glass house," 205
governance
    boards, processes for managing technology decisions, 89, 91
    business technology shapes business strategy, 78-81
    Holley, Jean, 193-195
    McFarlan, F. Warren, 75-76
    metrics, 84-86
    networked governance model, 90
    Palepu, Krishna, 91-92
    strategic visions, 83-84
Governance & Organization, XXIV, 15-16
governance models risk, 88

H-I

Hartert, Daniel (CIOs), 57-58
Henderson, John, 207
    business architecture, 37-39
Herman Miller SQA ("Simple, Quick and Affordable"), 4, 39-40
history of business technology, 17
Holley, Jean (governance), 193-195
HVB Americans, 44
identifying required business capabilities, 54-56
implementing BTM, 24-25
improvement, emphasis on, 139
increasing value, 192-193, 195-196
information, 11
information technology, 5
innovation
    emphasis on, 139
    principles of organization design, 101-102
Institute of Accountants in Glasgow, 210
integration risk, 88
Intel, value dials, 75, 84

intellectual capital-focused
investments, 36
investment risk, 88
IT, 5
IT Function Strategy, 55
ITfactsbiz.com, 188
ITIL (IT Infrastructure Library), 8
Ito, Hideo, 23

J-K-L

J. Lyons & Co., 209-210
Jans, Kees (convergence), 187-188

leaders, characteristics of, 206-208
leadership, 207
product leadership, 59
Rockart, John F., 17-18
leagile (learned agility), 46
leagility, 42
legacy systems, 171
LEO (Lyons Electronic Office),
209-210
leveraging
explorative capabilities and
dynamic leverage options,
65-66
stable platform resources with
exploitative capabilities, 62,
64-65
logic, developing
modular organizing logic, 104, 108
strategic sourcing logic, 108, 110
Luftman, Jerry N. (alignment),
200-202
Lyons Electronic Office (LEO), 209

M

management automation tools, 12
management processes, 10, 12
managing
business networks, 150, 152-153
compliance, 88
risk, 170, 179
technology decisions, 89, 91
Managing Technology
Investments, XXIV, 16
Approval and Prioritization, 17
Portfolio and Program
Management, 16

Project Analysis and Design, 17
Resource and Demand
Management, 19
market conditions, strategic
positions, 42
Matheys, Steve (convergence), 60,
62-63
Matula, Alan (portfolio management), 121-122
Mayor Fulbright, Harriet, XVIII
McFarlan, F. Warren
governance, 75-76
portfolio management, 125-126
measuring
business technology's contribution, 197-199
success, 203
metrics, 84-86, 182
assessing business value, 183-185
business value metrics, 74-75
categories of, 185
event-spawned metrics, 142
selecting, 185
Meyers, Ronald, XXII
Miller, Herman, 4
misalignment risk, 88
modular organizational units, 106
and governance network
types, 108
and value-creating process
types, 109
monitoring
business technology, 189, 191
operations and performance,
PPM, 131
Mystic, 184

N-O

net present value (NPV), 199
networked governance model,
90, 101
networks, real-time business networks (processes), 147, 149-150
Nobel Family Society, XIX
Nobel, Michael, XIX
normative models, 146
NPV (net present value), measuring business technology's contribution, 198

offshoring, 175-177
operational excellence, 59
operations, monitoring, 131
organization design, 111-112
    principles of
        coordination, 97-99, 101
        developing modular organiz-
            ing logic, 104, 108
        developing strategic sourcing
            logic, 108, 110
        relationships, 101-102
        three categories of processes,
            103-104
Organization Design and Change
    Management, 16
organization models, 105
organization structures, 95
    administrative forces, 96
    categories of processes, 103
    demand-side forces, 96
    supply-side forces, 96
organizational environment,
    systems risk, 166
organizational failures, 162
organizational models, 97
organizational structures, 10
organizational units, 108-109
Otis, REM, 186
outsourcing, 110, 173-174, 177
    communication, 177
    legal risks, 177
    location-related risks, 175
    P&G, 173
    risks, 163, 174
    standards, 176
    technical risks, 176

P

P&G (Procter & Gamble),
    outsourcing, 173
Pacioli, Luca, 210
Palepu, Krishna (governance), 91-92
partnering, 110
payoff of business technology, 202
people, Michael Westcott, 99-100
performance, monitoring, 131
perspective
    on business technology
        processes, 142-143
    enterprise-wide perspective of
        business technology, 77

planning and control risks, 167, 169
platform resources, leveraging
    exploitative capabilities, 62,
    64-65
PMBOK (Project Management
    Body of Knowledge), 8
Portfolio and Program
    Management. See PPM
portfolio management, 118. See
    also PPM
    Matula, Alan, 121-122
    McFarlan, F. Warren, 125-126
portfolio types, 123
portfolios, 123
    business technology portfolios,
        creating, 133
    enterprise portfolios, 130
    enterprise project portfolios, 124
    program-level portfolios, 125
    project-level portfolios, 124
    service delivery portfolios, 126
    technology asset portfolios, 124
Poussereau, Alain (alignment),
    66-67
PPM (Portfolio and Program
    Management), 16, 117-118
    analyzing information and
        developing strategies and
        plans, 130
    Approval and Prioritization, 128
    Business-Driven IT Strategy, 127
    Compliance and Risk
        Management, 126
    creating structures, defining
        taxonomies, and assigning
        responsibilities, 128-130
    decision making, 119
    gathering and categorizing
        information into enterprise
        portfolios, 130
    monitoring operations and
        performance, 131
    Resource and Demand
        Management, 128
    strategy, 119-121, 123
    principles of organization design
        categories of three processes,
            103-104
        coordination, 97-99, 101
        developing modular organizing
            logic, 104, 108

developing strategic sourcing
logic, 108, 110
relationships, 101-102
process approach, measuring
business technology's
contribution, 198
process improvement, 85
processes
Allen, William, 147-148
business technology processes,
140, 142-143
event-spawned metrics, 142
real-time business networks,
147, 149-150
rule-based business process
management, 142
service and customer
emphasis, 142
Sheinheit, Steven, 143-145
SOBEM, 146
Procter & Gamble (P&G),
outsourcing, 173
product leadership, 59
product-markets, 42
productivity enhancements,
business technology, 72-73
productivity paradox, 182
profitable opportunities,
discovering, 31
program-level portfolios, 125
Project Analysis and Design, 17
project complexity, risk, 166
Project Management Body of
Knowledge (PMBOK), 8
project-level portfolios, 124
pull driven, 43
push driven, 43

R

real-time business networks,
processes, 147, 149-150
regulatory compliance, 86, 88
relationship-focused investment, 37
relationships, principles of organization design, 101-102
REM (Remote Elevator
Monitoring), 186
renewal, 85
requirements risk, 166

Resouce and Demand
Management, PPM, 128
Resource and Demand
Management, 19
response innovation, 65
responsibilities, assigning (PPM),
128-130
return on investment (ROI), 192
risk, 158
Diamond, Lester, 161-163
managing, 170, 179
nature of risks in technology,
159-161, 163-164
organizational failures, 162
outsourcing, 163, 174
Schumacher, Leon, 171-173
sources of, 165
sourcing risks, 163
systems, 161, 164, 166-169
Willcocks, Leslie, 167-169
risk mitigation approaches, 178
Rockart, John F. (leadership), 17-18
ROI (return on investment), 192
roles
blurring of, 144
of BTM, 8
of business technology, 186, 188
Ross, Jeanne, 85, 95
rule-based business process
management, 142

S

Sarbanes-Oxley, 159, 188
Schumacher, Leon (uncertainty),
171-173
Schwab.com, 186
SCOR (Supply Chain Operations
Reference), 146
SDLC (system development life
cycle), 17
SEA (Strategic Enterprise
Architecture), XXIV, 20-21,
135, 137-138, 154
business networks, 151
and SOA, 151
Sears Home Services, 4, 38
selecting metrics, 185
sense and respond cycle, 190
sense-and-respond capability, 139

service delivery portfolios, 126
Service-Oriented Architecture
(SOA), 152
Service-Oriented Business Execution
Model (SOBEM), 145
services, 152
business technology processes, 142
Sheinheit, Steven (processes),
143-145
single-loop learning, 41
Slagboom, Rob, 208
organization models, 105
SOA (Service-Oriented
Architecture), 152
and SEA, 151
SOBEM (Service-Oriented
Business Execution Model),
145-146
Solow, Robert, 182
sources of risk, 165
sourcing, principles of organization
design, 101-102
sourcing risks, 163
spending, business technology, 73-74
Sperry, Roger, XXII
standards, 152
outsourcing, 176
statistical measurement
methods, 199
statistical methods, measuring
business technology's contribution, 198
status quo, 42
Strategic Planning and
Budgeting, 20
strategic actions
enabling through business
technology investments,
35-37, 39-40
exploitative actions, 32
exploratory actions, 33
Strategic and Tactical
Governance, 15
strategic learning, 41
Strategic Planning and
Budgeting, 35
strategic positions, 32, 51
business technology investment
changes, 47-48
establishing, 31-32

exploitation, 33-34
exploration, 34
market conditions, 42
required business capabilities,
57-59
strategic risk, 86
Strategic Sourcing and Vendor
Management, 20, 32
strategic visions, 83-84
strategies, 30-31
analyzing information and
developing strategies and
plans, 130
business strategy. *See* business
strategy
business technology shapes
business strategy, 78-81
PPM, 119-121, 123
Strategy & Planning, XXIV, 19-20
success, managing, 203
Sun Microsystems, 120
Supply Chain Operations
Reference (SCOR), 146
supply-side forces, organization
structures, 96
support, 144
synchronization, 7, 13-15
system development life cycle
(SDLC), 17
systems, risk, 161, 164, 166
planning and control risks,
167, 169
project complexity, 166
requirements risk, 166
team risk, 169
user involvement, 166

T

taxonomies, PPM, 128-130
TCO (total cost of ownership), 198
team risk, 169
technology
business technology, 5
effective technology, 12
nature of risks, 159-161, 163-164
Technology Architecture, 20, 137
technology asset portfolios, 124
technology decisions, processes for
managing, 89, 91

technology management domain, 8
Toshiba America, Inc., 23
total cost of ownership (TCO), 198
training, 192
transaction-focused investments, 36
transformation, 85
    business technology shaping
        business strategy, 81
Treacy, Michael, 58
trends in business technology,
    136-137

U-V

UPS, 169, 192
user involvement, systems risk, 166

value
    increasing value of business tech-
        nology, 192-193, 195-196
    making sense of value of busi-
        ness technology, 183
    metrics to assess business value,
        183-185
value dials, 75-76, 84
value discipline, 57, 60-61
value nets, 32
value types, 57, 59-60
value-creating process types
    and modular organizational
    units, 109
visioning, principles of organiza-
    tion design, 101-102

W-X-Y-Z

WACC (weighted average cost of
    capital), 199
Wal-Mart, 32, 169
    productivity enhancements, 73
weighted average cost of capital
    (WACC), 199
Weill, Peter, 95
Westcott, Michael (people), 99-100
"whole brain," XXII
Wiersema, Fred, 58
Willcocks, Leslie (risk), 167-169
Wrenn, Christopher (culture),
    43-45

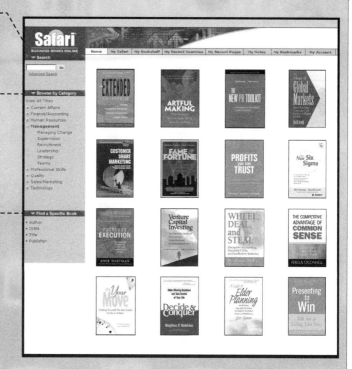

The Design of Things to Come
How Ordinary People Create Extraordinary Products
BY CRAIG M. VOGEL, JONATHAN CAGAN, AND PETER BOATWRIGHT

The iPod is a harbinger of a revolution in product design: innovation that targets customer emotion, self-image, and fantasy, not just product function. You'll read the hidden stories behind BodyMedia's SenseWear body monitor, Herman Miller's Mirra Chair, Swiffer's mops, OXO's potato peelers, Adidas' intelligent shoes, the new Ford F-150 pickup truck, and many other winning innovations. You'll meet the innovators, learning how they inspire and motivate their people, as they shepherd their visions through corporate bureaucracy to profitable reality. These design revolutionaries have a healthy respect for the huge cultural and economic forces swirling around them, but they've gotten past the fear of failure, in order to surf the biggest waves—and deliver the most exciting breakthroughs. Along the way, the authors deconstruct the entire process of design innovation, showing how it really works, and how today's smartest companies are innovating more effectively than ever before. *The Design of Things to Come* will fascinate you—whether you're a consumer who's intrigued by innovation or an executive who wants to deliver more of it.

ISBN 0131860828, © 2005, 272 pp., $26.95

Big Winners and Big Losers
The 4 Secrets of Long-Term Business Success and Failure
BY ALFRED A. MARCUS

What keeps great companies winning, year after year, even as yesterday's most hyped businesses fall by the wayside? It's not what you think—or what you've read. To find the real answers, strategic management expert Alfred Marcus systematically reviewed detailed performance metrics for the 1,000 largest U.S. corporations, identifying 3% who have consistently outperformed their industry's averages for a full decade. Many of these firms get little publicity: firms like Amphenol, Ball, Family Dollar, Brown and Brown, Activision, Dreyer's, Forest Labs, and Fiserv. But their success is no accident: they've discovered patterns of success that have largely gone unnoticed elsewhere. Marcus also identified patterns associated with consistently inferior performance: patterns reflected in many of the world's most well-known companies. Drawing on this unprecedented research, *Big Winners and Big Losers* shows you what really matters most. You'll learn how consistent winners build the strategies that drive their success; how they move towards market spaces offering superior opportunity; and how they successfully manage the tensions between agility, discipline, and focus. You'll learn how to identify the right patterns of success for your company, build on the strengths you already have, realistically assess your weaknesses, and build sustainable advantage one step at a time, in a planned and logical way.

ISBN 0131451324, © 2006, 432 pp., $27.99